Letting Go:

The Pathway
of
Surrender

Letting Go:
The Pathway
of
Surrender

David R. Hawkins, M.D., Ph.D.

VERITAS

Veritas Publishing
P.O. Box 3516
W. Sedona, AZ 86340 U.S.A
Phone: 928.282.8722 • Fax: 928.282.4789
www.veritaspub.com

Hardbound LCCN: 2012942251
Hardbound ISBN: 978-1-933885-98-8
Softbound ISBN: 978-1-933885-99-5

*Dedicated to removing the blocks to the
Higher Self on the path to Enlightenment*

CONTENTS

Contents

FOREWORD

This book provides a mechanism by which to unlock our innate capacities for happiness, success, health, well-being, intuition, unconditional love, beauty, inner peace, and creativity. These states and capacities are within all of us. They do not depend on any outer circumstance or personal characteristic; they do not require belief in any religious system. No single group or system owns inner peace, as it belongs to the human spirit by virtue of our origin. This is the universal message of every great teacher, sage, and saint: "The kingdom of heaven is within you." Dr. Hawkins says frequently, "What you are seeking is not different from your very own Self."

How can something innate to us—part and parcel of our true being—be so difficult to attain? Why all the unhappiness if we were endowed with happiness? If the "kingdom of heaven" is within us, why do we often "feel like hell"? How can we get free of the sludge of non-peace that makes our journey to inner peace seem so arduous, like molasses running uphill on a freezing cold day? It's nice to hear that peace, happiness, joy, love, and success are intrinsic to our human spirit. But what about all of the anger, sadness, despair, vanity, jealousy, anxieties, and daily little judgments that muffle the pristine sound of silence within us? Is there really a way to shake off the sludge and be free? Dance with unimpeded joy? Love all living things? Live in our greatness and fulfill our highest potential? Become a channel of grace and beauty in the world?

In this book, Dr. Hawkins offers a pathway to the freedom that we long for but find difficult to attain. It may sound counter-intuitive to get somewhere by "letting go"; however, he certifies from clinical and personal experience that surrender is the surest route to total fulfillment.

Many of us have been raised to correlate worldly and even spiritual accomplishment with "hard work," "keeping our nose to the grindstone," "living by the sweat of our brow," and other self-stringent axioms inherited from a culture steeped in the Protestant ethic. According to this view, success requires suffering, toil, and effort: "no pain, no gain." But where has all the effort and pain gotten us? Are we truly, deeply at peace? No. There is still the inner guilt, the vulnerability to someone's criticism, the wanting to be assured, and the resentments that fester.

If you're reading this book, you've probably already reached the end of your rope with the mechanism of effort. Perhaps you've seen that the more you pull on the rope to hitch yourself up to where you want to be, the more frazzled and frayed it becomes. Possibly, you might be wondering, "Isn't there an easier, better way?" Are you willing to let go of the rope? What would it be like to utilize the mechanism of surrender instead of the mechanism of effort?

I can share what it was like for a highly educated person who had already tried many different methods of self-improvement. Despite professional success, there were physical and emotional problems that never seemed to improve and, eventually, reached a breaking point. The encounter with Dr. David R. Hawkins and his writings catalyzed a healing effect that was unexpected and dramatic.

At first, there was skepticism. Having explored various spiritual, philosophical, and religious avenues with unfulfilling or only temporary results, I approached my study of Hawkins with the thought, "It will probably turn out like the rest." However, the conscientious seeker in me said, "I'll check it out. What have I got to lose?" So, I read *Power vs. Force: The Hidden Determinants of Human Behavior.* When the book was finished, there was the inner realization, "I'm a changed person from the one who picked up this book." That was in 2003. Now, many years later, the catalytic effect is still operating in all areas of life.

What convinced me of the truth of his work, ultimately, were the transformations in my own physical and nonphysical consciousness. There were empirical facts that I could not deny: the healing of an addiction that had been previously impossible to overcome, despite many sincere attempts; freedom from several allergies (pet dander, poison ivy, mold, hay fever); letting go of long-standing resentments, with a capacity to see the hidden gifts within the various life traumas I had been through; alleviation of several life-long fears and an anxiety disorder that had severely limited my career and personal life; resolution of several inner conflicts related to self-acceptance and life purpose. These major breakthroughs at the physical and non-physical levels were concretely observable not only by myself but by those around me. They would ask, "How do you explain the transformation?" Now, if faced with that question, I will suggest that they read this new book, *Letting Go: The Pathway of Surrender.* It lays out the pragmatics of the inner process of transformation that was experienced upon reading his earlier books.

Letting Go: The Pathway of Surrender provides the roadmap to a freer life for anyone who is willing to make the trip. Your life will be changed for the better if you apply the principles described in this book. They are not difficult to understand or to implement. They do not cost anything. They do not require special attire or travel to an exotic country. The major requirement for the journey is a willingness to let go of the attachment to your current experience of life.

As Dr. Hawkins explains, the "small" part of ourselves is attached to the familiar, no matter how painful or inefficient it is. It may seem bizarre, but our self with a small "s" actually enjoys an impoverished life and all the negativity that goes with it: feeling unworthy, being invalidated, judging others and ourselves, being inflated, always "winning" and being "right," grieving the past, fearing the future, nursing our wounds, craving assurance, and seeking love instead of giving it.

Are we willing to imagine a new life for ourselves, characterized by effortless success, freedom from resentment, gratitude for all that's happened to us, inspiration, love, joy, win-win resolutions, happiness, and creative expression? One of the biggest hurdles to happiness, he tells us, is the belief that it isn't possible: "There's got to be a catch"; "It's too good to be true"; "It can happen for others but not for me."

The gift of a person and teacher like Dr. Hawkins is that we see and experience a being who IS that happiness; who IS that boundless joy; who IS that unassailable peace. The book was written because he himself experienced the power of the mechanism it describes. To read about and be in the presence of such a liberated being gives us the catalyst, the hope, and the launch for our own inward trek. And so, despite the cynicism of the small self, there is the Self that beckons us on. We may first hear its call as coming from an advanced consciousness such as Dr. Hawkins, a teacher, a guide, or a sage who has realized the Self. Then, as we have our own experiences of truth, healing, and expansion, we hear the call as coming from an inner place. "The Self of the teacher and that of the student are one and the same," says Dr. Hawkins.

He radiates the truths of this book. As a serious seeker who saw much of contemporary spiritual writing as shallow, I wanted to verify the authenticity of this work. It was all-important to know: does this author speak from a true inner Realization? The answer is "Yes!" Close observations made during several years of interviews and visits confirmed the advanced state. In this book, he reminds us of the law of consciousness that says: We are all connected at the energetic level, and a higher vibration (such as love) has a powerful effect on a lower vibration (such as fear). I feel the truth of this law whenever I am with him; his energy field transmits healing love and profound peace. As he explains in this book, these higher states are available to all of us at any time.

No matter where we are in life, this book will illumine a "next step." The mechanism of surrender that Dr. Hawkins describes is applicable to the entire inner journey: from the letting go of childhood resentments to the final surrender of the ego itself. Thus, the book is equally useful for the professional interested in worldly success, the client in therapy seeking to heal emotional issues, the patient diagnosed with an illness, and the spiritual seeker devoted to Enlightenment. The important step for all of us, he advises, is to acknowledge that we have negative feelings as a consequence of our human condition, and to be willing to look at them without judgment. The high state of non-dual awareness may be our goal. But how do we handle the persistently dualistic "small self" that wants us to see ourselves as "better than" or "worse than" another?

In his previous ten books, Dr. Hawkins has described the non-dual state of Enlightenment with rare pristine awareness. As he says humorously at the start of many lectures, "We begin with the end." Indeed, in his lectures and books, he has thoroughly illuminated the highest states of consciousness that are the culmination of human inner evolution.

Now, in this book published in the latter part of his life, he is taking us back to our common starting point: acknowledging the existence of the small self. We must start where we are to get to where we want to go! If we want to go from here to there, we don't get there faster if we fool ourselves and say we are starting from nearby. By thinking we're closer than we are to the goal, we actually make the trip longer. As he explains in the book, it takes courage and self-honesty to see negativity and smallness in ourselves. Only when we can acknowledge the negativity that we've inherited from the human condition will we have the possibility to surrender and be free of it. We simply need to be willing to acknowledge and accept that part of our human experience. By accepting it, we can transcend it—and Dr. Hawkins shows us the way.

In this highly pragmatic book, he illumines a technique by which we can transcend the small self and break through to the freedom for which we long. This state of inner freedom and unalloyed happiness is our "birthright," he says. As we read, we draw encouragement and inspiration from the real-life clinical examples that he shares from his decades of psychiatric practice. In case after case, we see the power of surrender applied to nearly every area of life: relationships, physical health, work environments, recreational activities, spiritual process, family life, sexuality, emotional healing, and addiction recovery.

We learn that the answer to the problems we face is *within* us. By letting go of the inner blocks to it, the truth of our inner Self shines forth and the path to peace is revealed. Other spiritual teachers have emphasized the cultivation of inner peace as the only real solution to personal difficulties, as well as collective conflicts: "Inner disarmament first, then outer disarmament" (The Dalai Lama); "Be the change you want to see in the world" (Gandhi). The implication is clear. Because we are all part of the whole, when we heal something in ourselves, we heal it for the world. Each individual consciousness is connected to the collective consciousness at the energetic level; therefore, personal healing emerges collective healing. Dr. Hawkins may be the first to attempt to understand this principle in light of scientific and clinical applications. The crucial point is: by changing ourselves, we change the world. As we become more loving on the inside, healing occurs on the outside. Much like the rising of the sea level lifts all ships, so the radiance of unconditional love within a human heart lifts all of life.

. . . . .

Dr. David R. Hawkins is a world-renowned author, psychiatrist, clinician, spiritual teacher, and researcher of consciousness. Details of his extraordinary life are given in the "About the Author" section at the back of the book. His unique work effulges from a wellspring

of universal compassion and is dedicated to the alleviation of suffering in all dimensions of life. The gift of
Dr. Hawkins' work to human evolvement is beyond
what can be said about it.

The state of Enlightenment is totally complete in its
bliss, such that one would never leave it except out of
a total surrender of love to God and to one's fellow
human beings, to share the gift that was given. This
book on letting go, and all of his work in the world, is
the result of that surrender. As you will read in one of
the chapters, there was a very deep surrender that
allowed the resumption of his personal consciousness
in order to fulfill certain commitments in the world.
The state of oneness was not lost or left, but extraordinary love had to be directed toward the challenge of
verbalizing the ineffable. You will notice that some of
his pronouns do not fit grammatical convention—for
example, "our life"—yet they are true to the experience
of a spiritual state that knows the impersonal oneness
of all life. That Dr. Hawkins would re-enter the world
of logic and language in order to share a "Map of Consciousness" with us—so that we might also complete
our destiny—speaks volumes of his selfless love for
humanity. By showing us the way to liberation, Dr.
Hawkins gives us the chance of reaching it.

Thank you, Dr. Hawkins, for the gift of total surrender.

Fran Grace, Ph.D., editor.
Professor of Religious Studies and
Steward of the Meditation Room
University of Redlands, California
Founding Director, Institute for
Contemplative Life
Sedona, Arizona
June 2012

PREFACE

During many years of clinical psychiatric practice, the primary aim was to seek the most effective ways to relieve human suffering in all of its many forms. To this end, numerous disciplines of medicine, psychology, psychiatry, psychoanalysis, behavioral techniques, bio-feedback, acupuncture, nutrition, and brain chemistry were explored. Beyond these clinical modalities were philosophical systems, metaphysics, a multitude of holistic health techniques, self-improvement courses, spiritual pathways, meditative techniques, and other ways to expand one's awareness.

In all of these explorations, the mechanism of surrender was found to be of great practical benefit. Its importance necessitated the writing of this book to share with others what was clinically observed and personally experienced.

The previous ten books focused on advanced states of awareness and Enlightenment. Over the years, thousands of students at our lectures and Satsangs have asked questions that reveal the everyday obstacles to Enlightenment. It is pragmatic and helpful to share a technique that will facilitate their success in overcoming such obstacles: How to handle the vicissitudes of ordinary life, with its losses, disappointments, stresses, and crises? How to be free of negative emotions and their impact on health, relationships, and work? How to handle all of the unwanted feelings? The present work describes a simple and effective means by which to let go of negative feelings and become free.

The letting go technique is a pragmatic system of eliminating obstacles and attachments. It can also be called a mechanism of surrender. There is scientific proof of its efficacy, an explanation of which is included in one of the chapters. Research has shown the technique to be more effective than many other approaches currently available in relieving the physiologic responses to stress.

After researching most of the various stress-reduction and consciousness methods, this approach stands out for its sheer simplicity, efficiency, clinical efficacy, absence of questionable concepts, and rapidity of observable results. Its simplicity is deceptive and almost disguises the real benefit of the technique. Simply stated, it sets us free from emotional attachments. It verifies the observation made by every sage, that attachments are the primary cause of suffering.

The mind, with its thoughts, is driven by feelings. Each feeling is the cumulative derivative of many thousands of thoughts. Because most people throughout their lives repress, suppress, and try to escape from their feelings, the suppressed energy accumulates and seeks expression through psychosomatic distress, bodily disorders, emotional illnesses, and disordered behavior in interpersonal relationships. The accumulated feelings block spiritual growth and awareness, as well as success in many areas of life.

The benefits of this technique can, therefore, be described on various levels:

Physical:

The elimination of suppressed emotions has a positive health benefit. It decreases the overflow of energy into the body's autonomic nervous system, and it unblocks the acupuncture energy system (demonstrable by a simple muscle test). Therefore, as a person constantly surrenders, physical and psychosomatic disorders improve and frequently disappear altogether. There is a general reversal of pathologic processes in the body and a return to optimal functioning.

Behavioral:

Because there is a progressive decrease of anxiety and negative emotions, there is less and less need for escapism via drugs, alcohol, entertainment, and excessive sleep. Consequently, there is an increase in vitality, energy, presence, and well-being, with more efficient and effortless functioning in all areas.

Interpersonal Relationships:

As negative feelings are surrendered, there is a progressive increase of positive feelings that results in quickly observable improvement in all relationships. There is an increase in the capacity to love. Conflicts with others decrease progressively, so that job performance improves. The elimination of negative blocks allows vocational goals to be more easily accomplished, and self-sabotaging behavior based on guilt progressively diminishes. There is less and less dependence on intellectualism and a greater use of intuitive knowingness. With the resumption of personality growth and development, there is often the uncovering of previously unsuspected creative and psychic abilities, which are thwarted in all people by suppressed negative emotions. Of great importance is the progressive diminution of dependency, the bane of all human relationships. Dependency underlies so much pain and suffering; it includes even violence and suicide as its ultimate expression. As dependency diminishes, there is also a diminution of aggressiveness and hostile behavior. These negative feelings are replaced by feelings of acceptance and lovingness toward others.

Consciousness/ Awareness/ Spirituality:

This is an area that opens up by continuous use of the mechanism of surrender. The letting go of negative emotions means that the person experiences ever-increasing happiness, contentment, peace, and joy. There is an expansion of awareness, progressive realization, and experiencing of the real inner Self. The teachings of the Great Masters unfold from within as one's own personal experience. The progressive letting go of limitations allows the realization at last of one's true identity. Letting go is one of the most efficacious tools by which to reach spiritual goals.

Anyone can accomplish all of these ends, with gentleness and subtlety, as one silently surrenders throughout daily life. The progressive disappearance of negativity and its replacement by positive feelings and experiences is pleasurable both to watch and to experience. It is the purpose of this information to assist the reader in having those rewarding experiences.

David R. Hawkins, M.D., Ph.D.
Founding President,
Institute for Spiritual Research
Sedona, Arizona
June 2012

1

INTRODUCTION

While in contemplation one day, the mind said:

"What in the world is wrong with us?"
"Why doesn't happiness stay put?"
"Where are the answers?"
"How do we address the human dilemma?"
"Have I gone nuts or has the world gone crazy?"

The solution to any problem seems to bring only brief relief, for it is the very basis of the next problem.

"Is the human mind a hopeless squirrel cage?"
"Is everybody confused?"
"Does God know what He's doing?"
"Is God dead?"

The mind just kept chattering along:

"Does anybody have the secret?"

Don't worry—everybody's desperate. Some seem cool about it. "I can't see what all the fuss is about," they say. "Life seems simple to me." They are so scared they can't even look at it!

How about the experts? Their confusion is more sophisticated, wrapped in impressive jargon and elaborate mental construction. They have predetermined belief systems into which they try to squeeze you. It seems to work for a while and, then, it is just back to one's original state again.

It used to be that we could count on social institutions, but they have had their day; nobody trusts them any more. We now have more watchdogs than institutions. The hospitals are monitored by multiple agencies. Nobody has time for the patients, who get lost in the shuffle. Look down the corridors. There are no doctors or nurses. They are in the offices doing paperwork. The whole scene is dehumanized.

"Well," you say, "there have to be some experts who have the answers." When upset, you go to a doctor or psychiatrist, an analyst, a social worker, or an astrologer. You take up religion, get philosophy, take the Erhard Seminars Training (est), tap yourself with EFT. You get your chakras balanced, try some reflexology, go for ear acupuncture, do iridology, get healed with lights and crystals.

You meditate, chant a mantra, drink green tea, try the Pentecostals, breathe in fire, and speak in tongues. You get centered, learn NLP, try actualizations, work on visualizations, study psychology, join a Jungian group. You get Rolfed, try psychedelics, get a psychic reading, jog, jazzercise, have colonics, get into nutrition and aerobics, hang upside down, wear psychic jewelry. Get more insight, bio-feedback, Gestalt therapy.

You see your homeopath, chiropractor, naturopath. You try kinesiology, discover your Enneagram type, get your meridians balanced, join a consciousness-raising group, take tranquilizers. You get some hormone shots, try cell salts, have your minerals balanced, pray, implore, and beseech. You learn astral projection. Become a vegetarian. Eat only cabbage. Try macrobiotics, go organic, eat no GMO. Meet up with Native American medicine men, do a sweat lodge. Try Chinese herbs, moxicombustion, shiatsu, acupressure, feng shui. You go to India. Find a new guru. Take off your clothes. Swim in the Ganges. Stare at the sun. Shave your head. Eat with your fingers, get really messy, shower in cold water.

Sing tribal chants. Relive past lives. Try hypnotic regression. Scream a primal scream. Punch pillows. Get Feldenkraised. Join a marriage encounter group. Go to Unity. Write affirmations. Make a vision board. Get re-birthed. Cast the I Ching. Do the Tarot cards. Study Zen. Take more courses and workshops. Read lots of books. Do transactional analysis. Get yoga lessons. Get into the occult. Study magic. Work with a kahuna. Take a shamanic journey. Sit under a pyramid. Read Nostradamus. Prepare for the worst.

Go on a retreat. Try fasting. Take amino acids. Get a negative ion generator. Join a mystery school. Learn a secret handshake. Try toning. Try color therapy. Try subliminal tapes. Take brain enzymes, antidepressants, flower remedies. Go to health spas. Cook with exotic ingredients. Look into strange fermented oddities from faraway places. Go to Tibet. Hunt up holy men. Hold hands in a circle and get high. Renounce sex and going to the movies. Wear some yellow robes. Join a cult.

Try the endless varieties of psychotherapy. Take wonder drugs. Subscribe to lots of journals. Try the Pritikin diet. Eat just grapefruit. Get your palm read. Think New Age thought. Improve the ecology. Save the planet. Get an aura reading. Carry a crystal. Get a Hindu sidereal astrological interpretation. Visit a transmedium. Go for sex therapy. Try Tantric sex. Get blessed by Baba Somebody. Join an anonymous group. Travel to Lourdes. Soak in the hot springs. Join Arica. Wear therapeutic sandals. Get grounded. Get more prana and breathe out that stale black negativity. Try golden needle acupuncture. Check out snake gallbladders. Try chakra breathing. Get your aura cleaned. Meditate in Cheops, the great pyramid in Egypt.

You and your friends have tried all of the above, you say? Oh, the human! You wonderful creature! Tragic, comic and yet so noble! Such courage to keep on searching! What drives us to keep looking for an answer? Suffering? Oh, yes. Hope? Certainly. But there is something more than that.

Intuitively, we know that somewhere there is an ultimate answer. We stumble down dark byways into cul-de-sacs and blind alleys; we get exploited and taken, disillusioned, fed up, and we keep on trying.

Where is our blind spot? Why can't we find the answer?

> We don't understand the problem; that's why we can't find the answer.
>
> Maybe it's ultra simple, and that's why we can't see it.
>
> Maybe the solution is not "out there," and that's why we can't find it.
>
> Maybe we have so many belief systems that we are blinded to the obvious.

Throughout history, a few individuals have reached great clarity and have experienced the ultimate solution to our human woes. How did they get there? What was their secret? Why can't we understand what they had to teach? Is it really next to impossible or nearly hopeless? What about the average person who is not a spiritual genius?

Multitudes follow spiritual pathways, but scarce are the ones who finally succeed and realize the ultimate truth. Why is that? We follow ritual and dogma and zealously practice spiritual discipline—and we crash once again! Even when it works, the ego quickly comes in and we are caught in pride and smugness, thinking we have the answers. Oh, Lord, save us from the ones who have the answers! Save us from the righteous! Save us from the do-gooders!

Confusion is our salvation. For the confused, there is still hope. Hang on to your confusion. In the end it is your best friend, your best defense against the deathliness of others' answers, against being raped by their ideas. If you are confused, you are still free. If you are confused, this book is for you.

What's in the book? It tells of a simple method to reach great clarity and transcend your problems along the way. It's not by finding the answers, but by undoing the basis of the problem. The state reached by the great sages of history is available; the solutions are within us and easy to find. The mechanism of surrender is simple and the truth is self-evident. It works during daily life. There is no dogma or belief system. You verify everything for yourself, so you cannot be misled. There is no dependence on any teachings. It follows the dicta of "Know thyself"; "The truth shall set you free"; and "The kingdom of God is within you." It works for the cynic, the pragmatist, the religionist, and the atheist. It works for any age or cultural background. It works for the spiritual person and the non-spiritual person alike.

Because the mechanism is your own, nobody can take it away from you. You are safe from disillusionment. You will find out for yourself what is real and what are just the mind's programs and belief systems. While all of this is going on, you will become healthier, more successful with less effort, happier, and more capable of real love. Your friends will notice a difference; the changes are permanent. You aren't going to go for a "high" and crash later. You will discover there is an automatic teacher within yourself.

Eventually you will discover your inner Self. You always unconsciously knew it was there. When you come upon it, you will understand what the great sages of history were trying to convey. You will understand it because Truth is self-evident and within your own Self.

This book is written with you, the reader, constantly in mind. It is easy, effortless, and enjoyable. There is nothing to learn or memorize. You will become lighter and happier as you read it. The material will automatically start bringing you the experience of freedom as you read through the pages. You are going to feel the weights being removed. Everything you do will become more enjoyable. You are in for some happy surprises about your life! Things are going to get better and better!

It's okay to be skeptical. We've been taken down the primrose path before, so be as skeptical as you like. Indeed, it's advisable to avoid gushing enthusiasm. It is a setup for a letdown later. Therefore, rather than enthusiasm, quiet observation will serve you better.

Is there such a thing as something for nothing in

the universe? Oh, yes, most certainly there is. It's your own freedom which you have forgotten and don't know how to experience. What is being offered to you is not something that has to be acquired. It is not something that is new or outside of yourself. It is already yours and merely has to be reawakened and rediscovered. It will emerge of its own nature.

The purpose of sharing this approach is merely to put you in touch with your own inner feelings and experiences. In addition, there is much helpful information that your mind will want to know. The process of surrender will begin automatically, for it is the nature of the mind to seek relief from pain and suffering and to experience greater happiness.

CHAPTER

2

THE MECHANISM OF
LETTING GO

What is it?

Letting go is like the sudden cessation of an inner pressure or the dropping of a weight. It is accompanied by a sudden feeling of relief and lightness, with an increased happiness and freedom. It is an actual mechanism of the mind, and everyone has experienced it on occasion.

A good example is the following. You are in the midst of an intense argument; you are angry and upset, when suddenly the whole thing strikes you as absurd and ridiculous. You start to laugh. The pressure is relieved. You come up from anger, fear, and feeling attacked to feeling suddenly free and happy.

Think how great it would be if you could do that all of the time, in any place, and with any event. You could always feel free and happy and never be cornered by your feelings again. That's what this technique is all about: letting go consciously and frequently at will. You are then in charge of how you feel, and you are no longer at the mercy of the world and your reactions to it. You are no longer the victim. This is employing the basic teaching of the Buddha, which removes the pressure of involuntary reactivity.

We carry around with us a huge reservoir of accumulated negative feelings, attitudes, and beliefs. The accumulated pressure makes us miserable and is the basis of many of our illnesses and problems. We are resigned to it and explain it away as the "human condition." We seek to escape from it in myriad ways. The average human life is spent trying to avoid and run from the inner turmoil of fear and the threat of misery. Everyone's self-esteem is constantly threatened both from within and without.

If we take a close look at human life, we see that it is essentially one long elaborate struggle to escape our inner fears and expectations that have been projected upon the world. Interspersed are periods of celebration when we have momentarily escaped the inner fears, but the fears are still there waiting for us. We have become afraid of our inner feelings because they hold such a massive amount of negativity that we fear we would be overwhelmed by it if we were to take a deeper look. We have a fear of these feelings because we have no conscious mechanism by which to handle the feelings if we let them come up within ourselves. Because we are afraid to face them, they continue to accumulate and, finally, we secretly begin looking forward to death to bring all of the pain to an end. It is not thoughts or facts that are painful but the feelings that accompany them. Thoughts in and of themselves are painless, but not the feelings that underlie them!

It is the accumulated pressure of feelings that causes thoughts. One feeling, for instance, can create literally thousands of thoughts over a period of time. Think, for instance, of one painful memory from early life, one terrible regret that has been hidden. Look at all the years and years of thoughts associated with that single event. If we could surrender the underlying painful feeling, all of those thoughts would disappear instantly and we would forget the event.

This observation is in accord with scientific research. The Gray-LaViolette scientific theory integrates psychology and neurophysiology. Their research demonstrated that feeling tones organize thoughts and memory (Gray-LaViolette, 1981). Thoughts are filed in the memory bank according to the various shades of feelings associated with those thoughts. Therefore, when we relinquish or let go of a feeling, we are freeing ourselves from all of the associated thoughts.

The great value of knowing how to surrender is that any and all feelings can be let go of at any time and any place in an instant, and it can be done continuously and effortlessly.

What is the surrendered state? It means to be free of negative feelings in a given area so that creativity and spontaneity can manifest without opposition or the interference of inner conflicts. To be free of inner conflict and expectations is to give others in our life the greatest freedom. It allows us to experience the basic nature of the universe, which, it will be discovered, is to manifest the greatest good possible in a situation. This may sound philosophical, but, when done, it is experientially true.

Feelings and Mental Mechanisms

We have three major ways of handling feelings: suppression, expression, and escape. We will discuss each in turn.

1. Suppression and repression. These are the most common ways in which we push feelings down and put them aside. In repression, this happens unconsciously; in suppression, it happens consciously. We don't want to be bothered by feelings and, besides, we don't know what else to do with them. We sort of suffer through them and try to keep functioning as best as we can. The feelings that we select to be suppressed or repressed are in accord with the conscious and unconscious programs that we carry within us from social custom and family training. The pressure of suppressed feelings is later felt as irritability, mood swings, tension in the muscles of the neck and back, headaches, cramps, menstrual disorders, colitis, indigestion, insomnia, hypertension, allergies, and other somatic conditions.

When we *repress* a feeling, it is because there is so much guilt and fear over the feeling that it is not even consciously felt at all. It becomes instantly thrust into the unconscious as soon as it threatens to emerge. The repressed feeling is then handled in a variety of ways to ensure that it stays repressed and out of awareness.

Of these mechanisms used by the mind to keep the feeling repressed, denial and projection are perhaps the best-known methods, as they tend to go together and reinforce each other. Denial results in major emotional and maturational blocks. It is usually accompanied by the mechanism of projection. Because of guilt and fear, we repress the impulse or feeling, and we deny its presence within us. Instead of feeling it, we project it onto the world and those around us. We experience the feeling as if it belonged to "them." "They" then become the enemy, and the mind searches for and finds justification to reinforce the projection. Blame is placed on people, places, institutions, food, climatic conditions, astrological events, social conditions, fate, God, luck, the devil, foreigners, ethnic groups, political rivals, and other things outside of ourselves. Projection is the main mechanism in use by the world today. It accounts for all wars, strife, and civil disorder. Hating the enemy is even encouraged in order to become a "good citizen." We maintain our own self-esteem at the expense of others and, eventually, this results in social breakdown. The mechanism of projection underlies all attack, violence, aggression, and every form of social destruction.

2. Expression. With this mechanism, the feeling is vented, verbalized, or stated in body language, and acted out in endless group demonstrations. The expression of negative feelings allows just enough of the inner pressure to be let out so that the remainder can then be suppressed. This is a very important point to understand, for many people in society today believe that expressing their feelings frees them from the feelings. The facts are to the contrary. The expression of a feeling, first, tends to propagate that feeling and give it greater energy. Second, the expression of the feeling merely allows the remainder to be suppressed out of awareness.

The balance between suppression and expression varies in each individual depending on early training, current cultural norms and mores, and the media.

Expressing oneself is now in vogue as a result of a misunderstanding of the work of Sigmund Freud and psychoanalysis. Freud pointed out that suppression was the cause of neurosis; therefore, expression was mistakenly thought to be the cure. This misinterpretation became a license for self-indulgence at the cost of others. What Freud actually said, in classical psychoanalysis, was that the repressed impulse or feeling was to be neutralized, sublimated, socialized, and channeled into constructive drives of love, work and creativity.

If we dump our negative feelings on others, they experience it as an attack and they, in turn, are forced to suppress, express, or escape the feelings; therefore, the expression of negativity results in the deterioration and destruction of relationships. A far better alternative is to take responsibility for our own feelings and neutralize them. Then, only positive feelings remain to be expressed.

3. Escape. Escape is the avoidance of feelings through diversion. This avoidance is the backbone of the entertainment and liquor industries, and also the route of the workaholic. Escapism and avoidance of inner awareness is a socially condoned mechanism. We can avoid our own inner selves and keep our feelings from emerging by an endless variety of pursuits, many of which eventually become addictions as our dependency upon them grows.

People are desperate to stay unconscious. We observe how often people flick on the television set the minute they enter a room and then walk around in a dream-like state, constantly being programmed by the data poured into them. People are terrified of facing themselves. They dread even a moment of aloneness.

Thus the constant frantic activities: the endless socializing, talking, texting, reading, music playing, working, traveling, sightseeing, shopping, overeating, gambling, movie-going, pill-taking, drug-using, and cocktail-partying.

Many of the foregoing mechanisms of escape are faulty, stressful, and ineffective. Each of them requires increasing amounts of energy in and of itself. Enormous amounts of energy are required to keep down the growing pressure of the suppressed and repressed feelings. There is a progressive loss of awareness and an arrest of growth. There is a loss of creativity, energy, and real interest in others. There is a halting of spiritual growth and eventually the development of physical and emotional illness, disease, aging, and premature death. The projection of these repressed feelings results in the social problems, disorders, and the increase of selfishness and callousness characteristic of our present society. Most of all, the effect is the inability to truly love and trust another person, which results in emotional isolation and self-hatred.

In contrast to the above, what happens instead when we let go of a feeling? The energy behind the feeling is instantly surrendered and the net effect is decompression. The accumulated pressure begins to decrease as we constantly let go. Everyone knows that, when we let go, we immediately feel better. The body's physiology changes. There are detectable improvements in skin color, breathing, pulse, blood pressure, muscle tension, gastro-intestinal function, and blood chemistries. In the state of inner freedom, all bodily functions and organs move in the general direction of normalcy and health. There is an immediate increase in muscle power. Vision improves and our perception of the world and ourselves changes for the better. We feel happier, more loving, and more easygoing.

Feelings and Stress

There is much attention and publicity given to the subject of stress without a real understanding of its essential nature. It is said that we are more stress-prone than ever. What is the essential cause of stress? Certainly it is not the external precipitating factors. They are merely examples of the mechanism we described as projection. It is "they" or "it" that is thought to be the culprit when, in fact, what we are feeling is merely the letting out of the inner pressure of repressed emotions. It is these repressed feelings that make us vulnerable to external stress.

The real source of "stress" is actually *internal*; it is not external, as people would like to believe. The readiness to react with fear, for instance, depends on how much fear is already present within to be triggered by a stimulus. The more fear we have on the inside, the more our perception of the world is changed to a fearful, guarded expectancy. To the fearful person, this world is a terrifying place. To the angry person, this world is a chaos of frustration and vexation. To the guilty person, it is a world of temptation and sin, which they see everywhere. What we are holding inside colors our world. If we let go of guilt, we will see innocence; however, a guilt-ridden person will see only evil. The basic rule is that we focus on what we have repressed.

Stress results from the accumulated pressure of our repressed and suppressed feelings. The pressure seeks relief, and so external events only trigger what we have been holding down, both consciously and unconsciously. The energy of our blocked-off feelings re-emerges through our autonomic nervous system and causes pathological changes leading to disease processes. A negative feeling instantly causes a loss of 50% of the body's muscle strength and also narrows our vision both physically and mentally. Stress is our emotional reaction to a precipitating factor or stimulus. Stress is determined by our belief systems and their associated emotional pressures. It is not the external stimulus, then, that is the cause of stress, but our degree of reactivity. The more surrendered we are, the less prone we are to stress. The damage caused by stress is merely the result of our own emotions. The effectiveness of letting go and reducing the body's response to stress has been demonstrated in scientific studies (see Chapter 14).

Many stress-reduction programs offered today often miss the essential point. They try to relieve the after-effects of stress rather than remove the cause of the stress itself, or they concentrate on external events. This is like trying to reduce the fever without correcting the infection. For instance, muscle tension is the aftermath of anxiety, fear, anger, and guilt. A course in the techniques of muscle relaxation is going to be of very limited benefit. It would be far more effective, instead, to remove the source of the underlying tension, which is the repressed and suppressed anger, fear, guilt, or other negative feelings.

Life Events and Emotions

The rationalizing mind prefers to keep the true causes of emotion out of awareness and utilizes the mechanism of projection to do this. It blames events or other people for "causing" a feeling and views itself as the helpless innocent victim of external causes. *"They made me angry." "He* got me upset." *"It* scared me." *"World events* are the cause of my anxiety." Actually, it's the exact opposite. The suppressed and repressed feelings seek an outlet and utilize the events as triggers and excuses to vent themselves. We are like pressure-cookers ready to release steam when the opportunity arises. Our triggers are set and ready to go off. In psychiatry, this mechanism is called displacement. It is because we are angry that events "make" us angry. If, through constant surrendering, we have let go of the pent-up store of anger, it is very difficult and, in fact, even impossible for anyone or any situation to "make" us angry. The same, therefore, goes for all other negative feelings once they have been surrendered.

Because of social conditioning in our society, people even suppress and repress their positive feelings. Suppressed love results in the broken heart of the heart attack. Suppressed love re-emerges as excessive adoration of pets and various forms of idolatry. True love is free of fear and characterized by non-attachment. Fear of loss energizes undue attachment and possessiveness. For example, the man who is insecure about his girlfriend is very jealous.

When the pressure of suppressed and repressed feelings exceeds the individual's tolerance level, the mind will create an event "out there" upon which to vent and displace itself. Thus, the person with a lot of repressed grief will unconsciously create sad events in life. The fearful person precipitates frightening experiences; the angry person becomes surrounded by infuriating circumstances; and the prideful person is constantly being insulted. As Jesus Christ said, "Why do you see the splinter which is in your brother's eye, and do not feel the beam which is in your own eye (Matthew 7:3)?" All the Great Masters point us *within*.

Everything in the universe emits a vibration. The higher the vibration, the more power it has. Emotions, also, because they are energy, emit vibrations. These emotional vibrations impact the body's energy fields and reveal effects that can be seen, felt, and measured. Motion pictures using Kirlian photography, such as those done by Dr. Thelma Moss, show rapid fluctuations of the color and size of the energy field with changes of emotions (Krippner, 1974). The energy field has traditionally been called an "aura" and can be seen by people who have been born with or learned the ability to see vibrations of that frequency. The aura changes color and size with emotions. Muscle-testing also demonstrates the energy changes that accompany emotions, as our body's muscles instantly respond to positive and negative stimuli. Thus, our basic emotional states transmit themselves to the universe.

The mind has no dimensions or size and is not limited in space; therefore, the mind transmits its basic state via vibrational energy over an unlimited distance. This means that we routinely and unwittingly affect others by our emotional state and thoughts. Emotional patterns and their associated thought forms, for instance, can be picked up and received consciously by psychics at a great distance. This can be demonstrated experimentally, and the scientific basis for this has been a subject of great interest in advanced quantum physics.

Because emotions emit a vibrational energy field, they affect and determine the people who are in our lives. Life events become influenced by our repressed and suppressed emotions on the psychic level. Thus anger attracts angry thoughts. The basic rule of the psychic universe is that "like attracts like." Similarly, "love promotes love," so that the person who has let go of a lot of inner negativity is surrounded by loving thoughts, loving events, loving people, and loving pets. This phenomenon explains many scriptural quotations and common sayings that have puzzled the intellect, such as, "The rich get richer and the poor get poorer," and "Those who have, get." As a general rule, therefore, people who are carrying the consciousness of apathy bring poverty circumstances into their lives, and those with a prosperity consciousness bring abundance into their lives.

Because all living things are connected on vibrational energy levels, our basic emotional state is picked up and reacted to by all life forms around us. It is well known that animals can instantly read a person's basic emotional state. There are experiments demonstrating that even the growth of bacteria is affected by human emotions, and that plants register measurable reactions to our emotional state (Backster, 2003).

The Mechanism of Letting Go

Letting go involves being aware of a feeling, letting it come up, staying with it, and letting it run its course without wanting to make it different or do anything about it. It means simply to let the feeling be there and to focus on letting out the energy behind it. The first step is to allow yourself to have the feeling without resisting it, venting it, fearing it, condemning it, or moralizing about it. It means to drop judgment and to see that it is *just* a feeling. The technique is to be with the feeling and surrender all efforts to modify it in any way. Let go of wanting to resist the feeling. *It is resistance that keeps the feeling going.* When you give up resisting or trying to modify the feeling, it will shift to the next feeling and be accompanied by a lighter sensation. A feeling that is not resisted will disappear as the energy behind it dissipates.

As you begin the process, you will notice that you have fear and guilt over having feelings; there will be resistance to feelings in general. To let feelings come up, it is easier to let go of the reaction to having the feelings in the first place. A fear of fear itself is a prime example of this. Let go of the fear or guilt that you have about the feeling first, and then get into the feeling itself.

When letting go, ignore all thoughts. Focus on the feeling itself, not on the thoughts. Thoughts are endless and self-reinforcing, and they only breed more thoughts. Thoughts are merely rationalizations of the mind to try and explain the presence of the feeling. The real reason for the feeling is the accumulated pressure behind the feeling that is forcing it to come up in the moment. The thoughts or external events are only an excuse made up by the mind.

As we become more familiar with letting go, it will be noticed that all negative feelings are associated with our basic fear related to survival and that all feelings are merely survival programs that the mind believes are necessary. The letting go technique undoes the programs progressively. Through that process, the underlying motive behind the feelings becomes more and more apparent.

To be surrendered means to have no strong emotion about a thing: "It's okay if it happens, and it's okay if it doesn't." When we are free, there is a letting go of attachments. We can enjoy a thing, but we don't need it for our happiness. There is progressive diminishing of dependence on anything or anyone outside of ourselves. These principles are in accord with the basic teaching of the Buddha to avoid attachment to worldly phenomena, as well as the basic teaching of Jesus Christ to "be in the world but not of it."

Sometimes we surrender a feeling and we notice that it returns or continues. This is because there is more of it yet to be surrendered. We have stuffed these feelings all of our lives and there can be a lot of energy pushed down that needs to come up and be acknowledged. When surrender occurs, there is an immediate lighter, happier feeling, almost like a "high."

By continuously letting go, it is possible to stay in that state of freedom. Feelings come and go, and eventually you realize that you are not your feelings, but that the real "you" is merely witnessing them. You stop identifying with them. The "you" that is observing and is aware of what is happening always stays the same. As you become more and more aware of the changeless witness within, you begin to identify with that level of consciousness. You become progressively primarily the witness rather than the experiencer of phenomena. You get closer and closer to the real Self and begin to see that you had been duped by feelings all along. You thought that you were the victim of your feelings. Now you see that they are not the truth about yourself; they are merely created by the ego, that collector of programs which the mind has mistakenly believed are necessary for survival.

The results of letting go are deceptively quick and subtle, but the effects are very powerful. Often we have let go but think that we haven't. It will be our friends who make us aware of the change. One reason for this phenomenon is that, when something is fully surrendered, it disappears from consciousness. Now, because we never think of it, we don't realize that it has gone. This is a common phenomenon among people who are growing in consciousness. We are not aware of all the coal that we have shoveled; we are always looking at the shovelful we are handling right now. We don't realize how much the pile has gone down. Often our friends and family are the first ones to notice.

To keep track of progress, many people keep a chart of their gains. This helps to overcome the resistance that usually takes the form, "This isn't working." It is common for people who have made enormous gains to claim, "It just isn't working." We have to remind ourselves sometimes what we were like before we started this process.

Resistance to Letting Go

Letting go of negative feelings is the undoing of the ego, which will be resistant at every turn. This may result in skepticism about the technique, "forgetting" to surrender, a sudden upsurge of escapism, or venting feelings by expressing and acting out. The solution is simply to keep on letting go of the feelings you have about the whole process. Let the resistance be there but don't resist the resistance.

You are free. You don't *have* to let go. Nobody is forcing you. Look at the fear behind the resistance. What are you afraid of regarding this process? Are you willing to let go of that? Keep letting go of every fear as it arises, and the resistance will resolve.

Let's not forget that we are letting go of all the programs that have made us a slave and a victim for a long time. These programs have blinded us to the truth of our real identity. The ego is losing ground and will try tricks and bluffs. Once we start letting go, its days are numbered and its power is diminishing. One of its tricks is to go unconscious about the technique itself, for instance, to decide suddenly that the mechanism of surrender isn't working, things are still the same, it is confusing, and too hard to remember and do. This is a sign of real progress! It means that the ego knows we have a knife with which to cut ourselves free and it is losing ground. The ego is not our friend. Like "master control" in *Tron* (1982), it wants to keep us enslaved by its programs.

Letting go is a natural ability. It is not something new or foreign. It is not an esoteric teaching or somebody else's idea or a belief system. We are merely utilizing our own inner nature to get freer and happier. When letting go, it's not helpful to "think" about the technique. It's better, simply, just to do it. Eventually it will be seen that all thoughts are resistance. They are all images that the mind has made to prevent us from experiencing what actually *is*. When we have been letting go for a while and have begun experiencing what is really going on, we will laugh at our thoughts. Thoughts are fakes, absurd make-beliefs that obscure the truth. Pursuing thoughts can keep us occupied endlessly. We will discover one day that we are right where we started. Thoughts are like gold fish in a bowl; the real Self is like the water. The real Self is the space between the thoughts, or more exactly, the field of silent awareness underneath all thoughts.

We have had the experience of being totally absorbed in what we were doing, when we scarcely noticed the passage of time. The mind was very quiet, and we were simply doing what we were doing without resistance or effort. We felt happy, maybe humming to ourselves. We functioned without stress. We were very relaxed, although busy. We suddenly realized that we never needed all those thoughts after all. Thoughts are like bait to a fish; if we bite at them, we get caught. It's best not to bite at the thoughts. We don't need them.

Inside of us, but out of awareness, is the truth that "I already know everything I need to know." This happens automatically.

Paradoxically, one resistance to surrendering is due to the effectiveness of the technique. What happens is that we keep letting go when life is not going too well and we are beset by unpleasant emotions. As we finally surrender our way out of it and all is well, then we stop letting go. This is a mistake because, as good as we may feel, there is usually more to it. Take advantage of the higher states and the momentum of letting go. Keep on going because it will get better and better all the time. Letting go gains a certain momentum. It is easy to keep it going once it is started. The higher we feel, the easier it is to let go. That's a good time to reach down and let go of some things (suppressed and repressed "garbage") that we wouldn't want to tackle if we were in the dumps. There is always a feeling to be let up and surrendered. When we are feeling good, the emotions are merely subtler.

Sometimes you will feel stuck with a particular feeling. Simply surrender to the feeling of being stuck. Just let it be there and don't resist it. If it doesn't disappear, see if you can let go of the feeling in bits and pieces.

Another block that may occur is the fear that if we let go of a desire for something, we won't get it. It is often beneficial to look at some commonly held beliefs and let go of them right in the beginning, such as: (1) We only deserve things through hard work, struggle, sacrifice, and effort; (2) Suffering is beneficial and good for us; (3) We don't get anything for nothing; (4) Things that are very simple aren't worth much. Letting go of some of these psychological barriers to the technique itself will allow an enjoyment of its effortlessness and ease.

3

THE ANATOMY OF EMOTIONS

There are numerous complicated psychologies of the human emotions. They often involve considerable symbology and references to mythology, and they are based on hypotheses that are hotly debated. As a result, there are various schools of psychotherapy with their different aims and methods. Simplicity is one of the earmarks of truth, and so we will describe a simple, workable, testable map of the emotions that can be verified by subjective experience, as well as by objective testing.

The Goal of Survival

Whichever psychology is studied reveals that the primary human goal, superseding all others, is survival. Every human desire seeks to ensure one's personal survival and the survival of one's identified groups, such as family, loved ones, and country. Humans fear, most of all, the loss of the capacity to experience. To that end, people are interested in the survival of the body because they believe that they *are* the body and, therefore, they need the body to experience their existence. Because people view themselves as separate and limited, they are stressed by their sense of lack. It is common for humans to look outside of themselves for the satisfaction of their needs. This leads them to experience themselves as vulnerable because they are insufficient unto themselves.

The mind is, therefore, a survival mechanism, and its method of survival is primarily the use of emotions. Thoughts are engendered by the emotions and, eventually, emotions become shorthand for thoughts. Thousands and even millions of thoughts can be replaced by a single emotion. Emotions are more basic and primitive than mental processes. Reason is the tool the mind uses to achieve its emotional ends. When used by the intellect, the basic underlying emotion is usually unconscious or at least out of awareness. When the underlying emotion is forgotten or ignored and not experienced, people are unaware of the reason for their actions and they develop all kinds of plausible reasons. In fact, they frequently do not know why they are doing what they are doing.

There is a simple way to become conscious of the underlying emotional goal behind any activity through use of the question, "What for?" With each answer, "What for?" is asked again and again until the basic feeling is uncovered. An example would be the following. A man wants a new Cadillac. His mind gives all the logical reasons but logic doesn't really explain it. So he asks himself, "What do I want the Cadillac for?" "Well," he says, "it is to achieve status, recognition, respect, and solid citizen success status." Again: "What do I want status for?" "Respect and approval from others," he might say, "and to ensure that respect." Again: "What do I want respect and approval for?" "To have the feeling of security." Again: "What do

I want security for?" "To feel happy." The continual
question, "What for?," reveals that basically there are
feelings of insecurity, unhappiness, and lack of fulfillment. Every activity or desire will reveal that the basic
goal is to achieve a certain feeling. There are no other
goals than to overcome fear and achieve happiness.
Emotions are connected with what we believe will
ensure our survival, not with what actually will. Emotions themselves are actually the cause of the basic
fear that drives everyone to seek security constantly.

The Scale of Emotions

For simplicity and clarity, we will utilize the scale of
emotions that corresponds with the levels of consciousness. A thorough presentation of consciousness
levels, their scientific basis, and practical applications
is found in *Power vs. Force: The Hidden Determinants
of Human Behavior* (Hawkins, [1995], 2012).

Briefly, everything emits energy, either positive or
negative. Intuitively, we know the difference between
a positive person (friendly, genuine, considerate) and
a negative one (greedy, deceitful, hateful). The energy
of Mother Teresa was obviously different from the
energy of Adolf Hitler; most people's energy is somewhere in between the two. Music, places, books, animals, intentions, and all of life emit an energy that can
be "calibrated" as to its essence and its degree of truth.

"Like goes to like." The different energies constel-
late in "attractor patterns" or "levels of consciousness."
The Map of Consciousness (see Appendix A) provides
a linear, logarithmic view of this nonlinear energetic
terrain. Each level of consciousness (or attractor pattern) is calibrated on a logarithmic scale of energetic

power, ranging from 1–1000. The level of Full Enlightenment (1000), at the top of the Map, represents the
highest level attainable in the human realm; it is the
energy of Jesus Christ, the Buddha, and Krishna. The
level of Shame (20) is at the bottom, close to death,
representing bare survival.

The level of Courage (200) is the critical point that
marks the shift from negative to positive energy. It is
the energy of integrity, being truthful, empowerment,
and having the capacity to cope. The levels of consciousness below Courage are destructive, whereas the
levels above it are life-supportive. A simple muscle-test
reveals the difference: negative stimuli (below 200)
instantly weaken the muscle, and positive stimuli
(above 200) instantly strengthen the muscle. True
"power" strengthens; "force" weakens. Above the level
of Courage, people seek us out because we give
energy to them ("power") and we have goodwill
towards them. Below the level of Courage, people
avoid us because we take energy from them ("force")
and we want to use them for our own material or
emotional needs.

Here, we delineate the basic scale, starting from
the higher energies down to the lower:

Peace (600): This is experienced as perfection, bliss,
effortlessness, and oneness. It is a state of non-duality
beyond separateness and beyond the intellect, as in
the "peace that passeth all understanding." It is
described as Illumination and Enlightenment. It is rare
in the human realm.

Joy (540): Love that is unconditional and unchanging,
despite circumstances and actions of others. The world
is illuminated by exquisite beauty, which is seen in all

things. The perfection of creation is self-evident. There is closeness to unity and discovery of Self; compassion for all; enormous patience; the feeling of at-oneness with others and a concern for their happiness. A sense of self-completion and self-sufficiency prevails.

Love (500): A way of being that is forgiving, nurturing, and supportive. It does not proceed from the mind; rather, it emanates from the heart. Love focuses on the essence of a situation, not the details. It deals with wholes, not particulars. As perception is replaced with vision, it takes no position and sees the intrinsic value and lovability of all that exists.

Reason (400): This aspect differentiates humans from the animal world. There is the ability to see things in the abstract, to conceptualize, to be objective, and to make rapid and correct decisions. Its enormous utility is problem solving. Science, philosophy, medicine, and logic are expressions of this level.

Acceptance (350): This energy is easy-going, laid back, harmonious, flexible, inclusive, and free of inner resistance. "Life is good. You and I are good. I feel connected." It meets life on life's terms. There is no need to blame others or blame life.

Willingness (310): This energy subserves survival by virtue of a positive attitude that welcomes all expressions of life. It is friendly, helpful, wants to assist, and seeks to be of service.

Neutrality (250): This is a way of life that is comfortable, pragmatic, and relatively free of emotionality. "It's okay either way." It is free of rigid positions, nonjudgmental, and noncompetitive.

Courage (200): This energy says, "I can do it." It is determined, excited about life, productive, independent, and self-empowered. Effective action is possible.

Pride (175): "My way is the best way," says this level. Its focus is achievement, desire for recognition, specialness, and perfectionism. It feels "better than . . ." and superior to others.

Anger (150): This energy overcomes the source of fear by force, threats, and attack. It is irritable, explosive, bitter, volatile, and resentful. It likes to "get even," as in "I'll show you."

Desire (125): It is always seeking gain, acquisition, pleasure, and "getting" something outside oneself. It is insatiable, never satisfied, and craving. "I have to have it." "Give me what I want, and give it to me now!"

Fear (100): This energy sees "danger," which is "everywhere." It is avoidant, defensive, preoccupied with security, possessive of others, jealous, restless, anxious, and vigilant.

Grief (75): There is helplessness, despair, loss, regret, and the feeling, "If only I had . . ." Separation. Depression. Sadness. Being a "loser." Mournful, as in "I can't go on."

Apathy (50): This energy is characterized by hopelessness, playing dead, being a "drain" to others, being immobilized, and the feelings: "I can't" and "Who cares?" Poverty is common.

Guilt (30): In this energy field, one wants to punish and be punished. It leads to self-rejection, masochism, remorse, "feeling bad," and self-sabotage. "It's all my fault." Accident-proneness, suicidal behavior, and projection of self-hatred onto "evil" others are common. It is the basis of many psychosomatic illnesses.

Shame (20): Characterized by humiliation, as in "hanging your head in shame." It is traditionally accompanied by banishment. It is destructive to health and leads to cruelty toward self and others.

In general, we can say that the lower end of the scale is associated with lower vibrational frequencies: lower energy, lower power, poorer life circumstances, poorer relationships, less abundance, less love, and poorer physical and emotional health. Because of the low energy, such needy people drain us on all levels. They tend to be avoided and find themselves surrounded by people on the same level (e.g., in jail).

As we let go of negative feelings, there is a progressive movement up the scale to Courage and then beyond, with increasing effectiveness, success, and more effortless abundance. We tend to seek out such people. We say they are "high." They give off life energy to all living things around them. Animals are attracted to them. They have a green thumb and positively influence the lives of all with whom they come in contact. At the level of Courage, the negative feelings have not all disappeared, but now we have sufficient energy to handle them because we've re-owned our power and self-adequacy. The fastest way to move from the bottom to the top is by telling the truth to ourselves and to others.

The energy levels are also traditionally associated with the body energy centers that are sometimes referred to as "chakras." The chakras are energy centers through which "kundalini energy" is said to flow, once it is awakened at the level of Courage (200). The energy centers (chakras) can be measured by a variety of clinical techniques and sensitive electronic instruments. On the Map of Consciousness, the chakras calibrate as follows: Crown (600), Third Eye (525), Throat (350), Heart (505), Solar Plexus (275), Sacral or Spleen (275), Base or Root Chakra (200). When we relinquish negative feelings, the energy in our higher chakras increases. For instance, instead of habitually "venting our spleen" (second chakra), we are now described as "all heart" (fifth chakra).

This energy system has a direct impact on the physical body. The energy in each chakra flows out through channels called "meridians" to the whole energy body, which is like a blueprint to the physical body. Each meridian is associated with a particular organ, and each organ is associated with a particular emotion. A negative emotion throws off the energy balance of its associated acupuncture meridian and related organ. For instance, depression, despair, and melancholy are associated with the liver meridian, so these emotions tend to interfere with liver function. Every negative feeling impairs a body organ and, as the years go by, that organ becomes diseased and eventually fails to function.

The lower our emotional state, the more negatively we influence not only our own lives but also all of life around us. The higher the emotional level of evolution, the more positive our life becomes on all levels, and we support all life around us. As negative emotions are acknowledged and surrendered, we get freer and move up the scale, eventually experiencing predominantly positive feelings.

All lower emotions are limitations and blind us to the reality of our true Self. As we surrender our way up the scale and near the top, a new type of experience begins to happen. At the very top of the scale, there occurs the realization of one's true Self and the varying levels of Illumination. The main importance of this is to note that, as we get higher and freer, what the world calls spiritual awareness, intuition, and growth of consciousness occur. This is the common experience of all who surrender their negative feelings. They become more and more conscious. That which is impossible to see or experience at lower levels of consciousness becomes self-evident and stunningly obvious at higher levels.

Understanding Emotions

According to scientific findings, all thoughts are filed in the mind's memory bank under a filing system based upon the associated feeling and its finer gradations (Gray–LaViolette, 1982). They are filed according to feeling tone, not fact. Consequently, there is a scientific basis for the observation that self-awareness is increased much more rapidly by observing feelings rather than thoughts. The thoughts associated with even one feeling may literally run into the thousands. The understanding of the underlying emotion and its correct handling is, therefore, more rewarding and less time-consuming than dealing with one's thoughts.

In the beginning, if one is unfamiliar with the whole subject of feelings, it is often advisable to begin merely by observing them without any intention of doing anything about them. In this way, some clarification will occur about the relationship between feelings and thoughts. After there is more familiarity, some experimentation can then occur. For instance, certain areas of thoughts that tend to recur can be set aside and the feeling associated with them identified. The feeling can then be worked with by first accepting that it is there, without resisting it or condemning it. And then one begins to empty out the energy of the feeling directly by letting it be what it is until it runs out. Somewhat later, the former thoughts can now be looked at and their character will be observed to have changed. If the feeling has been totally surrendered and let go, usually all thoughts associated with it will have disappeared entirely and been replaced by a concluding thought which handles the matter quickly.

For example, there was the case of a man who misplaced his passport shortly before going to a foreign country. As the scheduled date of departure drew closer and closer, his inner panic mounted. His mind raced wildly, trying to think where the passport could have been misplaced. He searched high and low. He tried various mental tricks to no avail. He berated himself: "How could I have been so stupid as to lose a passport? Now there isn't time to get another one!" As the fateful day approached, he faced a real dilemma: no passport, no trip. Missing the trip had a lot of negative consequences because it was both business and pleasure, and it would have created a difficult situation. Finally, he remembered to do the letting go technique.

He sat down and asked himself: "What is the basic feeling that I've been ignoring?" To his surprise, the basic feeling that came up was grief. The grief was associated with not wanting to be separated from someone he dearly loved. There was also an associated fear of loss of the relationship, or at least the weakening of it due to his absence. As he let go of the grief and the associated fear, he suddenly felt at peace about the matter. He also concluded that if the relationship couldn't handle a two-week absence, it wasn't worth all that much anyway; so, there was really nothing at risk. As soon as he felt at peace, he instantly remembered where the passport was. In fact, it was in a place so simple and obvious that only unconscious blocking could explain why he had not remembered it. Needless to say, all of the thousands of thoughts about the missing passport, the failed trip and the potential consequences instantly disappeared. His emotional state became one of gratitude and happiness instead of frustration.

Letting go can be very useful in everyday life situations, but its use in life crises can be crucial in preventing and alleviating large amounts of suffering. In a life crisis there is usually an overwhelm of emotion. The crisis has tapped into one of our major areas of suppressed or repressed feelings. In this situation the problem is not one of identifying the emotion but how to handle the overwhelm.

Handling Emotional Crises

Because this is a very difficult problem for most people, some details are needed. There are several techniques to help move through emotional disaster much more quickly, and with a better end result, than allowing it to run out on its own. Recall the usual mechanisms that the mind consciously uses to handle emotions, which are suppression (or repression), expression, and escape. These are deleterious only when they are used without conscious intent. In an overwhelm, it is often advisable to utilize them, but doing so *consciously*. The purpose of this maneuver is to reduce the sheer overwhelming quantity of the emotion itself so that it can be disassembled and let go of in bits and pieces (this process is described below). Thus, in this case, it is all right *consciously* to push away as much of the emotion as we are capable of at the moment. The emotion can be reduced in intensity by sharing the feeling with close friends or mentors. By merely expressing the feeling, some of the energy behind it is reduced. It is also alright in this circumstance consciously to utilize escape mechanisms, such as going out in a social situation to get some distance from the upset, playing with the dog, watching television, going to the movies, playing music, making love, or whatever one's habit is under the circumstances. When the feeling has been reduced in its sheer quantity and intensity, it is best to start letting go of small aspects of the situation rather than the overall situation and the accompanying emotion itself.

To illustrate this point, let's take the example of a man who loses his job after many years with a company, and is now in an overwhelm of despair. By utilizing the three mechanisms already described, some of the emotion can be reduced. What he can look at, then, are some of the small trivia about the job. For instance, could he let go of wanting to have lunch where he always had lunch with his business colleagues? Could he let go of wanting to park his car in the parking space he always had in the past? Could he let go of wanting to ride up in the same elevator? Could he let go of the attachment to his desk? Could he let go of the attachment to the secretary and her friendliness toward him? Could he let go of the attachment to his computer? Could he let go of seeing the same boss every day? Could he let go of his feeling of familiarity with the background noises in the office?

The purpose of surrendering these smaller aspects of losing a job, which may seem trivial, is that it gets the mind into the letting go mode. The letting go mode takes us up to the level of Courage; the negative feelings have been acknowledged and worked through; consequently, they've lost their charge. Suddenly there is the awareness that we have the courage to face the situation, recognize our feelings, and do something about them. As the trivia are surrendered, curiously, the main event becomes less and less oppressive. The reason for the phenomenon is that, when we use the mechanism of surrender on one emotion, we are surrendering on all emotions at the same time. It is as though all emotions have the same underlying energy, so that to surrender in one direction surrenders feelings which appear, on the surface, to be in an opposite direction. This is a matter of clinical experience; it must be tried personally in order to believe it.

After utilizing the above four methods (suppression, expression, escape, surrender of smaller aspects), a fifth now becomes apparent. Every strong emotion is really a composite of a number of subsidiary emotions and the total emotional complex can be disassembled. Thus, for instance, the man who has lost his job initially has an overwhelming feeling of despair; but, as he begins to surrender around the periphery, and as he diminishes his overwhelm through consciously utilizing escape, suppression, and expression, he now realizes that there is also anger. He sees that the anger is associated with pride. There is a lot of anger in the form of resentment. There is self-invalidation, which is a form of anger expressed against himself. There is also considerable fear. Thus these associated emotions can now be addressed directly. For instance, he can start letting go of the fear that he won't find another job. When that fear is acknowledged and let go, all the alternate possibilities that exist will become suddenly apparent to him. And, as he surrenders pride, he will quickly see that he is not faced with economic disaster, as he had thought. Thus, as the disassembled emotional complex is taken apart into its component parts, each component part now has less energy and can be surrendered individually.

As we come out of the overwhelm, it will be remembered that a certain portion of the emotion was purposely suppressed or escaped. It can now be re-examined, so that it no longer does residual harm, such as ending up in bitterness, unconscious guilt, or lower self-esteem. Fragments of the emotional complex may recur for a period of time, even years; however, because they are now small fragments, each can be handled as it arises. At least the crisis situation will have been passed through safely and consciously.

Handling a crisis from the emotional rather than the intellectual level will shorten its duration dramatically. In the case of someone who loses a job, handling it from the intellectual level will produce thousands of thoughts and hypothetical scenarios. The person suffers through many sleepless nights due to the racing thoughts about the situation as the mind reviews it over and over again. All of this is fruitless. Until the underlying emotion is surrendered, the thoughts will be engendered endlessly. We all know of people who have had an emotional crisis many years ago and, to this day, have not recovered. It has totally colored their life, and they have paid a big price for their lack of know-how in handling the underlying emotions. There are numerous benefits to handling a life crisis successfully. For one thing, the amount of suppressed or repressed emotion is now much less. The crisis has forced it up to be relinquished and, therefore, the amount that is left in the reservoir is much less. There is a greater feeling of self-esteem and confidence because there is the awareness that one can survive and handle whatever life will bring. There is an overall reduction of the fear of life, a greater feeling of mastery, greater compassion for the suffering of others, and an increased ability to help them through similar circumstances. Paradoxically, after a life crisis, there often is a period of variable duration of peace and calmness, sometimes approaching the level of mystical experience. The "dark night of the soul" frequently precedes states of heightened awareness.

One of the best-known examples of this paradox is illustrated by persons who have had near-death experiences. There are now many books on the subject that reveal a certain commonality. Once the worst of all possible fears—the dread and shock of death—has been faced, it is superseded by a profound sense of serenity, peace, oneness, and immunity from fear. Many such persons develop extraordinary abilities, become healers, develop psychic awareness, and advanced states of spiritual illumination. They experience major leaps in growth and the sudden appearance of new talents and capacities. Thus, every life crisis carries within it the kernels of a reversal, a renewal, an expansion, a leap in consciousness, and a letting go of the old and a birth of the new.

Healing the Past

When we look at our lives, we will see the residual of past life crises which are still unresolved. Thoughts and feelings about the events tend to occur and color our perception, and we will note that they have disabled us in certain areas of life. At that point, it is wise to ask ourselves if it is worth paying the continuing cost. Now that we have some mechanisms by which to handle these residuals, they can be uncovered. The residual feelings can be investigated and let go of so that a healing can take place. This brings us to another emotional healing technique that becomes powerful once the major event has passed. That is to place the event in a different context, to see it from a different perspective, and to hold it in a different paradigm with a different significance and meaning.

It is said that most people spend their lives regretting the past and fearing the future; therefore, they are unable to experience joy in the present. Many of us have assumed that this is our human fate, our lot, and the best that we can do is "grin and bear it." Philosophers have sometimes made hay out of this negativistic, pessimistic approach and developed whole systems of nihilism. These philosophers, some of whom have become celebrated over the years, are obviously mere victims of painful emotions that they did not handle and which triggered endless intellectualization and elaboration. Some spent their entire lifetime constructing sophisticated intellectual systems to justify what is glaringly obvious as a simple suppressed emotion.

One of the most effective tools for handling the past is the creation of a different context. What this means is that we give it a different meaning. We take on a different attitude about the past difficulty or trauma, and we acknowledge the hidden gift in it. The value of this technique was first recognized in psychiatry by Viktor Frankl. He explained the approach—which he called "Logotherapy"—in his famous book, *Man's Search for Meaning*. His clinical and personal experience demonstrated that emotional events and traumatic occurrences will change considerably and be healed if a new meaning is placed around them. Frankl told of his own experience in the Nazi concentration camps wherein he came to see his physical and psychic suffering as an opportunity to achieve inner triumph. "Everything can be taken from a man but one thing: the last of the human freedoms—to choose one's attitude in any given set of circumstances, to choose one's own way" (Frankl, [1959] 2006). Frankl re-contextualized the horrific circumstances to hold profound meaning for the human spirit.

Every life experience, no matter how "tragic," contains a hidden lesson. When we discover and acknowledge the hidden gift that is there, a healing takes place. In the example of the man who lost his job, after some time had passed, he looked back and saw that his former job was stunting, that he had been in a rut. Frankly, the job had given him an ulcer. Prior to losing the job, he had seen only the pleasures from it. Once outside of the situation, he began to see the costs that he had been paying—physically, mentally, and emotionally. After losing the job, he was open to discovering new abilities and new talents; in fact, he began a new, more promising career.

So, life events are opportunities to grow, expand, experience, and develop. In some cases, it seems in retrospect that there was actually this unconscious purpose behind the event, as though our unconscious knew that something important had to be learned and, painful as it was, it was the only way it could be brought into experience. This is part of the psychology of the psychoanalyst Carl Jung, who concluded after a lifetime of study, that there is an inborn drive in the unconscious toward wholeness, completeness, and realization of the Self, and that the unconscious will devise the ways and means of bringing this about, even if they are traumatic to the conscious mind.

Jung also said that in the unconscious there was an aspect of ourselves called the "shadow." The shadow is all the repressed thoughts, feelings and concepts about ourselves that we do not want to face. One benefit of a crisis is that it often brings us into familiarity with our shadow. It makes us more human and more whole to realize what we share with all of humanity. All the stuff that we thought "they" were guilty of is equally in ourselves. Thus, when it is brought up to conscious awareness, acknowledged, and surrendered, it no longer unconsciously runs us. Once the shadow has been acknowledged, it loses its power. All that is necessary is merely to recognize that we have certain forbidden impulses, thoughts, and feelings. Now, they can be handled with a "So what?"

Passing through a life crisis, then, makes us more human, more compassionate, more accepting and understanding of ourselves and others. We no longer have to indulge in making others wrong or making ourselves wrong. Handling an emotional crisis leads to greater wisdom and results in lifetime benefits. Fear of life is really the fear of emotions. It is not the facts that we fear but our feelings about them. Once we have mastery over our feelings, our fear of life diminishes. We feel a greater self-confidence, and we are willing to take greater chances because we now feel that we can handle the emotional consequences, whatever they might be. Because fear is the basis of all inhibitions, mastery over fear means the unblocking of whole avenues of life experience that previously had been avoided.

Thus, the man who successfully handles the crisis of losing a job will never again experience that same fear. He will, therefore, be more creative on the next job, willing to take the necessary risks to make it a success. He begins to see how that haunting fear of job loss had severely limited his performance in the past, made him fearful and cautious, and cost him his self-esteem due to his kowtowing and compliance with his superiors.

One benefit from a life crisis is greater self-awareness. The situation is overwhelming, and we are forced to stop all of our diversionary games, take a good look at our life situation, and re-evaluate our beliefs, goals, values, and life direction. It is an opportunity to re-evaluate and let go of guilt. It is also an opportunity for a total shift in attitude. Life crises, as we pass through them, confront us with polar opposites. Shall we hate or forgive that person? Shall we learn from this experience and grow, or resent it and become bitter? Do we choose to overlook the other person's shortcomings and our own, or instead do we resent and mentally attack them? Shall we withdraw from a similar situation in the future with greater fear, or shall we transcend this crisis and master it once and for all? Do we choose hope or discouragement? Can we use the experience as an opportunity to learn how to share, or shall we withdraw into a shell of fear and bitterness? Every emotional experience is an opportunity to go up or down. Which do we choose? That is the confrontation.

We have the opportunity to choose whether we want to hang on or let go of emotional upsets. We can look at the cost of hanging on to them. Do we want to pay the price? Are we willing to accept the feelings? We can look at the benefits of letting go of them. The choice we make will determine our future. What kind of a future do we want? Will we choose to be healed, or will we become one of the walking wounded?

In making this choice, it is well to look at the payoff we get from hanging on to the residuals of a painful experience. What are the satisfactions we are getting? How little are we willing to settle for? Anger. Hatred. Self-pity. Resentments. They all have their cheap little payoff, that little inner satisfaction. Let's not pretend that it's not there. There is a weird, quirky pleasure when we hang on to pain. It certainly satisfies our unconscious need for the alleviation of guilt through punishment. We get to feel miserable and rotten. The question then arises, "But for how long?"

Take, for example, a man who had not spoken to his brother for twenty-three years. Neither of them could remember what the incident was about; it had been long forgotten. But they were in the habit of not speaking, and so for twenty-three years they paid the price of missing each other's company, affection, togetherness in family matters, and all the shared experiences and love they could have had. When the man learned about the mechanism of surrender, he began to let go of his feelings about his brother. Suddenly, he broke out in tears of grief, realizing all that had been lost over the years. By forgiving his brother, he triggered a similar response in the brother, and the two were reunited. Then, one of the brothers flashed back on the incident. It had been an argument over a pair of tennis shoes. Over one pair of tennis shoes they had paid a price extending over twenty-three years! Had the man not learned the technique of letting go, he might well have gone to his grave with the same resentment. So the question is, "How long do we want to go on suffering? When are we willing to give it up? When is enough enough?"

The part of us that wants to cling to negative emotions is our smallness. It is the part of us that is mean, petty, selfish, competitive, cheap, conniving, mistrusting, vindictive, judgmental, diminished, weak, guilty, ashamed, and vain. It has little energy; it is depleting, demeaning, and leads to the lowering of self-respect. It is the small part of us that accounts for our own self-hatred, unending guilt, and seeking for punishment, sickness, and disease. Is that the part with which we want to identify? Is that the part we want to energize? Is that the way we want to see ourselves? Because if that's the way we see ourselves, that's the way others will see us.

The world can only see us as we see ourselves. Are we willing to pay those consequences? If we see ourselves as cheap and petty, it's unlikely that we'll be at the top of the company list for a raise.

The price of holding on to smallness can be demonstrated with muscle testing. The procedure is fairly simple (Hawkins, [1995], 2012). Hold in mind a mean, petty thought and have someone press down on your arm while you resist; notice the effect. Now choose the exact opposite view. Picture yourself as being generous, forgiving, loving, and experiencing your inner greatness. Instantly, there will be an enormous increase in muscle strength indicating a surge of positive bio-energy. Smallness brings weakness, sickness, disease, and death. Do you really want that? Letting go of negative feelings can be accompanied by another very healthy maneuver which will greatly assist your inner transformation, and that is to stop resisting the positive emotions.

Enhancing Positive Emotions

The corollary to letting go of negative feelings is to stop resisting the positive ones. Everything in the universe has its opposite; therefore, in the mind, every negative feeling has its counterpart between smallness and greatness, whether we are constantly aware of its existence at any given moment or not.

A good and very illuminating exercise is to sit down and look at the feeling that is directly opposite the negative one that we are experiencing and begin to let go resisting it. Let's say, for instance, that a friend's birthday is coming up and we are feeling resentful and stingy; therefore, we just can't seem to get out to shop for a present, and the day is getting closer. The exact opposite feelings are those of forgiveness and generosity. We just start looking for the feeling of forgiveness within ourselves and stop resisting it. As we keep letting go of our resistance to being a forgiving person, it is often surprising that it will come up with a surge. We will begin to recognize that part of our nature has always been willing and wanting to forgive, but we didn't dare chance it. We thought we might appear foolish. We thought we were punishing the other person by holding the resentment, but we have actually been suppressing love. In the beginning, we may not consciously feel this specifically about our friend, but we will begin to notice that we do have this aspect to our personality. As we keep surrendering our resistance to love, we will notice that within ourselves there is something that wants to express itself through sharing and giving, letting the past go and burying the hatchet. There is a desire to make a friendly gesture; we want to heal the separation, to repair the wound, to make good the wrong, to express gratitude, and to take a chance on being thought a fool.

The purpose of this exercise is to locate within ourselves that which can only be described as greatness. Greatness is the courage to overcome obstacles. It is the willingness to move to a higher level of love. It is the acceptance of others' humanness and having compassion for their suffering by putting ourselves in their shoes. Out of the forgiveness of others come self-forgiveness and the relief of guilt. The real payoff we get is when we let go of our negativity and choose to be loving; we are the ones who benefit. We are the ones who gain from the real payoff. With this increased awareness of who we really are comes the progressive invulnerability to pain. Once we compassionately accept our own humanness and that of others, we are no longer subject to humiliation, for true humility is a part of greatness.

Out of the recognition of who we really are comes the desire to seek that which is uplifting. Out of it arises a new meaning and context for life. When that inner emptiness, due to lack of self-worth, is replaced by true self-love, self-respect and esteem, we no longer have to seek it in the world, for that source of happiness is within ourselves. It dawns on us that it cannot be supplied by the world anyway. No amount of riches can compensate for an inner feeling of poverty. We all know of the many multimillionaires who try to compensate for their inner sense of hollowness and lack of inner worth. Once we have contacted this inner Self, this inner greatness, this inner completion, contentment, and true sense of happiness, we have transcended the world. The world is now a place to enjoy, and we are no longer run by it. We are no longer at the effect of it.

When we utilize these techniques of relinquishing the negative and surrendering resistance to the positive, sooner or later we come into a sudden, comprehensive awareness of our true dimension. Once this has been experienced, it will never be forgotten. The world will never intimidate us again as it once did. There may be continued compliance with the ways of the world out of sheer habit, but the inner drivenness, the inner vulnerability, and the inner doubt is now gone. Outwardly, the behavior may appear the same but, inwardly, the causes for it are now totally different. The end result of the conscious handling of emotions is invulnerability and imperturbability. Our inner nature is now bullet proof. We are able to go through life with balance and grace.

4

APATHY AND DEPRESSION

Apathy is the belief, "I can't." It is the feeling that we cannot do anything about our situation and no one else can help. It is hopelessness and helplessness. It is associated with such thoughts as: "Who cares?"; "What's the use?"; "It's boring"; "Why bother?"; "I can't win anyway." This is the role exhibited by Eeyore, the glum character in "Winnie the Pooh" cartoons who says: "Oh well. Won't do any good anyway." Discouragement. Defeat. Impossible. Too hard. All alone. Give up. Isolated. Estranged. Withdrawn. Cut off. Desolate. Depressed. Depleted. Unfulfilling. Pessimistic. Careless. Humorless. Meaningless. Absurd. Pointless. Helpless. Failure. Too tired. Despair. Confused. Forgetful. Fatalistic. Too late. Too old. Too young. Mechanical. Doomed. Negative. Forlorn. Useless. Lost. Senseless. Bleak. Blasé.

The biologic purpose of apathy is to summon aid, but part of the feeling is that no help is possible. Much of the world's population is functioning on the level of apathy. For them, there is no hope that they will be able to meet their basic needs, nor will help be forthcoming from elsewhere.

The average person is often apathetic in a number

of areas in life, but only periodically faces overwhelming apathy about their whole life situation. Apathy indicates a lack of life energy and is close to death. This was observed during the World War II blitz of London. Infants were removed to nurseries and remote safe sections of England where their physical, nutritional, and medical needs were well attended. However, the infants developed apathy and began to fail; they lost their appetites and the death rate was high. It was discovered that apathy resulted from a lack of nurturing and emotional closeness to a mothering figure. It was an emotional state and not a physical one. Without love and affection, they lost the will to live.

In our country, we see depressed economic areas where an entire local population goes into apathy. When people from such areas appear on the television news, it is often with such comments as, "When the welfare check runs out, I guess we just face starvation; there's no hope for us."

Feelings of apathy about the letting go technique itself may appear as resistances. These may take the form of attitudes and thoughts such as: "It won't work anyway"; "What's the difference?"; "I'm not ready for this yet"; "I can't feel"; "I'm too busy"; "I'm tired of letting go"; "I'm too overwhelmed"; "I forgot"; "I'm too depressed"; "I'm too sleepy." The way out of apathy is to remind ourselves of our intention, which is to get higher and freer, to become more effective and happy, and to let go of the resistance to the technique itself.

"I Can't" vs. "I Won't"

Another way out of apathy is to look at the payoff we are getting out of the apathetic attitudes. The payoff may be in the face-saving excuses to cover up what is actually fear. Since in reality, we are very capable beings, most "I can'ts" are really "I won'ts." Behind the "I can'ts" or the "I won'ts" is frequently a fear. Then, when we look at the truth of what is behind the feeling, we have already moved up the scale from apathy to fear. Fear is a higher energy state than apathy. Fear at least begins to motivate us into action and, in that action, we can again surrender fear and move up to anger or pride or courage, all of which are higher states than apathy.

Let's take a typical human problem and trace how the mechanism of surrender works to free us from an inhibition. Public speaking is one of the most common inhibitions. On the level of apathy in this arena, we say: "Oh, I can't possibly speak in public. It is way too overwhelming. Nobody will want to hear me anyway. I don't have anything worth saying." If we remind ourselves of our intention, we will see that the apathy is merely covering up fear. Now, the thought of speaking in public is frightening, not hopeless. This brings about a certain clarity. The facts are not that we "can't," but merely that we are "afraid."

As this fear comes up and is let go, we become aware of the fact that we have a desire to do the very thing that we fear. Now when looking at the desire, which is blocked by fear and perhaps compounded by some grief over lost opportunities in the past, anger arises. At this point, we have already moved from apathy, to grief, to desire, and up to anger. In anger there is much more energy and capacity for action. Anger often takes the form of resentment, such as resentment that we agreed to the public speaking and now feel obligated to do it.

There is also anger about our fear, which has blocked accomplishment in the past, and the anger leads to a decision to do something about it. This decision might take the form of a public speaking course. When we sign up for a public speaking course, we have already moved up to the energy of pride in that we have finally taken the bull by the horns and are doing something about it. On the way to the speaking course, again more fear will arise. As this is constantly acknowledged and surrendered, we become aware that we have courage in our capacity at least to face our fears and take action to overcome them.

The level of courage has a lot of energy. That energy takes the form of letting go of residual fear, anger, and desire, so that in the middle of the speaking class, we suddenly experience acceptance. With acceptance there is the freedom from resistance, which had taken the form previously of fear, apathy, and anger. Now, we begin to experience pleasure. There is the self-confidence of acceptance, "I can do it." On the level of acceptance, there is greater awareness of others, so that in the speaking class, we become aware of the pain, suffering, and embarrassment of others in the class and begin to be concerned about them.

With the emergence of this compassion towards others, there is a loss of self-consciousness. With the emergence of selflessness come moments of peace. On the way home from the class, we experience an inner contentment, a feeling that we have grown, that we have shared with others. In the experience of sharing, we have forgotten ourselves for a few moments and have been more concerned with the happiness of someone else. We take pleasure in the accomplishments of others. In this state, there is a transforming grace, the discovery of our inner compassion, a feeling of connectedness with others, and a compassion for their suffering. With the full development of this progression, we might then share with others how we had a fear of public speaking, the steps we took to overcome it, the success we experienced, the increase of our self-esteem, and the positive changes in our relationships.

This entire progression is the basis of a great deal of the power of self-help groups: the sharing of inner experiences from the lowest to the highest levels on the scale of emotions. That which in the beginning seemed formidable and overwhelming has now been surmounted and handled, with the resultant increase of aliveness and well-being. This increase in self-esteem then spills over into other areas of life, and the increase in confidence results in greater material abundance and capability in vocational functioning. On this level, love takes the form of sharing and encouraging others, and our activities are constructive instead of destructive. The energy radiated out is then positive and attractive to others, resulting in a constant positive feedback.

Once we have experienced this progression up the scale of emotions in any one particular area, we now begin to realize that it can be done in other areas of limitation in our lives. Behind all of the "I can'ts" are merely "I won'ts." The "I won'ts" mean "I am afraid to" or "I am ashamed to" or "I have too much pride to try, for fear I might fail." Behind that is anger at ourselves and circumstances engendered by pride. Acknowledging and letting go of these feelings brings us up to courage and, with that, finally acceptance and an inner peacefulness, at least as it regards the area which has been surmounted.

Apathy and depression are the prices we pay for having settled for and bought into our smallness. It's what we get for having played the victim and allowed ourselves to be programmed. It's the price we pay for having bought into negativity. It's what results from resisting the part of ourselves that is loving, courageous, and great. It results from allowing ourselves to be invalidated by ourselves or others; it is the consequence of holding ourselves in a negative context. In reality, it is only a definition of ourselves that we have unwittingly allowed to happen. The way out is to become more conscious.

What does it mean, "to become more conscious"? To begin with, becoming more conscious means to start looking for the truth for ourselves, instead of blindly allowing ourselves to be programmed, whether from without or by an inner voice within the mind, which seeks to diminish and invalidate, focusing on all that is weak and helpless. To get out of it, we have to accept the responsibility that we have bought into the negativity and have been willing to believe it. The way out of this, then, is to start questioning *everything*.

There are many models of the mind. One of the most recent has been that of the computer. We can look at the mind's concepts, thoughts, and belief systems as programs. Because they are programs, they can be questioned, cancelled, and reversed; positive programs can replace negative ones if we so choose. The smaller aspect of ourselves is very willing to accept negative programming.

If we look at the source of our thoughts, begin to identify their origins, and stop the vanity of labeling them as "mine" (and therefore sacrosanct), we notice that thoughts can be looked at objectively. We see that their origins were often the early childhood training from parents, family, and teachers, as well as dribbles and drabbles of information we picked up from playmates, newspapers, movies, television, radio, church, novels, and the automatic input from our senses. All of this went on unwittingly without our having exercised any conscious choice. Not only that, but out of our unconsciousness, ignorance, innocence, and naïveté, plus the nature of the mind itself, we ended up as the composite of all the negative garbage prevalent in the world. Furthermore, we concluded that it applied to us personally. As we become more aware, we begin to realize that we have a choice. We can stop giving authority to all the mind's thoughts, begin to question them, and find out if there is really any truth in them for ourselves.

The feeling state of apathy is associated with the belief, "I can't." The mind doesn't like to hear it, but in reality most "I can'ts" are "I won'ts." The reason the mind doesn't want to hear this is because "I can't" is a cover-up for other feelings. These feelings can be brought to awareness by posing the hypothetical question to oneself, "Is it true that I *won't* rather than that I *can't*? If I accept that 'I won't,' what situations will be brought up and how do I feel about them?"

As an example, let's say we have a belief system that we can't dance. We say to ourselves: "Perhaps that's a cover-up. Maybe the truth is that I don't want to and I won't." The way we can find out what the feelings are is to envision ourselves as going through the process of learning to dance. As we do that, all of the associated feelings now start to come up: embarrassment, pride, awkwardness, the sheer effort of learning a new skill, and the reluctance about the time and energy involved. As we replace "I can't" with "I won't," we uncover all of these feelings, which can then be surrendered. We see that learning to dance means we have to be willing to let go of pride. We look at the cost and ask ourselves, "Am I willing to continue to pay this price? Would I be willing to let go of the fear of not succeeding? Would I be willing to let go of resisting the effort required? Would I be willing to let go of the vanity so that I could allow myself to be awkward as a learner? Could I let go of my stinginess and smallness and be willing to pay for the lessons and give the time?" As all of the associated feelings are surrendered, it becomes very clear that the real reason is unwillingness—not incapacity.

It must be remembered that we are free to acknowledge and surrender our feelings, and we are free not to surrender. As we examine our "I can'ts" and find out that they are really "I won'ts," it doesn't mean that we have to let go of the negative feelings that result in the "I won'ts." We are perfectly free to refuse to let go. We are free to hang on to negativity as long as we want. There is no law that says we have to give it up. We are free agents. But it makes a big difference in our self-concept to realize that "I won't do something" is quite a different feeling than to think that "I'm a victim and I can't." For instance, we can choose to hate somebody if we want. We can choose to blame them. We can choose to blame circumstances. But being more conscious and realizing that we are freely choosing this attitude puts us in a higher state of consciousness and, therefore, closer to greater power and mastery than being the helpless victim of a feeling.

Blame

One of the biggest blocks to overcome in getting out of depression and apathy is that of blame. Blame is a whole subject in itself. Looking into it is rewarding. To begin with, there are a lot of payoffs to blame. We get to be innocent; we get to enjoy self-pity; we get to be the martyr and the victim; and we get to be the recipients of sympathy.

Perhaps the biggest payoff of blame is that we get to be the innocent victim and the other party is the bad one. We see this game played out in the media constantly, such as the endless blame games dramatized in a multitude of controversies, mudslinging, character assassinations, and lawsuits. In addition to the emotional payoff, blame has considerable financial benefits; therefore, it is a tempting package to be the innocent victim, as it is often financially rewarded.

There was a famous example of this in New York City many years ago. A public conveyance accident occurred. People poured out of the front door of the vehicle, then gathered in a small crowd, furnishing their names and addresses for future financial benefit. Bystanders quickly caught on to the game and secretly climbed into the back of the vehicle, so that they could then emerge from the front as injured, "innocent victims." They hadn't even been in the accident, but they were going to collect a reward!

Blame is the world's greatest excuse. It enables us to remain limited and small without feeling guilty. But there is a cost—the loss of our freedom. Also, the role of victim brings with it a self-perception of weakness, vulnerability, and helplessness, which are the major components of apathy and depression.

The first step out of blame is to see that we are *choosing* to blame. Other people who have had similar circumstances have forgiven, forgotten, and handled the same situation in a totally different way. We earlier saw the case of Viktor Frankl, who chose to forgive the Nazi prison guards and to see a hidden gift in his experience at the concentration camps. Because others, such as Frankl, have chosen not to blame, that option is also open to us. We have to be honest and realize that we are blaming because we choose to blame. This is true, no matter how justified the circumstances may appear to be. It is not a matter of right or wrong; it is merely a matter of taking responsibility for our own consciousness. It is a totally different situation to see that we *choose* to blame rather than to think that we *have* to blame. In this circumstance, the mind often thinks, "Well, if the other person or event is not to blame, then *I* must be." Blaming others or ourselves is simply not necessary.

The attraction of blame arises in early childhood as a daily occurrence in the classroom, playground, and at home among siblings. Blame is the central issue in the endless court proceedings and lawsuits that characterize our society. In truth, blame is just another one of the negative programs that we have allowed our mind to buy because we never stopped to question it. Why must something always be someone's "fault"? Why must the whole concept of "wrong" be introduced to the situation in the first place? Why must one of us be wrong, bad, or at fault? What seemed like a good idea at the time may not have turned out well. That's all. Unfortunate events may have just happened.

To overcome blame, it is necessary to look at the secret satisfaction and enjoyment we get out of self-pity, resentment, anger, and self-excuses, and to begin to surrender all of these little payoffs. The purpose of this step is to move up from being a victim of our feelings to choosing to have them. If we merely acknowledge and observe them, begin to disassemble them, and surrender the component parts, then we are consciously exercising choice. In this way, we make a major move out of the morass of helplessness.

It is helpful in overcoming resistance and taking responsibility for our negative programs and feelings to see that they come from the small aspect of ourselves. It is the very nature of the smallest part of ourselves to think negatively, so there's an unconscious tendency to agree readily to its limited viewpoint. But that is not the whole of our beingness; for outside and beyond the smaller self is our greater Self. We may not be conscious of our inner greatness. We may not be experiencing it, but it is there. If we let go of our resistance to it, we can begin to experience it. Depression and apathy, therefore, result from the willingness to hang on to the small self and its belief systems, plus the resistance to our Higher Self, which consists of all of the opposites of the negative feelings.

It is the nature of the universe that everything in it is represented by its equal and opposite. Thus, the electron's equal and opposite is the positron. Every force has an equal and opposite counter-force. Yin is compensated for by Yang. There is fear but there is also courage. There is hatred but its opposite is love. There is timidity but there is also bravery. There is stinginess but also generosity. In the human psyche, every feeling has its opposite. The way out of negativity is, therefore, the willingness to acknowledge and let go of negative feelings and, at the same time, the

willingness to let go of resisting their positive opposite. Depression and apathy are the result of being at
the effect of the negative polarity. How does this work
in everyday life?

Let's look again at the example of someone's birthday that is approaching quickly. Because of things that
have happened in the past, we have resentments and
feel unwilling to do anything for the birthday. Somehow, it just seems impossible to get out and shop for a
birthday present. We resent having to spend the
money. The mind conjures up all kinds of justifica-
tions: "I don't have time to shop"; "I can't forget how
mean she was"; "She should apologize to me first." In
this case, two things are operating: clinging to the negative and the smallness in ourselves, and resisting the
positive and the greatness in ourselves. The way out
of apathy is to see, first of all, that "I can't" is an "I
won't." In looking at the "I won't," we see that it is
there because of negative feelings and, as they come
up, they can be acknowledged and let go. It is also
apparent that we are resisting positive feelings. These
feelings of love, generosity, and forgiveness can be
looked at one by one.

We can sit down and imagine the quality of generosity and let go resisting it. Is there something generous within ourselves? In this case, we may not be
willing to apply it to the birthday person in the beginning. What we can begin to see is the existence of such
a quality as generosity within our consciousness. We
begin to see that, as we let go resisting the feeling of
generosity, there is generosity. We do, in fact, enjoy giving to others under certain circumstances. We begin to
remember the positive flood of feeling that comes upon
us when we express gratitude and acknowledge the

gifts that others have given us. We see that we have really been suppressing a desire to forgive and, as we let go of the resistance to being forgiving, there emerges the willingness to let go of the grievance. As we do this, we stop identifying with our small self and become consciously aware that there is something in us that is greater. It is always there but hidden from view.

This process is applicable in all negative situations. It enables us to change the context by which we perceive our current situation. It enables us to give it a new and different meaning. It lifts us up from being the helpless victim to the conscious chooser. In the example given, it doesn't mean that we have to rush out and buy a birthday gift. But it does mean that we are now aware that we are in our current position out of choice. We have total freedom, with greater latitude of action and choice. This is a much higher state of consciousness than the helpless victim who is trapped by a past resentment.

One of the laws of consciousness is: *We are only subject to a negative thought or belief if we consciously say that it applies to us.* We are free to choose not to buy into a negative belief system.

How does this work in everyday life? Let's take a common example. The newspapers report unemployment is at a record high. The television news commentator states: "No jobs are available." At this point, we are free to refuse to buy into the negative thought form. We can say instead, "Unemployment does not apply to me." By refusing to accept the negative belief, it now has no hold over our own life.

Examples from personal experience reveal that, during periods of high unemployment such as after World War II, there was no problem getting a job. As a matter of fact, one could have two or even three jobs at the same time: dishwasher, waiter, bellhop, cab driver, bartender, factory worker, greenhouse worker, and window-washer. This was the consequence of a belief system that said: "Unemployment applies to others but not to me," and "Where there's a will, there's a way." There was also a willingness to relinquish pride in return for employment.

Another example is that of belief systems having to do with epidemic diseases. A few years ago, fourteen acquaintances were observed closely during an epidemic of flu. Of the fourteen people, eight came down with the flu, but six did not. What is important here is not that eight people came down with the flu, but that six did not! In any epidemic, there are people who do not "catch it." Even during the depths of the depression, there were still people who became wealthy and even millionaires. The thought of poverty was "catching" in those days, but somehow those people did not buy into it; therefore, it did not apply to them. For negativity to apply to our life, we must first subscribe to it and, secondly, give it the energy of belief. If we have the power to make negativity manifest in our life, obviously our mind also has the power to make its converse come true.

Choosing the Positive

One surprising effect of the willingness to let go of our inner negativity is the discovery that the polar opposite of the negative feelings exists. There is an inner reality that we can term our "inner greatness" or "Higher Self." It has much more power than the inner negativity. In return for letting go of the payoffs that we were

getting from the negative position, we are now surprised by the positive payoffs that stem from the
power of our positive feelings. For example, when we
let go of blame, we experience forgiveness.

Our Higher Self, which we might say is the composite of our higher feelings, has almost unlimited
capabilities. It can create employment opportunities. It
can create situations for the healing of relationships. It
has the power to create the opportunity for loving
relationships, financial opportunities, and physical
healing. As we stop giving authority and energy to all
of the negative programs that stem from our own
thinking, we stop giving away our power to others
and begin to own it back again. This results in a rise of
self-esteem, the return of creativity, and the opening of
a positive vision of the future that replaces fearfulness.

We can experiment with someone with whom we
have a poor relationship due to our holding of resentments. We can sit down and say to ourselves that this
will merely be an experiment. The purpose for this,
we tell ourselves, is strictly to learn; that is, we want to
become familiar with the laws of consciousness and to
watch the phenomena that occur. We acknowledge the
payoffs we have been getting from our negative feelings. We surrender each component and, at the same
time, let go resisting that within us which would be
willing to heal the relationship. At this point, it is not
necessary to have any personal contact with the other
person. We are doing this experiment for our own
sake and not for them.

As we look within ourselves, we ask, "What is the
anger covering up?" Underneath the anger, we are
likely to find fear. Aside from the fear, we also find
jealousy. We find competitiveness and all the other lit-

tle components of the feeling complex that have blocked the relationship. The simultaneous letting go of the negative and letting go of resisting the positive result in a shift of inner energies, and there is an accompanying subtle change in our self-esteem. Letting go of our resistance to the willingness to have something positive happen in the relationship is all that is necessary. We can then just sit back and watch what occurs. In this experiment, we are not interested in whether or not the other person "gets it." We are only interested that *we* get it. We are only interested in moving our own position in the matter and, then, we just watch what happens. A very rewarding experience usually ensues, which will take different forms depending on the circumstances.

Another cause for apathy is the residual of a previously experienced traumatic overwhelm which has not been resolved. The mind projects on to the future with the expectation that the past will be repeated. When we discover this unconscious dynamic, we can choose to look again at the emotional complex, disassemble it into its component parts, let go of the negative aspects, and let go of our resistance to the positive ones. As we do this, our perspective of the future changes. We can forgive ourselves that, at the time of the previous emotional overwhelm, we simply didn't know how to handle it. There were a lot of residuals that left us emotionally disabled at that time. But, because in the unconscious mind there is no such thing as time, we can choose at any time in the present to heal the past event. As we go through our own emotional healing for our own sake, that past event now begins to take on a different meaning. Our Higher Self begins to create a new context for it. We can see the hidden gift. We can end up acknowledging with gratitude that it gave us a new opportunity to learn, to grow, and to acquire wisdom.

One of the most common areas in which we see this emotional crippling is after divorce. All too often it is followed by bitterness and the impaired capacity to create a new loving relationship. The unwillingness to let go of the blame continues the emotional crippling, which can go on for years, or even a lifetime.

When we come upon bitterness, what we have really discovered is an unhealed area in our own emotional makeup, and the effort that we put into healing it will bring enormous rewards. In any situation which involves suffering, we have to ask ourselves: "How long am I willing to pay the cost? What were the karmic propensities to begin with? How much blame is enough? Is there a time to call an end to it? How long will I hang on to it? How much sacrifice am I willing to pay to the other person for their wrongs, real or imaginary? How much guilt is enough? How much self-punishment is enough? When will I give up the secret pleasure of the self-punishment? When does the sentence come to an end?" When we really examine it, we will always find that we have been punishing ourselves for ignorance, naïveté, innocence, and lack of inner education.

We can ask ourselves: "When was I ever trained in the techniques of emotional self-healing? When I went to school, did they teach me courses on consciousness? Did anybody ever tell me that I had the freedom to choose what went into my mind? Was I ever taught that I could refuse all of the negative programming? Did anybody ever tell me the laws of consciousness?" If not, why beat ourselves up about having innocently believed certain things? Why not stop beating our-selves up right now?

We all did what we thought was best in the moment. "It seemed like a good idea at the time" is what we can say about our past actions and those of others. We've all been unwittingly programmed without our conscious assent. Out of our confusion, ignorance, and naïveté, we bought into the negative programs. We let them run us. But now we can choose to stop. We can choose a different direction. We can choose to become more aware, more conscious, more responsible, and more discerning. We can refuse to sit there like a blank tape recorder, taking in every program the world hands us. The world is only too willing to exploit our naiveté and play upon our smallness, with all of its vanities and fears.

When we become aware of how we were manipulated, exploited, and taken in, anger is going to come up. Be ready to handle it. It's okay to be angry. It's better to be angry than apathetic by a long shot. In anger, we have a lot of energy. We can do something about it. We can take action. We can change our mind. We can reverse direction. Then, it's easy to jump from anger to courage. On the level of courage, we can see it, examine it, and observe how it all happens.

We begin to see that our smallness was a bill of goods that we bought. In that investigation, we will stumble upon our own inner innocence. When we rediscover it, we can let go of a lot of guilt. When the guilt goes, necessity for self-punishment goes with it, and that lifts us right out of apathy and depression. We can choose to revalidate ourselves, our value, and our worth. And we can see how others were programmed just as we were. They, too, were doing what they thought was best at the time. We don't have to blame them or ourselves any more. We can give up the whole blame game as obsolete and ineffectual.

The Company We Keep

Another valuable technique for getting out of apathy, depression, and situations which are predominantly being run by the thought, "I can't," is to choose to be with other persons who have resolved the problem with which we struggle. This is one of the great powers of self-help groups. When we are in a negative state, we have given a lot of energy to negative thought forms, and the positive thought forms are weak. Those who are in a higher vibration are free of the energy from their negative thoughts and have energized positive thought forms. Merely to be in their presence is beneficial. In some self-help groups, this is called "hanging out with the winners." The benefit here is on the psychic level of consciousness, and there is a transfer of positive energy and relighting of one's own latent positive thought forms. In some self-help groups this is called "getting it by osmosis." It is not necessary to know *how* it happens, but merely that it *does* happen.

It is common to witness this phenomenon. For instance, in our society most people have been trained to be logical and left-brained in their orientation. However, some people from birth are right-brain oriented. Such right-brain persons are characterized by greater powers of intuition, creativity, telepathic communication, and awareness of thought forms and energy vibrations. Frequently included among these capabilities is the capacity to see the bio-energy field around the human body called the aura. When in the presence of people with this capacity, it becomes possible to share that capacity.

This was true even as a skeptical, logical, left-brain male scientist who was in the company of people with a capacity to see auras. Upon following their instructions on how to see the aura, surprisingly, there was indeed a visible field of light around people's heads. In particular, the aura around one man seemed to be almost like "ectoplasm" hung predominantly over his left ear. On the right side of the head, however, there was practically nothing to be seen. To know whether this phenomenon was real and not coming from the imagination, it was confirmed by poking someone nearby who was adept at seeing auras. She also saw an aura that was very wide on one side and practically absent on the other.

The capacity to see auras was available only when in the presence of others with that capacity. Upon leaving the instructional situation where there had been people who could see auras, the capacity was no longer there. In the following years, when in the company of friends who could see auras, the capacity returned. One time, in the presence of a woman psychologist at a clinic—whose job was that of psychic diagnosis by means of observing people's auras and their changing color patterns—there suddenly was the capacity not only to see auras, but also to see them in their scintillating colors and watch the aura change in response to fluctuating emotions. Just by talking with her, that capacity was suddenly available.

It is as though when we are in the proximity of the auras of people with certain capacities, some transfer of ability can take place. Simply put, we are either positively or negatively influenced by the company we keep. It is unlikely that we will overcome an inhibition if we choose to be in the company of others who have our same problem.

This phenomenon was evident in the case of a divorced woman who came for a consultation. She wanted to know whether or not she should have psychotherapy. Her complaints were a recurrent ulcer and migraine headaches. As the story unfolded, great bitterness over an unfortunately traumatic divorce came forth. She had joined a consciousness-raising feminist group, she said. She described this particular group as almost completely made up of divorced women who were bitter, angry, and hateful of men. As a group, they were getting a lot of payoff from their negativity. In reality, their lives were forlorn and rather pathetic, as they struggled to regain their self-esteem through extremes and marked emotional imbalance.

After listening to her story and investigating her life circumstances, it was suggested that instead of psychotherapy, she follow one simple recommendation for a period of three months. If it didn't work, then, she could reassess the need for psychotherapy. The recommendation was merely to discontinue her association with the group and with her bitter, divorced friends and, instead, seek the company of people who had successfully re-established relationships despite former divorces.

At first she resisted and claimed that she had nothing in common with these group members. Then she acknowledged two basic facts. First, it was far more energy-saving to foster relationships with positive people. Secondly, one of the laws of consciousness is that "like goes to like"; bitterness attracts bitterness, whereas love attracts love. She asked herself, "Where has my bitterness taken me? Have I gotten anything out of it that is positive and helpful?" As time progressed, she stopped spending time with her group and began to pursue relationships with healthier, more balanced people.

In the company of happier people, she had an exhilarated awareness of how much negativity she was holding inside of herself. She began to be aware that she was consciously holding negativity and choosing to hold it, and she began to look at the cost of such negativity. Her whole social life changed. She became smiling and happier. Her migraine headaches disappeared. Eventually, she fell in love again and joked that falling in love was the best cure she had ever discovered for an ulcer!

If we find ourselves in the state of apathy, we can discover the underlying program by asking ourselves what we are trying to prove. Are we trying to prove that life is rotten? That this is a hopeless world? That it wasn't our fault? That one can't find love? That happiness is impossible? What are we trying to justify? How much are we willing to pay to be "right"? As we acknowledge and let go of the feelings that arise in response to these questions, the answers begin to appear.

5

GRIEF

Grief is an experience common to us all. In grief, we feel that things are too difficult; we'll never make it; we are unloving and unlovable. We have thoughts such as, "All the years I've wasted." It is a feeling of sadness and loss. Loneliness. The feeling of "if only." Regret. Feelings of abandonment, pain, helplessness, and hopelessness. Nostalgia. Melancholy. Depression. Longing. Irretrievable loss. Heartbrokenness. Anguish. Disappointment. Pessimism.

Grief can be precipitated by the loss of a belief system, a relationship, a capacity or role, a hope about ourselves, or an overall attitude toward our life, external circumstances, or institutions. It's the feeling: "I'll never get over this. This one is too difficult. I tried, but nothing helps." There is a feeling of vulnerability to pain and suffering, and so we see a great deal of it in the external world to reinforce and justify our own inner feeling. There is a crying for someone to help because we can't do anything about it, and we feel that maybe someone else can do it for us. This is in contradistinction to apathy, where there is a feeling that no one can help.

Allowing the Grief

Most of us carry a great deal of suppressed grief. Men especially are prone to hide that particular feeling, as it is considered unmanly and un-masculine to cry. Most people are afraid of the amount of grief they have suppressed; they are terrified that they will be swamped and overwhelmed by it. People will say, "If I were ever to start crying, I would never stop"; "There is so much grief in the world, grief in my life, grief in my family and friends"; "O, the untold tragedies of life! All of the disappointments and smashed hopes!" Suppressed grief is responsible for many psychosomatic conditions and health-related complaints.

Instead of suppressing the feeling, if it is allowed to come up and be relinquished, we can quickly jump from grief to acceptance. The continuing grief over a loss is due to the resistance to accepting that state and allowing the grief to expend itself. The persistence of a feeling is due to the resistance to allowing it to be relinquished (e.g., "Cry me a river"). Once we accept the fact that we can handle grief, we are already up into pride. The feeling of "I can do it" and "I can handle it" brings us to courage. With the courage to face our inner feelings and let them go, we thus move on to the levels of acceptance and eventually peace. When we let go of a lot of grief we have been holding over the years, our friends and family will notice a change in our facial expression. Our step will be lighter and we will look younger.

Grief is time-limited. This fact gives us the courage and willingness to face grief. If we don't resist the feeling of grief and totally surrender to it, it will run out in about 10–20 minutes; then it will stop for variable lengths of time. If we keep surrendering to it every time it comes up, then it will eventually run out. We just allow ourselves to experience it fully. We only have to tolerate an overwhelming grief for 10–20 minutes, and then all of a sudden it will disappear. If we resist the grief, then it will go on and on. Suppressed grief can go on for years.

In facing grief, we often have to acknowledge and let go of our shame and embarrassment about having the feeling in the first place. For men this is especially so. We have to relinquish our fear of the feeling and our fear of being swamped and overwhelmed by it. It helps to realize that letting go of the resistance to the feeling moves us quickly through it. Traditionally, women have said out of their own experience and wisdom: "A good cry makes me feel better." Many a man has been surprised when he learned the truth of this.

Experientially, there was the surprising and almost immediate relief from a pounding headache as soon as the grief about a past situation was allowed to come up. As the grief surfaced, there was the sentence, "Men don't cry." After letting go of the masculine pride about crying, then up came a fear that the crying would never stop once it was allowed to start. As soon as that fear was gone, then there was anger. It was anger at a society that forces men to suppress their feelings, and anger at the notion that men are not even supposed to have feelings. With the letting go of that anger, the level of courage was reached, and then the needed crying could be allowed. Not only was there relief from the headache but, when the torrent of sobs subsided, a profound peacefulness settled. Henceforth, the subject did not have to be avoided.

Once a man has fully let the grief come up and totally freed himself from that suppressed energy, he is peaceful and his view of his own masculinity changes. He realizes that his masculinity is now more complete. He is still just as much of a man, but now he is a man who can also be in touch with and handle his own feelings. Consequently, he is more adequate, more capable, more well-rounded, more understanding, more mature, more capable of relating to and understanding others, more compassionate, and more loving.

The psychological basis of all grief and mourning is attachment. Attachment and dependence occur because we feel incomplete within ourselves; therefore, we seek objects, people, relationships, places, and concepts to fulfill inner needs. Because they are unconsciously utilized to fulfill an inner need, they come to be identified as "mine." As more energy is poured into them, there is a transition from identifying with the external objects as "mine" to being an actual extension of "me." Loss of the object or person is experienced as a loss of our own self and an important part of our emotional economy. Loss is experienced as a diminution of the quality of ourselves, which the object or person represented. The more emotional energy invested in the object or person, the greater will be the feeling of loss and the greater the pain associated with the undoing of the bonds of dependence. Attachment creates a dependency, and dependency, because of its nature, intrinsically carries with it a fear of loss.

Within each person, there is the child, parent, and adult. When grief comes up, it is rewarding to ask, "Within myself, is it the child, parent, or adult that is the source of this feeling?" For example, the "child" within a person is scared that something will happen to a beloved dog. It wonders, "How will I make it?" The inner adult also feels grief, but the adult accepts the inevitable. The little kitty or doggie is not immortal. The adult in us regretfully accepts that impermanency is a reality of life. We accept that our youth is not permanent, that many romantic relationships are not life-long, and that our dog will one day die.

Handling Loss

Because of the nature of attachment, the first state preceding the actual experiencing of loss is that of fear of loss. This is usually defended in one of two ways. One is to increase the intensity of the attachment by ever-persistent attempts to strengthen the bonds. This approach is based on the fantasy that "the greater the bond, the less likelihood of loss." However, this is the very maneuver that often precipitates loss in personal relationships, because the other person struggles to be free of the possessive attachment and the amount of restrictive control they feel being placed upon them. Thus, because what we hold in mind tends to manifest, the fear of a loss can, paradoxically, be the mechanism of bringing about that loss.

The second way that fear of loss is handled is by the psychological mechanism of denial which is, in common language, called "playing ostrich." We see this around us every day in its various forms of refusing to face the inevitable. All the warning signs are there, but the person does not take heed. Thus, the man who is obviously in the process of losing his job tends not to notice. The partners in a marriage that is going down the drain take no corrective action. The person with a serious disease ignores all of the symptoms and avoids medical attention. The politicians fail to look at social problems, hoping they will go away. Whole countries are oblivious to the precarious state of existence (e.g., 9-11 attack). The motorist ignores the ominous warning signals of a misbehaving engine. We have all experienced regret that we didn't pay attention to the warning signals of trouble ahead.

To handle the fear of loss, we have to look at what purpose the external person or object serves in our life. What emotional need is being fulfilled? What emotions would arise were we to lose the object or the person? Loss can be anticipated, and we can handle the various fears associated with the sense of loss by disassembling the emotional complexes that they represent, and letting go of the individual component feelings.

Let's say, for example, that you have a pet dog to which you have been attached for many years. It is obvious that old Rover is getting older. You find that you don't like to think about his advanced age, feeling uncomfortable at the prospect of his death and putting it out of mind. As you catch yourself doing this, you realize that these feelings are warning signals and that you are not handling the emotional situation. And so, you ask yourself, "What purpose is the dog serving in my life? What is his emotional service to me?" Love, companionship, devotion, amusement, and diversion. "Will losing the dog leave these personal emotional needs unfulfilled?" In looking at this, some of the fear can be acknowledged and relinquished. Once the fear is let go, you don't have to resort to denial and pretend to yourself that Rover will live forever.

Another emotion associated with grief and mourning

is that of anger. The loss of that which is important frequently brings up a feeling of rage, which may be projected onto the world, society, individuals and, ultimately, God, who is held to be responsible for the nature of the universe. Anger results from prior refusal to accept the fact that all relationships and possessions in this life are transitory. Even the physical body, which is our biggest attachment, eventually has to be relinquished, as everyone is aware.

We feel that what has become important or comforting to us is a permanent attachment. Consequently, when that illusion is threatened, there is anger, resentment, and self-pity, feelings which can result in chronic bitterness. "Impotent rage" is associated with the desire to change the nature of the world and the impossibility of doing so. In facing this fact of existence, a major loss can therefore bring about a shift in our philosophical position. One major loss can awaken us to the nature of all attachments and all relationships, or we may again deny the obvious fact that all relationships are transitory and furiously re-intensify existing bonds to compensate for the loss.

A part of handling denial of the inevitability of loss is seeing through attempts at manipulation. In fantasy, the mind tries to develop tactics so as to avoid the loss. This may take the form of becoming "gooder" or more hard-working, more honest, more persevering, or more loyal. In religious persons, this may take the form of trying to manipulate God by promises and bargains. In relationships, it may take the form of over-compensatory behavior. The spouse becomes ever more dutiful, loving, and attentive in an attempt to prevent a breakup. The inattentive husband suddenly starts bringing home gifts and flowers instead of getting to the root cause of the problem.

When the denial breaks down, the manipulations have not worked, and the fear has been passed through, then the depression itself, the actual process of mourning and grief, takes place. All of these emotional stages can be worked through much more rapidly by the process of letting go, in which the inevitability of the emotion of grief is surrendered to and replaced by a willingness to let go of resistance and let the process pass through and complete itself. There can be a decision to let go of resisting the grief. Instead of denial and resistance, you plunge into it and get over it. You have a "good cry" over old Rover or the lost relationship.

Associated with the feeling of grief is always a variable amount of guilt. This is based on the fantasy that the loss represents a punishment or that a different attitude or behavior would have prevented it from happening. Unless it is relinquished, the guilt can then recycle and refuel the anger and rage. The unacknowledged and unrelinquished rage may be projected onto others in the environment in the form of blame. Blame projected onto other relationships may, then, compound the loss by bringing about further loss.

This happens frequently between marital partners as a result of the death of a child. It has been reported that the divorce rate among parents who have lost children is as high as 90%. Because of the projection of blame, a severe loss is then compounded by another severe loss—that of a marital partner. An example of this type of reaction is the case of a forty-year-old woman. She had an excellent marriage for twenty years with an attentive, dutiful husband. Her youngest son developed leukemia. When he died, she went into grief and mourning and, more importantly, developed a rage reaction. It took the form of hatred. She hated the doctors; she hated the hospital; she hated God; she hated her husband and the existing children. Her rage became so uncontrollable that she became physically violent and threatening. Several times the police had to be called to control her violent behavior. Finally the other children left home out of fear of the chaos, physical abuse, and menacing emotional states. Her husband left no stone unturned in trying to help her with the rage, but she vented her fury upon him as well, violently attacking him on several occasions. Finally, in desperation and despair, he was driven from the home. The chaotic situation ultimately ended in a divorce in which the woman lost her home. It was almost five years before the rage subsided, at which time the woman had destroyed her whole life and now had to start over from scratch, rebuilding a new life.

When all the negative emotions have been worked through, surrendered to and let go of, relief finally occurs, and the former suffering is replaced by acceptance. Acceptance is different from resignation. In resignation there are still residuals of the previous emotion left. There is reluctance and a delaying of the true recognition of the facts. Resignation says, "I don't like it, but I have to put up with it."

With acceptance, resistance to the true nature of the facts has been relinquished; thus, one of the signs of acceptance is serenity. With acceptance, the struggle is over and life begins anew. The energies that were bound up in the previous negative emotion are now freed up, so that the healthier aspects of the personality are now re-energized. The creative aspects of the mind develop opportunities for new life situations and further options for growth and experience, accompanied by a new sense of aliveness. A well-known and widely-practiced teaching is the Serenity Prayer of the 12-Step groups:

God, Grant me the
Serenity to accept the things I cannot change, the
Courage to change the things I can, and the
Wisdom to know the difference.

Failure to work through any of the various emotions associated with mourning and loss can result in chronic stuckness in any of its components. Thus, it can result in prolonged depression, and prolonged states of denial in which the death of the person is actually denied. Chronic guilt or refusal to work through the emotions associated with loss can result in delayed grief reaction and physical disease. The mechanisms behind this process are explained in a later chapter on the relationship between mind and body. The suppressed energy of the unrelinquished emotions reemerges through the body's endocrine and nervous system as an energetic imbalance, which impairs the flow of life energy through the body's acupuncture meridians. This results in pathologic changes in various organs. It is a well-known fact that the death rate among the bereaved is much higher than that of the general population, especially in the first year or two following the death of a spouse.

One source of grief-related guilt is anger at the loved one for departing. This is often suppressed because it seems irrational to the conscious mind. The virtues of the departed loved one are enhanced and exaggerated in fantasy, and this discrepancy compounds the guilt. How could we be angry at such a wonderful person? There is guilt about being angry at God, the author of the universe, for having allowed the tragic event to take place.

A sixty-year-old woman came into the office with multiple physical complaints. She had asthma attacks, allergies, bronchitis, frequent episodes of pneumonia, and all kinds of breathing difficulties. During psychotherapy, it was revealed that her mother had died 22 years previously, and she stated that, curiously, she had had no reaction to her mother's death. Oddly, although it was her responsibility, she had not ordered a head stone to be placed on her mother's grave. From information given, it was obvious that she had had an extremely dependent relationship with her mother, about whom she was ambivalent because of the mother's refusal to fill all of her dependency needs.

It took many months for her to work through her massive denial, which was associated with guilt over her anger at her mother for leaving her. That anger was directed inwardly at herself in the form of disease, which also expressed her helplessness and her wish to cry out for her mother. The suppressed desire to cry for the mother-loss led to a constant feeling that she could not breathe. She hated herself for the love/hate feelings for her mother, and the sum total of all her repressed emotions had reemerged in the form of her multiple respiratory symptoms and complaints ("psychosomatic" illness). As she worked through the delayed mourning, the reaction to grief and loss began to surface. The extent of her resistance to working through these emotions and how that resistance had resulted in her physical symptoms became very clear to her. Eventually, she went for additional professional training to become a therapist working with the dying in a hospice program.

Preventing Grief

From the nature of the processes we have described, it becomes apparent that severe mourning, loss, and the pathological reactions that may ensue can be prevented by early recognition, and by preemptive surrender of the associated feelings while they are still mild and can be handled without excessive suffering.

As we have seen, the basis of all mourning and loss is attachment, plus the denial of the transitory nature of all relationships. We can begin by looking at our lives, identifying those areas of attachment, and asking ourselves: "What internal needs are they satisfying? What feeling would come up if I were to lose them? How can my inner emotional life be balanced so as to decrease the extent, degree, and number of attachments on external objects and people?" The greater our attachment to that which is outside of ourselves, the greater is our overall level of fear and vulnerability to loss. We can ask ourselves why we feel so incomplete. "Why am I so empty within myself that I have to search for solutions in the form of attachment and dependency on others?"

We can begin to look at our own inner areas of immaturity. Specifically, we need to examine: "Where am I looking to get love rather than to give it?" The more loving we are, the less vulnerable we are to grief and loss, and the less we need to seek attachments. When we have acknowledged and let go of all negative feelings, and we have graduated from smallness to the recognition of our greatness so that our internal joy comes from the pleasure of giving and loving, then we are really invulnerable to loss. When the source of happiness is found *within*, we are immune to the losses of the world.

When we take a critical look at our life, we see all of the attachments and escapes into which we have fallen. Each one represents a potential future source of pain and suffering. The really important areas should be closely examined. Let's take, for example, the failure to face these issues in the commonly seen, so-called retirement syndrome. Traditionally, this may occur in women when the job of raising young children comes to an end with their maturity and leaving home ("empty nest syndrome"), and with a man when he reaches retirement age or loses his job, or through some physical disablement is unable to carry on his previous work. The reaction that typically occurs in middle age is due to the many years of pre-existing denial. There is often a lack of facing the inevitable and making plans for other life activities that would gratify the same inner needs which, in these cases, are feelings of self-esteem, importance, the wanting to feel needed and significant, and the need to make a contribution and be productive.

Anticipation of the inevitable and preparing for it now bring relatively minor discomfort compared to traumatic grief and loss at a later date. We can look at our major love relationships and honestly examine them. To what degree do they subserve our selfish inner needs? To what degree are we really using the other person to exploit them for our own gain? To what degree are they merely subserving our happiness? To find out, all we need to do is ask ourselves: "If their happiness were best served by leaving me, how would I feel about it?" This reveals the degree to which we are trying to restrict and control the other person—which is attachment and not love.

Over two thousand years ago, the Buddha made the observation that the basis of all human suffering was due to desire and attachment, and human history has merely proven the truth of his teaching. What is the solution to that dilemma? As we can see, it is only the small aspect of oneself that becomes attached. The smaller self buys into the frightened, inadequate set of programs that we have unwittingly allowed to run us. The purpose of letting go is to de-energize these programs so that they no longer run us; then, we are free to expand into the greater awareness of our Higher Self.

That part of us to which we refer as our "greater Self" loves rather than seeks love. Consequently, there comes the awareness that we are at all times surrounded by love, which is unlimited. Love is automatically attracted to the person who is loving.

By constantly letting go of our negative feelings, we thus cure present pain and prophylactically prevent the occurrence of future pain. Fear is replaced by trust and with it comes a profound sense of wellbeing. Immunity to grief of loss occurs when we replace dependence on the small self (the personality) with dependence on the Self (the Divinity within). We look for security to the Self, which is eternal, instead of to the small self, which is transitory.

6

FEAR

The many faces of fear are familiar to us all. We have felt free-floating anxiety and panic. We have been paralyzed and frozen by fear, with its accompanying palpitations and apprehension. Worries are chronic fears. Paranoia is its extreme. In milder forms of fear, we are merely uneasy. When it is more severe, we become scared, cautious, blocked, tense, shy, speechless, superstitious, defensive, distrustful, threatened, insecure, dreading, suspicious, timid, trapped, guilty, and full of stage fright. There is fear of pain and suffering, fear of living, fear of loving, fear of closeness, fear of rejection, fear of failure, fear of God, fear of hell, fear of damnation, fear of poverty, fear of ridicule and criticism, fear of being trapped, fear of inadequacy, fear of danger, fear of disapproval, fear of boredom, fear of responsibility, fear of making a decision, fear of authority, fear of punishment, fear of change, fear of loss of security, fear of violence, fear of losing control, fear of feelings themselves, fear of manipulation, fear of being found out, fear of heights, fear of sex, fear of being on our own and being responsible, and fear of fear itself.

There is, moreover, a cause of fear of which many

people are unaware: the fear of retaliation. This fear arises from the desire to strike out, to hit back, and to attack. As we let go of fear, we find that behind it, there is often anger at the object of fear itself. The willingness to let go of the fear and overcome it already moves us up to the next level, which is anger. The fact that we can face this combination of fear/anger feelings and surrender it moves us instantly up to pride and courage.

The Fear of Public Speaking

One excellent experiment is to let go of the fear of fear itself. When we stop being afraid of fear, we notice that it is just a feeling. In fact, fear is far more tolerable than depression. Surprisingly, to a person who has been in bad depression, the re-emergence of fear is welcomed. It is better to feel scared than hopeless.

To understand how fear is self-reinforcing, we have to stop and look at another one of the laws of consciousness: *What one holds in mind tends to manifest.* What this means is that any thought which we consistently hold in mind and consistently give energy to will tend to come into our life according to the very form in which our mind has held it. Thus, fear engenders fearful thoughts. The more we hold these thoughts in mind, the more likely the feared event will happen in our life, which again reinforces our fear.

As a medical intern, there was a fear of public speaking. At the very thought of getting up in front of medical colleagues to present a patient's case, the voice would fail out of sheer fright. Because of holding that fear, the inevitable situation arose that necessitated having to present the case of a patient to the staff meeting. After reading a few paragraphs of the case history, the voice began to falter and get weaker and eventually stopped. The very fear that had been held in mind came to pass and, of course, that occurrence reinforced a fear of public speaking and brought on apathy about it. Henceforth, for many years, the limiting belief system operated: "I can't speak in public. I'm just not a public speaker." Any and all speaking occasions were avoided, with the consequent loss of self-esteem, avoidance of activities, and limitation of vocational goals.

As the years passed, the fear took a somewhat different form. The belief system was: "I don't want to speak, because I might be a boring and bad speaker." Finally, an occasion arose where it was necessary to speak in a public meeting. There was the opportunity to sit down and find the courage to face the fear. The inner dialogue was: "What's the worst possible thing that could happen? Well, you could be terribly boring." This brought to mind all the boring speeches given by others, and then it became possible to accept that a boring speech was actually common and certainly not the end of the world. There was a letting go of the pride and vanity behind that fear. Yes, it just might happen that the speech would be terribly boring.

The fateful day finally arrived. The paper was written out so all that was needed was to read it. Yes, it would have been far more interesting to give it extemporaneously, but there was an acknowledgement and acceptance of the fear, and so the speech was written out beforehand. The moment arrived to ascend the podium. Despite the inner fear and reading the speech in a flat monotone voice, the feat was accomplished. Afterwards some friends said, "That was technically a good paper but, boy, it sure was boring." The inner self, however, didn't care; it was jubilant that there had been the courage and acceptance to face the situation and actually do it. The fact that it was boring was irrelevant. What was important was that it was done at all. Self-esteem increased because the fear and inhibition had been overcome, and speaking engagements no longer had to be avoided. In fact, the practice developed to begin all presentations with a warning to the audience, "I am one of the most boring speakers around and, in fact, I can be quite tedious." Surprisingly, this brought a laugh from the audience. Their laughter signified acceptance of our common humanness, and so the fears were lifted.

It was discovered that humor is valuable in public speaking. It is a way of just being at one with the humanness of the audience and discovering their compassion. Once we are united with them in compassion, we can feel their encouragement as they cheer us on. We love them for relieving our fear and accepting us, and they love us back for doing the very thing that they themselves fear. Once this evolution through the levels of emotion is made, there is an enjoyment of public speaking. We find out that part of the mind can be quite funny when the occasion arises.

Eventually, with complete surrender, reading a prepared speech dropped off and the speaking became extemporaneous. With more experience, the public speaking improved, which engendered more speaking engagements. This allowed the accomplishment of many vocational goals that heretofore had been thwarted. There were appearances in the national media, such as talk shows on television. It is a long step from being too frightened even to read a case history in front of a few interns to enjoying one-self speaking on a television network to millions of viewers on *The Barbara Walter's Show.*

We all derive great benefit from liberating ourselves out of a fearful inhibition into successful functioning, because that learning process automatically spills over into many other areas of our life. We become more capable, freer and happier and, with that, there is an inner peace of mind.

The Healing Effect of Love

Fear is so pandemic in our society that it constitutes the predominant ruling emotion of our world, as we know it. Fear was also the predominant emotion among the thousands of patients treated during the decades of clinical practice. Fear is so extensive and takes so many forms that there are not enough pages in this book to enumerate all of its varieties.

Fear is associated with our survival, and so it is given a special accord in our minds. For most people, fear is so all-pervasive that their life really constitutes one giant set of compensatory devices to conquer their fears. However, even this does not suffice, so that the media present us over and over again with fearful situations, as in this morning's news: "Terrorist group threatens to poison our food supply." Such headlines are constant, as though to give the mind further opportunities to master that most dreaded of all emotions. As the lyrics of the song put it, "We are caught between a fear of living and a fear of dying."

When all the mind's compensatory devices fail and fear spills forth into consciousness as overt anxiety attacks or phobias, the person is labeled as having an anxiety neurosis. It is informative to note that the tranquilizer Valium is the biggest selling drug in America.

Fears tend to escalate. Thus, the typical patient with phobias shows a progressive extension of the fear into more and more avenues of life, leading to further and further restrictions of activity, and, in severe cases, to total immobilization. This was the case of a patient named Betty.

Betty was thirty-four years old, but she looked much older because she was thin and drawn. She entered the office carrying armloads of paper bags, which were later found to contain 56 different bottles of health store preparations, vitamins, nutritional supplements, plus several bags of special food. Her fear had started out as a germ phobia and soon everything around her seemed to be possibly contaminated with germs. She had many health fears of contracting contagious diseases, which had progressed now to a fear of cancer. She believed every scare story she read, so she was afraid of nearly every food, the air she breathed, and getting sunshine on her skin. She wore white clothes because she was afraid of dyes in the materials.

In the office, she would never sit down because she was afraid that the chair might be contaminated. Whenever she needed a prescription, she asked that it be written from the middle of the prescription pad which had not been touched. Furthermore, she wanted to tear the page from the pad herself; she didn't want me to touch it because possibly I had gotten germs from shaking hands with the last patient. She wore white gloves at all times. She requested to be treated by telephone as she was too afraid of making the trip to the office again.

The following week on the telephone, she said that

she was afraid to get up. She would call from home while still in bed because now she was afraid to go out on the streets. She had developed a fear of muggers, rapists, and air pollution. At the same time, she was afraid to stay home in bed for fear that she might get worse and, to compound all her other fears, she was afraid that she was losing her mind. She was afraid that the medication wouldn't help her and that it might have side effects, but she was afraid not to take it for fear that she would not get better. Now she said that she had a fear that she might choke on the pills and had stopped taking even her health pills, much less the prescribed medication.

Her fears were so paralyzing that every therapeutic maneuver was totally stymied. She wouldn't allow me to talk to her family. She was afraid they would find out that she was seeing a psychiatrist and think she was crazy. I was totally baffled and racked my brain for weeks on how I could possibly help her. Finally, I let go. I experienced the relief of surrender in that I just totally gave up: "There is absolutely nothing I can do to help her. The only thing left to do is just to love her."

And, so, that's what I did. I just thought of her lovingly, and frequently I sent her loving thoughts. I gave her as much love as I could possibly give when we talked on the telephone and, finally, after a couple of months of "loving therapy," she got sufficiently better to come to the office. As time went on, she improved and her fears and inhibitions began to diminish, though she never did develop any insight. She was too afraid of talking about psychological matters, she said, and so over the months and eventually years of treatment, the only thing I ever did was to love her.

This case illustrates a concept that we previously

presented in the chapter on apathy; that is, a higher vibration, such as love, has a healing effect on a lower vibration, such as that in the patient's case, fear. This love is the mechanism of reassurance, and very often we can quiet another person's fears by our mere physical presence, and by the loving energy that we project to them and with which we surround them. It is not what we say, but the very fact of our presence that has the healing effect.

We can learn another one of the laws of consciousness: *Fear is healed by love.* This is the central theme of the series of books by psychiatrist Jerry Jampolsky (e.g., *Love is Letting Go of Fear*). This was also the basis of the healing that went on at the Attitudinal Healing Center in Manhasset, Long Island, of which I was co-founder and medical advisor. Attitudinal healing has to do with group interaction with patients who have fatal and catastrophic illnesses, and the whole process of healing has to do with the letting go of fear and replacing it with love.

This is the same mechanism of healing demonstrated by the great saints and illumined healers, whose very presence has the power to heal because of the intense vibration of love which they radiate. This healing power—the basis of spiritual healing—is also transmitted by loving thoughts. The multitudes of people down through recorded history who have healed by just this kind of love are legendary. In recent history, for instance, Mother Teresa is credited with healing great numbers of people by these very mechanisms of unconditional love and illumined presence. To people who are unfamiliar with the laws of consciousness, these types of cures seem miraculous. But to those who are familiar with the laws of consciousness, such phenomena are commonplace and to be expected. High levels of consciousness are in themselves capable of healing, transforming, and enlightening others. The value of the surrendering mechanism is that, by letting go of the blocks to love, our capacity to love increases progressively, and loving energy has the capacity to heal ourselves as well as others.

The only drawback to these types of healings is that often the healing is sustained while in proximity to a person capable of radiating high levels of love, but the illness returns when people leave that presence, unless they themselves have learned to elevate their own consciousness.

"Well," you might ask, "if sending loving thoughts has a healing power, how come we see all the sick people in hospitals, whose families are so solicitous? Why does the love of the family not heal the patient?" The answer is to look at the kinds of thoughts that are being sent by the family to the patient. As you examine them, you will find that they are primarily thoughts of anguish and fear, accompanied by guilt and ambivalence.

We might picture love to be like the sunlight and negative thoughts like the clouds. Whereas our higher, greater Self is like the sun, all the negative thoughts, doubts, fears, anger, and resentments that we hold dim the light of the sun and, finally, the light comes through only weakly. It was Jesus Christ who said that we all, with faith, potentially have the power to heal. The saint, or person of high consciousness, is by definition one who has removed the clouds of negativity and radiates the full healing power of the sun. That is also why saintly beings have such magnetic power that they attract multitudes to their physical presence.

As an example, when the late Indian saint Sri Ramana Maharshi had a birthday, 25,000 people stood in the sweltering tropical sun shoulder-to-shoulder in one solid mass to celebrate his presence and wish him well.

As we consistently let go of resisting our fears and allow them to be surrendered, the energy that was tied up in the fear is relinquished and now becomes available to shine forth as the energy of love. Therefore, unconditional love has the greatest power of all, and that love is the power of the celebrated saints. Unconditional love is also the power of the mother and of the father, the presence of whom is so essential to the children's learning to love as they grow. It was Sigmund Freud who observed that the most fortunate thing that can happen to us growing up is to be our mother's favorite child.

What about those of us who did not have the fortunate experience of being bathed in unconditional love as we grew up? There is the commonly held belief that if we did not have this experience, then we are somehow scarred or crippled for life; actually, this is not so. A person who has experienced a great deal of love in early life has fewer fears and a head start, but this love is intrinsic within all of us. By the very nature of our being and by the very nature of the life energy that flows through us and empowers us to breathe and to think, we all have that same vibrational energy level of love within us.

If, in looking at ourselves, we see that we have allowed the experience of our own nature to become blocked off by extensive fears, then we can rediscover the love within us by utilizing the mechanism of surrender and, thus, letting go of the clouds of negativity.

By rediscovering this inner love, we rediscover the true source of happiness.

Owning the "Shadow"

One of the blocks to emotional development is the fear of what lies buried in our unconscious. Carl Jung called this area, which we are unwilling to look at and to own, the "shadow." He said that the self cannot become healed and whole unless we look at and acknowledge the shadow. This means that buried within us all, in what Jung called the "collective unconscious," is everything that we most dislike admitting about ourselves. The average human, he said, would much rather project his shadow onto the world and condemn it and see it as evil, thinking that his problem is to battle with evil in the world. In actuality, the problem is merely to acknowledge the presence of such thoughts and impulses in ourselves. By acknowledging them, they become quiet. Once they are quiet, they no longer unconsciously run us.

In looking at our fears of the unknown, which are really fears of what is in the depths of the unconscious, it is useful to have a sense of humor. Once looked at and acknowledged, the shadow no longer has any power. In fact, it is only our fear of these thoughts and impulses that give them any power. Once we become acquainted with our shadow, we no longer have to project our fears upon the world, and they begin to evaporate rapidly.

What makes the endless television programs, which are concerned with mayhem and its various forms, so attractive? It is because what is being acted out on the screen, where it is safe, are all the forbidden unconscious fantasies in our own psyche. Once we are willing to look at the same movies on the TV screen of our own minds and see whence they really originate, the attraction of such "entertainment" disappears. People who have acknowledged the content of their own shadow have no interest in crime, violence, and fearful disasters.

One of the blocks to becoming acquainted with the fears in one's own mind is the fear of the opinions of others. The wanting of their approval goes on inside of our minds in a constant fantasy. We identify with the opinions of others, including authority figures, and coalesce this in such a way that we hear it as our own opinion of ourselves.

In looking at fears, then, it is well to remember that Carl Jung saw this reservoir of the forbidden inside the shadow as a part of the *collective unconscious.* The term collective unconscious means that *everybody* has these thoughts and fantasies. There is nothing unique about any of us when it comes to the way we symbolize our emotions. Everybody secretly harbors the fear that they are dumb, ugly, unlovable, and a failure.

The unconscious mind is not polite. It thinks in gross concepts. When it thinks of the phrase "Murder the bum!," the unconscious literally means that. Look deep within yourself the next time somebody cuts you off in traffic, and picture what you would really do to that person if you were strictly honest with yourself and did not censor the image coming to mind. You'd like to run them off the road, wouldn't you? Pulverize them. Push them off the cliff. Isn't that right? That's the way the unconscious thinks.

The reason that a sense of humor is useful is because these images are comical once we look at them. There is nothing awful about it; it is just the way the unconscious handles images. It doesn't mean that you are a rotten person or that you are potentially a criminal. It just means that you have gotten honest and faced how the human animal mind operates in this dimension. There is no point in getting melodramatic, self-critical, or tragic about it. The unconscious is crude and uncivilized. While your intellect went to prep school, your unconscious remained in the jungle where it is still swinging in the trees! Looking at the shadow side is not a time to get prissy or squeamish. It's not a time to take it literally either, because the symbols of the unconscious are just that: they are symbols, and they are primitive in nature. If worked with consciously, they can empower us rather than inhibit us.

It takes a lot of energy to keep the shadow buried and to suppress our multitude of fears. The result is energy depletion. On the emotional level, it is expressed as an inhibition of the capacity to love.

In the world of consciousness, like goes to like, so that fear attracts fear just as its corollary is true that love attracts love. The more fear we hold, the more fearful situations we attract to our life. Each fear requires additional energy to create a protective device until, finally, all of our energy is drained into our extensive defensive measures. The willingness to look at a fear and work with it until we are free of it brings about immediate rewards.

Each of us has within us a certain reservoir of suppressed and repressed fear. This quantity of fear spills into all areas of our life, colors all of our experience, decreases our joy in life, and reflects itself in the musculature of the face so as to affect our physical appearance, our physical strength, and the condition of health in all of the organs in the body. Sustained and chronic fear gradually suppresses the body's immune system. With kinesiologic testing, we can instantly demonstrate that a fearful thought causes a major reduction in muscle power and deranges the energy flow down the body's energy meridians to the body's vital organs. Although we know that it is totally damaging to our relationships, health, and happiness, we still hang on to fear. Why is that?

We have the unconscious fantasy that fear is keeping us alive; this is because fear is associated with our whole set of survival mechanisms. We have the idea that, if we were to let go of fear, our main defense mechanism, we would become vulnerable in some way. In reality, the truth is just the opposite. Fear is what blinds us to the real dangers of life. In fact, fear itself is the greatest danger that the human body faces. It is fear and guilt that bring about disease and failure in every area of our lives.

We could take the same protective actions out of love rather than out of fear. Can we not care for our bodies because we appreciate and value them, rather than out of fear of disease and dying? Can we not be of service to others in our life out of love, rather than out of fear of losing them? Can we not be polite and courteous to strangers because we care for our fellow human beings, rather than because we fear losing their good opinion of us? Can we not do a good job because we care about the quality of our performance and we care about our fellow workers? Can we not perform our job well because we care about the recipients of our services, rather than just the fear of losing our jobs or pursuing our own ambition? Can we not accomplish more by cooperation, rather than by fearful competition? Can we not drive carefully because we have a high regard for ourselves and care for our welfare and those who love us, rather than because we fear an accident? On a spiritual level, isn't it more effective if, out of compassion and identification with our fellow human beings, we care for them, rather than trying to love them out of fear of God's punishment if we don't?

Guilt

One particular form of fear is what we call guilt. Guilt is always associated with a feeling of wrongness and potential punishment, either real or in fantasy. If punishment is not forthcoming in the external world, it expresses itself as self-punishment on an emotional level. Guilt accompanies all of the negative emotions and, thus, where there is fear, there is guilt. If you think a guilty thought and have somebody test your muscle strength, you will see that the muscle instantly goes weak. Your cerebral hemisphere has become desynchronized and all of your energy meridians are thrown out of balance. Nature, therefore, says that guilt is destructive.

If guilt is so destructive, then why are there such paeans of praise allotted to it? Why do so-called experts view guilt as beneficial? For example, a psychiatrist wrote a magazine article in praise of guilt, declaring: "Guilt is good for you." He then qualified the statement with "appropriate guilt." Let's look at what guilt is really all about and see if we agree or not.

When you cross the street, you look both ways to see if a car is coming. How did this come about? When you were a child, you were told that it was "bad" to cross the street. Thus, we see that guilt is really a substitute for a sense of reality in a mind that is undeveloped, such as that of a child. It is a learned behavior which is purportedly pragmatic: to prevent further error or the repetition of a mistake. Ninety-nine percent of guilt has nothing whatsoever to do with reality. In fact, the most pious, meek, and harmless individuals are often riddled with guilt. Guilt is really self-condemnation and self-invalidation of our worth and value as a human being.

Guilt is as prevalent as fear, and we feel guilty no matter what we are doing. A part of our mind says that we really ought to be doing something else. Or, whatever we are actually doing at the moment, we ought to be doing "better." We "should" be getting a better golf score. We "should" be reading a book instead of watching television. We "should" make love better. Cook better. Run faster. Grow taller. Be stronger. Be smarter. Be more educated. In between the fear of living and the fear of dying is the guilt of the moment. We seek to escape it by remaining unaware of it through suppression, repression, projecting it onto others, and escapism.

Remaining unconscious of guilt (repression), however, does not solve it. The guilt re-emerges in the form of self-punishment and through accidents, misfortune, loss of jobs and relationships, physical disease and sickness, tiredness, exhaustion, and the multiple ways the ingenious mind figures out how to bring about the loss of pleasure, joy, and aliveness.

Guilt represents death just as love represents life. Guilt is part of the smaller self and underlies our willingness to believe negative things about ourselves. The happiness and joy of the day is instantly destroyed by one negative remark from a family member, friend, or neighbor. Physical disease is unlikely to exist without guilt, and guilt is a denial of our inner intrinsic innocence.

Why do we buy into so much garbage? Is it not because of our very innocence? Is it not because, as we grew up, we trusted that what others were telling us was the truth? And even currently, do we still trust what others are telling us is the truth? Is it not so that we have bought into ten thousand lies and are willing to buy another ten thousand out of the naïveté of our inner innocence? Is not that inner innocence the very reason for our exploitability? In fact, when we look deep within ourselves, is it not because of our very innocence that we believe ourselves to be guilty?

It is because of our own inner innocence that we have bought into all the negativity of the world and allowed it to kill our aliveness, destroy our awareness of who we really are, and sell us the pathetic little smallness for which we have settled. Is not ours the innocence of the newborn that cannot defend itself and, with no capacity for discernment, could only allow itself to be programmed, like a computer?

To see this means to become conscious. We hear of consciousness-raising programs and weekend seminars to expand our consciousness. What does this mean? To get some new complicated formulas? To get programmed with somebody else's idea of mystical truth?

Most of the consciousness programs boil down to this essential point: become aware of what we are buying into, what we are accepting daily. Let's look at what we have already been programmed with and begin to question it, disassemble it, and let it go. Let's wake up and free ourselves from being exploited and enslaved by the negative programming of the world. We will see it for what it is, which is an attempt by others to control us; exploit us; extract our money, our services, our energy, our loyalties; and capture our mind. The mechanisms whereby this comes about were so beautifully exemplified in the movie, *Tron,* in which the very function of "master control" was to enslave by progressive programming.

When we see the truth of how programming happens, we will see that we are the pure, blank computer. We are the innocent space in which the programming is occurring. When we look at all of this, we are going to get angry. Anger is better than resignation, apathy, depression, and grief! It means to take charge of our mind instead of handing it to the television set, the newspaper, the magazines, the neighbors, the conversations in the subway, the chance remarks of the waitress, the garbage in and the garbage out. What went into our memory banks was garbage, and when we see this, we will have much less fear. We will enjoy starting to let the feelings come up, seeing them for what they are, clearing out all of the garbage, and letting it all go.

Once we have looked deep within ourselves and found that innate inner innocence, we will stop hating ourselves. We will stop condemning ourselves and stop buying into the condemnation of others and their subtle attempts to invalidate our worth as human beings. It's time to re-own our own power and stop giving it away to every passing scammer who jiggles our fears and shakes loose some money out of our pocketbook or enslaves us to their cause, living off of our energy. It's easy to get away from all that fear because we have the power of choice now.

We fear that the inner voyage of discovery will lead us to some dreadful, awful truth. In its programming of our minds, this is one of the barriers that the world has set up to prevent us from finding out the real truth. There is one thing the world does not want us to find out and that is the truth about ourselves. Why? Because then we will become free. We can no longer be controlled, manipulated, exploited, drained, enslaved, imprisoned, vilified, or disempowered. Therefore, the inner voyage of discovery is cloaked over with an aura of mystery and foreboding.

What is the real truth about this voyage? The real truth is that, as we go within and discard one illusion after another, one falsehood after another, one negative program after another, it gets lighter and lighter. The awareness of the presence of love becomes stronger and stronger. We will feel lighter and lighter. Life becomes progressively more effortless.

Every great teacher since the beginning of time has said to look *within* and find the truth, for the truth of what we really are will set us free. If what is to be found within ourselves were something to feel guilty about, something that is rotten, evil and negative, then all the world's great teachers would not advise us to look there. On the contrary, they would tell us to avoid it at all costs. We will discover that all of the things the world calls "evil" are right on the surface; they are right on the top, as the superficial, outer thin layer. Beneath these errors is mistakenness. We are not rotten—only ignorant.

As the quantity of guilty fear and the energy accompanying it are relinquished, we will notice that physical diseases and symptoms begin to disappear. The capacity to love ourselves in the form of increased self-esteem returns and with it comes the capacity to love others. Being freed from guilt brings about a renewal of life energy. This can be dramatically witnessed in many people who are converted through religious experience. The sudden freedom from guilt through the mechanism of forgiveness is responsible for thousands of recoveries from serious and advanced diseases. Whether or not we agree with their religious concept is immaterial. What is important to notice is that the alleviation of guilt is accompanied by a resurgence of life energy, well-being, and physical health.

When it comes to healing ourselves and increasing our own emotional health, it "pays to be paranoid." We become aware of all the guilt-mongers in our life and their deleterious influences.

We can ask ourselves, could we not achieve the same motivation or behavior out of love rather than out of fear and guilt? Is guilt the only reason we don't stab our neighbor? Why couldn't it be that we would refuse to stab our neighbor because we love and care for him as a fellow human being who is intrinsically innocent and who is struggling to grow, but may make mistakes along the way just as we, ourselves, have done? Would not following religious teachings, whatever they are, be more effective if done out of love and appreciation, rather than out of guilt and fear? We can ask ourselves, what do we really need guilt for anyway? What possible service do we get out of it? Are we so miserably stupid that we behave only out of guilt? Are we so unconscious? Cannot consideration for the feelings of others replace guilt as a motivation for appropriate human behavior?

As we examine these issues and look at their social origins, we see that the Middle Ages are far from over. The Inquisition has merely taken on newer and subtler forms of cruelty. We have unwittingly bought into a system of negativity that is currently running the planet. To make wrong and to make guilty is really a form of cruelty, is it not? We have allowed others to program us with methods of self-torture, and we can see that we have retaliated by inviting others to torture themselves in return. We have allowed ourselves to be manipulated by guilt, and we turn it around and use that same mechanism of guilt to try to exploit and control others.

The degree to which we have not allowed ourselves to experience the reality of our true Self is represented by our resentment toward those who have actually done so. We resent their aliveness in the areas in which we feel disabled. This sobering truth is represented by the story of the man who walks along the beach and comes upon a fisherman with a pail full of crabs. He says to the fisherman, "You'd better put a cover on that pail or the crabs will get out." "Well, no," said the wise old fisherman. "There is no need for that. You see, as one crab crawls up the side of the pail to get out, the other crabs reach up and grab him and pull him back down. So there's no need for a cover."

As we keep letting go, getting lighter, and becoming freer, we will, unfortunately, see that the nature of the world is like that pail of crabs. And, then, the full extent of its negativity becomes apparent. When we become totally aware of the bill of goods that we have been sold, it is very likely that we will feel anger and a strong desire to become liberated from the constraints of negativity.

7

DESIRE

This emotion may range from a mild wanting to an obsessive, driven craving for something or someone. It is also expressed as greed, obsession, hunger, envy, jealousy, clinging, hoarding, ruthlessness, fixation, frenzy, exaggeration, over-ambition, selfishness, lust, possessiveness, control, glamorization, insatiability, and acquisitiveness. "Never satisfied." "Never enough." "Must have." The underlying quality of this emotion is its drivenness. When we are at the effect of desire, we are no longer free. We are controlled by it, run by it, enslaved and led about by the nose by it.

Here again, the essential point of freedom is whether we have chosen consciously to fulfill a certain want, or whether we are just being blindly run by unconscious programs and belief systems.

Desire as an Obstacle

There is often a lack of understanding of the function of wanting and desire. The main illusion is seen in the statement, "The only way that I'll get what I want is by desiring it; if I let go of my desire, then I won't get what I want." Actually, the opposite is true. Desire, especially strong desire (e.g., cravingness), frequently blocks our getting what we want.

Why is this so? Actually, the way something comes into our life is because we have chosen it. It was the result of our intention, or we made a decision for it. It has come into our life *in spite of desire*. The desiring was actually the obstacle to its achievement or acquisition. This is because desire literally means, "I do not have." In other words, if we say that we desire something, we are saying that it isn't ours. When we say that it isn't ours, we put a psychic distance between ourselves and what we want. This distance becomes the obstacle that consumes energy.

The impossible becomes possible as soon as we are totally surrendered. This is because wanting blocks receiving it and results in a fear of not getting it. The energy of desire is, in essence, a denial that what we want is ours for the asking.

This is a different way of looking at achieving goals than the one we are used to from the programming of our world. We are used to picturing ambition and success as being associated with hard work and the classical "Protestant ethic" virtues. These include self-sacrifice, asceticism, great expenditure of effort and endeavor, keeping our nose to the grindstone, tightening our belt, buckling down, and all the grimness of hard work. When we look at this whole picture, it sounds arduous, doesn't it? Well, it is. It involves struggle, and the struggle results from the block we have put in our own way because of desire.

Let's compare the arduous lower consciousness way of achieving goals with a higher state of consciousness in which we have acknowledged and let go of the desire, and are in a freer state. In a freer state, that which is chosen manifests in our life effortlessly. We surrender the emotion of desire and, instead, merely choose the goal, picture it lovingly, and allow it to happen because we see that it is already ours.

Why is it already ours? In a lower state of consciousness, the universe is seen as negative and denying, frustrating, and reluctant. It is like a bad, stingy parent. In a higher state of consciousness, our experience of the universe changes. It now becomes like a giving, loving, unconditionally approving parent who wants us to have everything we want, and it is ours for the asking. This is creating a different context. It is giving the universe a different meaning.

Although the world may be stingy and hostile to other people, there is no reason why we should buy into this paradigm. When we buy into it, we make it that way in our own life. As we experience the letting go of desires, we begin to see that what we have chosen will come into our life almost magically. "What we hold in mind tends to manifest." As was said before, during times of supposed high unemployment, some people are not only employed but have two or three jobs.

This was a shockingly new way of looking at the world when it was first encountered. There was the hope that it was true, but also a skepticism that said, "This just isn't possible on a pragmatic level." A strict "Protestant ethic" background made it hard to believe; nonetheless, the willingness was there to be open-minded enough to give it a try. Here was the initial experience with letting go of desire.

Personal goals were written down, followed by a letting go of the desire for them. It sounds paradoxical but that is the process: identify the goals and then let go of wanting them. One goal that had been held in mind for several years was an apartment in New York City, because work commitments required a lot of commuting and money spent on hotel rooms. A small apartment in the city—a so-called *pied-à-terre*—would be the economical solution. "Apartment in New York City" was written down as a goal. When utilizing this way of achieving goals, we include all of the details, as impossible as they may seem to the rational mind to achieve. So, the ideal apartment was detailed: reasonably priced, on Fifth Avenue in the 70s block, right next to an entrance to Central Park, at least eight or nine floors up and in the rear so that the street noise would be minimized, and not any bigger than about two and a half rooms.

The next day at work, it was busy as usual, with a big caseload, meetings, and patient visits. In between the meetings and patients, the feeling of wantingness for the apartment would be acknowledged and let go. And, as the day progressed, the apartment was actually forgotten. At 4:30 P.M., after the last patient, there was suddenly the impulse to drive into the city. Despite the fact that it was ostensibly rush hour, the road was clear and the drive took only half an hour. The car cruised to about 73rd and Lexington, pulling up to the nearest real estate office. Rather magically, there happened to be a parking space open right in front of the real estate office. The real estate officer, upon hearing the tongue-in-cheek announcement that an apartment on Fifth Avenue was desired, looked with surprise and said, "Well, you are certainly in luck! Exactly one hour ago we listed the only apartment for rent on all of Fifth Avenue, at 76th Street, on the ninth floor. It's the rear apartment, two and a half rooms, and the rent is reasonable (rent-controlled at $500.00 a month). It has just been painted and you can move in any time." So we walked over and viewed the apartment. It fit the description of the goal exactly. The lease was signed on the spot! Thus, within 24 hours of trying the letting go technique on a specific personal goal, the goal was a reality. It had been something that was almost impossible to find, and yet it happened exactly as pictured, effortlessly, and with no negative emotions. It was an easy and joyous experience.

This is not an unusual experience but a typical one, because in this case the desire was moderate and could, without much effort, be totally surrendered. By being totally surrendered, this means that it was okay if the apartment happened, and it was okay if it didn't. Because of being totally surrendered, the impossible became possible, manifesting itself effortlessly and rapidly.

We can all doubt this mechanism and look back at things that we wanted and that were achieved through ambition, desire, craving, and even obsessive, frenzied wanting. The mind says, "Well, what if I had let go of the desire for those things? If it weren't for the desire, how would I have gotten them?" The truth is, we could have gotten them anyway, only without anxiety (fear of not getting), without all the energy expenditure, without all the effort, without all the trial and error, and without all the hard work.

"Well!" the mind says, "if we got it effortlessly, how about the pride of achievement? Wouldn't we have to sacrifice that?" Well, yes, we would have to relinquish the vanity of all that sacrifice and hard work that we put into it. We would have to give up the sentimentality about the self-sacrifice and all the pain and suffering we went through to achieve our goals. This is a

peculiar perversion in our society, isn't it? If we suddenly become successful almost effortlessly, then people are envious. It really annoys them that we didn't
have to go through all kinds of anguish, pain, and suffering to get there. Their mind believes that such
anguish is the cost that must be paid for success.

Let's look at this belief. If it weren't for the negative
programming that made us believe otherwise, why
should we go through any cost of pain and suffering
to achieve anything in our life? Isn't that a rather sadis-
tic view of the world and the universe?

Other blocks to the achievement of our wants and
desires, of course, are unconscious guilt and smallness. Peculiarly, the unconscious will allow us to have
only what we think we deserve. The more we hang on
to our negativity and the small self-image that results,
the less we think we deserve, and we unconsciously
deny ourselves the abundance which flows so easily to
others. That is the reason for the saying, "The poor get
poorer and the rich get richer." If we have a small
view of ourselves, then what we deserve is poverty,
and our unconscious will see to it that we have that
actuality. As we relinquish our smallness and revalidate our own inner innocence, and as we let go of
resisting our generosity, openness, trust, lovingness,
and faith, then the unconscious will automatically start
arranging life circumstances so that abundance begins
to flow into our life.

Having—Doing—Being

As we free ourselves out of lower states of consciousness such as apathy and fear, we come into wantingness. What was formerly an "I can't" and impossible

now becomes possible. The general progression of the levels of consciousness, as we go from the lowest to the highest, is to move from havingness to doingness to beingness. At the lower levels of consciousness, it is what we *have* that counts. It is what we *have* that we want. It is what we *have* that we value. It is what we *have* that gives us our self-image of worth and position in the world.

Once we have proven to ourselves that we can have, that our basic needs can be fulfilled, that we have the power to provide for our own needs and those of others who are dependent upon us, the mind begins to become more interested in what it is that we *do*. Then, we move to a different social set in which what we *do* in the world is the basis of our value and how others rate us. As we move up in lovingness, our doingness is less and less preoccupied with self-service and becomes more and more oriented to being of service to others. As our consciousness grows, we see that service, which is lovingly oriented toward others, automatically results in the fulfillment of our own needs. (This does not mean sacrifice. Service is not sacrifice.) Eventually, we become convinced that our own needs are automatically fulfilled by the universe, and our actions become almost automatically loving.

At that point, it is no longer what we do in the world but what we *are* that counts. We have proven to ourselves that we can have what we need, that we can do almost anything, given the willingness. And now what we *are*, within ourselves and to others, becomes most important. People now seek our company, not because of what we *have*, not because of what we *do* and society's labels, but because of what we have *become*. Because of the quality of our presence, people just want to be around us and experience us. Our social description changes. We are no longer the person who has a fashionable apartment or big car or a bric-a-brac collection, nor are we labeled as the President of the So-and-So Corporation or a member of the Board of Directors of some organization. Now we are described as a splendid person, as somebody whom people just have to meet, just have to know. We become described as a charismatic person.

This level of beingness is typical of self-help groups. In self-help groups, no one is interested in what others do in the world or what they have. They are only interested in whether or not we have achieved certain inner goals, such as those of honesty, openness, sharingness, lovingness, willingness to help, humility, genuineness, and awareness. They are interested in our quality of beingness.

Glamour

Glamour is a very useful subject to understand. Once we understand it, it greatly facilitates the letting go of desires. The book called *Glamour: A World Problem* (1950), by Alice Bailey, presents the whole subject expertly.

If we look at something that we want, we can begin to distinguish between the thing itself versus the aura, patina, flash, and attractive magnetic effect of a quality that can best be described as "glamour." It is this disparity between what a thing is in itself, and the glamour that we have attached to it, which leads to disillusionment. So often we have chased some goal and, then, when we have achieved it, we are disappointed. That is because the thing itself does not coincide with our pictures of it. Glamour means that we have attached sentimentality or we have made it bigger than life. We have projected onto a thing a magical quality that somehow leads us to believe that, once we acquire it, we will magically achieve some higher state of happiness and satisfaction.

This happens very often with vocational goals. The man works year after year striving to become president of the company or become important and prominent in some other way. When he gets there, he expects to experience all the satisfaction and the glamour associated with that level of achievement: the kowtowing by employees, the flashy cars, the prominent office, the labels, the titles, and the exclusive addresses. But what he finds is that all of these things are superficial. They are very inadequate compensation for the agonizing energy drain and daily grind that, in reality, the position necessitates. While he pictured that he would get admiration, what he often finds at the top levels is viciousness, competitiveness, envy, and the endless fawning and dishonest manipulations that occur to people in power, including the paranoid attacks by competitors. He finds that his energy is so drained that he has no energy left over for his personal life; his relationships are impaired. His wife complains that he is too exhausted to make love, too depleted to give her the energy she needs, too worn-out to be a good father, and too tired even to enjoy a favorite recreational activity.

The same thing occurs with women in the traditionally feminine areas of achievement. A woman thinks, for instance, if she gets a certain designer dress for the party that the dress is going to bring her attention, adulation, and admiration, and that it will win her a certain social status. With much sacrifice, she spends a great deal of money and effort on the dress, running back and forth for fittings. But what happens? At the dinner party, there are a few passing comments on her dress and that's the end of it. Nobody dances with her any more than usual. She is not more prominent than she was before the party. No more genuine attention is paid to her than previously. She gets some hostile, envious looks from other women who recognize what she probably paid for the dress. During the evening, she has the usual argument with her escort, and they go home in the car barely speaking to each other, the same as in the past.

As women make gains in the corporate and political arenas, they face the disappointment that accompanies longed-for, glamorized leadership roles in the public. What was predicted to enhance prestige and esteem instead brings criticism, envy, and hostility—even from other women. The experience of achieving their goal is often not what they thought it was going to be. There is endless judgment of a woman's public persona and dress, and she may have the gnawing feeling of inner worry that she has failed her family by going for professional fulfillment. "Winning" is sometimes not as liberating as glamour would want us to believe.

Emotional goals are also glamorized by sentimentality and emotionalism. A certain excitement is projected onto the emotional event (e.g., a reunion, a first date, or being elected president of one's class). It is made to seem more important than it really is in the overall course of events. After the event passes, life goes on the same and disappointment ensues.

Glamorization, of course, is starkly obvious in

advertising. Here we see it *sui generis*. The cowboy is the glamorization of masculinity, and the ballet dancer is the glamorization of femininity. Men are attracted by personality, not the brand; thus, the cowboy represents the glamorized male who is rugged, cool, suave, and in control. The consumer projects onto the product that it will give him those desired personality traits.

Glamorization is living at a fantasy level. Therefore, when we proceed to let go of a desire, we must dissect away that which is exaggeration, fantasy, and romanticization. Once we have relinquished the glamour, it will be relatively easy to surrender the desire itself. If you let go of the romanticization of the cowboy, for example, then the cigarette or the cheeseburger that he was handling in the commercial will lose its appeal. In fact, much to our surprise, we will find over and over again that the desire was attached to the glamorous fantasy; there was no reality in it in the first place. Because there was no reality in it, the world is constantly selling us dishonesty, catering to our desire for that romantic, glamorized aspect. It promises to make us more important than we really are. Glamour at that level of dishonesty is a fake.

The mind protests: "Do I have to give up all that glamorous excitement? Do I have to let go of my pictures of emotional gratification and excitement?" The answer is obviously "No." We don't have to give them up at all. And we can achieve the goals effortlessly and easily once we are conscious of what we are choosing. We can have them directly. We can be attractive, but we won't get it in a fake way such as driving a certain style of car. We will get it by letting go of our smallness and owning our greatness, thereby reflecting it out into the world. We can easily become that exciting person whom people are eager to know. Just choose to be that person and let go of the block of desiring to be that way. We can have what we want directly without detouring through some fraudulent promise that will lead us into frustration and disappointment.

The way to become that exciting person whom people want to know is very easy. We simply picture the kind of person we want to be and surrender all the negative feelings and blocks that prevent us from being that. What happens, then, is that all we need to have and to do will automatically fall into place. This is because, in contrast to *having* and *doing*, the level of *being* has the most power and energy. When it is given priority, it automatically integrates and organizes one's activities. This mechanism is evidenced in the common experience, "What we hold in mind tends to manifest."

The Power of Inner Decision

These are not philosophical positions but practical processes that can be proven through experience. It is easy to experiment with these concepts and watch the automatic results take place. Because of the mind's tendency to want to attribute credit elsewhere, other than to the power of our own consciousness, it is good to keep a diary to write down goals that we would really like to achieve and then check them off and make follow-up notes. Why? Because it will take a while before we believe that it is truly our own power that is accomplishing these ends.

Here is an interesting example of the denial of inner power. A man, who was desperate for a job and pretty frantic about it, was instructed on how to apply the letting go technique to his job situation. Because he was of a religious nature, he was advised to forget about getting a job, to turn it over to God, and to surrender his desire in the matter while staying open to what might happen. A week later, he recounted: "Well, the day after I surrendered wanting a job, nothing happened. Then I got a long-distance phone call from my brother-in-law, and I am going to be joining his firm. If it weren't for my brother-in-law, I never would have gotten a job. It's a good thing I didn't wait for God!"

This is a good example of what the mind has a tendency to do. It was his own surrender, of course, that brought in the call from his brother-in-law. He so frantically desired the job that the desire was blocking the fulfillment of that goal. When he let go of wanting a job, it quickly appeared within 24 hours. But the propensity of the mind is to disown one's own power and project it elsewhere onto the world. This is why people in their own estimation think they are powerless. They have the power, but they have merely projected it onto external forces. We are all powerful beings who have become unconscious of our own power; we have denied and projected it onto others out of guilt and our own sense of smallness.

The majority of what happens in our lifetime is the result of some decision we have made somewhere in the past, either consciously or unconsciously. Because this is so, it is very simple, then, to see our past decisions by looking at our life and tracking backwards.

This principle is demonstrated by a woman who came for psychotherapy. She needed treatment because, in her words, "My relationships never work out." She had one unsatisfactory love affair after another and was always left feeling used and abused. She was full of resentment, self-pity, and depression. The problem, of course, was given in her opening sentence, "My relationships never work out."

Because we deny the power of our own mind, we don't see the glaringly obvious. It is very curious how we have become so unaware. Here is a woman who has the answer sitting right there, but she does not see that it is the answer. She really doesn't see the power of her own belief system. Our mind is so powerful that, if we hold in mind a single thought such as, "My relationships never work out," then that is most likely going to happen in our life. Our unconscious genie, which can only take orders and not make decisions, sees to it that our relationships don't work out.

Of course, she got a lot of payoffs from her disappointing relationship history. She got to experience self-pity, resentment, jealousy, envy, and all those gratifications that the small self feeds on endlessly. If we look at the small part of ourselves, we will see that this is the kind of thing in which it just loves to wallow. The small self glorifies in how miserable life is, how tough luck is, how rotten our experiences have been and how mean people have been to us. But we pay a big price when we listen to this set of programs.

The corollary is obviously true. If our mind, by its decision, has the power to make negative things happen in our life, then it has equal power in the opposite, positive direction. We can choose all over again. This time we can choose the positive. We can cancel the old programs, and we can do that by beginning to relinquish the gratification we were getting out of the negative payoffs.

Now that we have looked at the subject a bit, we

can come up with the term that most aptly describes this set of emotions: "selfishness." The mere use of the word instantly sets up a resistance due to guilt. We all feel guilty because of selfishness. This puts us in an impossible position because, in order to carry out what the world has taught us, we have to indulge in the very thing for which it then condemns us: selfishness. To look at the subject, let's first make a decision that we are not going to beat ourselves up about it and get into the self-indulgence of guilt. That's what guilt is, really, isn't it? Self-indulgence.

Instead, let's look at the term "selfishness" as merely describing the collective motivations and modes of operation of the small self that is a genetic aspect of the mind which, due to our own naïveté, we allowed ourselves to be programmed with, and which we are now resolved to de-program in reverse, like the "uninstall" command on a computer.

The reason to let go of selfishness is not because of guilt. Not because it's a "sin." Not because it's "wrong." All such motivations come from lower consciousness and self-judgment. Rather, the reason to let go of selfishness is simply because it is impractical. It doesn't work. It's too costly. It consumes too much energy. It delays the accomplishment of our goals and the realization of our wants. Because of its very nature, the small self is the creator of guilt and its self-perpetuator; that is, out of guilt we strive to accomplish and achieve success. Then, when we achieve success, we feel guilty because we have it. There is no winning of the guilt game. The only solution is to give it up, to let it go.

Our mind would like to make us think that guilt is laudatory, and the guilt-mongers of the world love to make an idol of it. Which is more important: to feel guilty or to change for the better? If somebody owes us money, would we rather they feel guilty about it or pay us the money? If we intend to feel guilty, we should at least consciously choose it instead of being unwittingly run by it.

When we move from being selfish with a small "s," we move into being Selfish with a capital "S." We move from our smaller self to our greater Self. We move from weakness to power, and from self-hatred and pettiness to lovingness and harmony. We move from strife to ease, and from frustration to accomplishment.

In summation, then, instead of the motivation of selfishness and desire, we can much more effortlessly bring into our life that which we want by envisioning what we wish to have happen. We do this by declaration of our intention, by acceptance, by decision, and by the act of consciously choosing.

8

ANGER

Anger may vary all the way from rage to mild resentment. It includes revenge, outrage, indignation, fury, jealousy, vindictiveness, spite, hatred, contempt, wrath, argumentativeness, hostility, sarcasm, impatience, frustration, negativity, aggression, violence, revulsion, meanness, rebellion, explosive behavior, agitation, abusiveness, abrasiveness, smoldering, sullenness, pouting, and stubbornness. These variations of anger are well exemplified by the daily news on television.

Anger may come up about the technique of surrender itself. Anger that one is expected to let go of feelings that, in the past, have been valued. Anger at the fear of loss. Anger at feelings in general. Anger at a feeling that does not relinquish immediately.

There is a lot of energy in anger; therefore, we may actually feel energized when we are irritated or angry. One of the tricks people learn is to move up quickly from apathy and grief into anger, and then to jump from anger to pride, and then on into courage. In anger, there is the energy for action. This results in doingness in the world. When the "have-nots" of the world become energized by desire and move up to anger over what they lack, that anger moves them into the actions necessary to fulfill their dreams for a better life.

The quantity of suppressed anger in the population can be verified quickly by seeing how popular violence is in the media, where the viewers are presented with a vicarious experience of letting out their anger in the form of beatings, shootings, stabbings, lynchings, killings of various "bad guys."

We typically feel so much guilt about anger that we find it necessary to make the object of our anger "wrong" so that we can say our anger is "justified." Few are the persons who can take responsibility for their own anger and just say, "I am angry because I am full of angriness."

Using Anger Positively

It is common for people to repress their anger, aggression, and inner hostility; they view it as unpleasant, undignified, and even as a moral failure or spiritual setback. They do not realize that repressed anger is nonetheless the energy of anger and, if not acknowledged and worked through, it will have deleterious consequences to their health and overall progress. The intention behind anger is negative, and it will have similar consequences even if it is not expressed.

A helpful approach is to view the energy of anger positively and to use it to fire up our ambitions and our actions in a useful way. For instance, let's say that we are angry at our boss. We feel resentful. He never seems to acknowledge our abilities or efforts. But we know it's unwise to express anger and resentment. It would very likely result in the loss of our job or at least bring on the continued resentment of the boss. At best, the expression of anger would result in a tacky situation. Instead, we can make a decision to use that energy in a constructive way in our own behalf. It can be the inspiration for us to create a project that, because of its excellence, proves our point. It might be the energy for us to move up and out of a situation that is unsatisfactory. We can utilize that energy to create new job opportunities or find a better job, form a committee, improve our employment situation, start a union, or whatever we think would benefit our personal goals.

In personal relationships, the same opportunity exists. The anger can be utilized to inspire us to improve our communication skills, take a course on interpersonal relationships, or enroll in a self-improvement program. The anger can inspire us to rededication, to put forth greater clarity of effort, and to actually do a better job. In this way, the situation can result in recommitment. It can inspire us to look within ourselves and relinquish all the negative feelings, via acceptance. Instead of being mad about it, we can accept it.

Self-Sacrifice

There are many sources of anger. We have already mentioned that very often a complex of angry feelings is connected with fear, and the anger disappears when we let go of the fear. Another source of anger is that of pride, and especially that aspect of pride called vanity. Frequently, it is our personal pride that feeds and propagates the anger.

One source of pride is connected with self-sacrifice. If our relationships with others are associated with our small self in the form of sacrifice, then we are setting ourselves up for later anger, because the other person is usually unaware of our "sacrifice" and is, therefore, unlikely to fulfill our expectations.

An example of this comes from a day in the life of a typical traditional marriage. The wife spends the entire day working hard at cleaning the house, meticulously looking after the plants, bringing in flowers, rearranging some furniture, and doing all she can to make the house look beautiful. When the husband comes home, he doesn't say a word about the house or even seem to notice. Instead, he is exhausted from a day at work, and he recounts its various trials and tribulations. In his mind, he is thinking of all the self-sacrifices he has made: the irate customers, the arduous drive through commuter traffic, the irritable boss, and the pressure of deadlines. He is thinking of all that he has done for his wife and family. While he is thinking of all this hardship, she is feeling a mounting resentment that he hasn't acknowledged her efforts, and she goes back in her mind over all the sacrifices she made that day. She could have gone out for lunch with friends. She could have finished reading the book that she is enjoying. She could have watched her favorite program on television. Instead, she did all of this for him, and now he is making no comment on the results of her efforts. As both harbor their grudges, resentments, and frustrations, their inner anger mounts; it is expressed as coolness and detachment as they escape into television for the evening and go to bed silently to brood over their grievances. This is such a typical American home scene that it is almost banal to repeat it here. Yet, its commonness speaks of its learning value to us; we can examine it and try to unravel this decline of a relationship.

That which we want, desire, and insist upon from another person is felt by them as pressure. They will, therefore, unconsciously resist. In the above example, both persons are looking for acknowledgment. They want it, desire it, but block it in each other. Each side feels pressured and, consequently, resistant. The resistance is because pressure is always felt by us as a denial of our choice. It is felt as emotional blackmail. The unconscious formula goes, "Give me what I want or I will punish you by withdrawal, anger, pouting, sulking, and resentment." We all resent feeling emotionally blackmailed. We all know the resistance we feel when we become aware that somebody is fishing for a compliment, and the same resistance goes on unconsciously as well as consciously.

When we are motivated by self-sacrifice, we are pressuring the other person. Even if we force an acknowledgment, it will be a disgruntled one. A forced compliment does not satisfy. Part of the anger here arises from the pride of self-sacrifice. We have a certain secret vanity about what we are doing for others, and our pride of achievement makes us vulnerable to anger when our "sacrifice" is not recognized.

The way to offset this anger is to acknowledge and relinquish the pride, surrender our desire for the pleasure of self-pity and, instead, view our efforts on behalf of others as *gifts*. We can experience the joy of being generous with others as its own reward.

Acknowledgment

One of the great secrets of relationship is acknowledgment. The behavior of others toward us always includes a hidden gift. Even if that behavior appears

negative, there is something in it for us. Very often that
something appears in the form of a signal to us to
become more aware. Let's say, for example, that somebody calls us "stupid." Our natural response is one of
anger. We can use the energy of that anger consciously: "What is that person asking me to become
more aware of?" If we ask ourselves the question, we
may come to the realization that we were being self-
centered; we were being uncaring; we were failing to
acknowledge them; and we were not being conscious
and aware of what was going on in the relationship.

If we constantly follow this procedure, we will
come to the awareness that everyone in our life is acting as a mirror. They are really reflecting back to us
what we have failed to acknowledge within ourselves.
They are forcing us to look at what needs to be
addressed. What aspect of our smaller self needs to be
relinquished? This means that we have to constantly let
go of our pride in order to undo anger, so that we can
be grateful for the continual opportunities of growth
with which we are presented in the course of everyday experience.

To do this, we have to resist the temptation to
indulge in making ourselves and others "wrong." If we
look at the "small self" aspect of ourselves, we will see
that making ourselves and others "wrong" is one of its
favorite activities (e.g., politics and the media). This is
because the small self is ignorant of better ways to
accomplish our goals. It does not see the alternative,
which is choosing to change a situation out of free
choice.

One way we force ourselves out of unsatisfactory
situations is by making ourselves or the situation
"wrong." Instead of merely choosing to find a better

job, for instance, our smaller self makes the job, the boss, and fellow workers "wrong." Because of the picture of wrongness, the situation now becomes intolerable, and we are forced to change it. How much easier it would have been had we just simply chosen to move on to a better situation. However, because of our sense of obligation, guilt is very often the block to this simpler way. In other words, because of what has benefited us in a situation, we feel guilty about leaving it. So the unconscious ingeniously has created the whole mechanism of wrongness to force us out of dead-end situations. This often happens in interpersonal relationships where we feel that we have to make the other person "wrong" in order to justify leaving them. Resorting to the mechanism of wrongness is simply a denial of our own freedom to choose.

One source of anger stems from the unacknowledged acts of the love that we have expressed to others. Love in this context means the everyday simple forms of lovingness that go on in every human relationship in the form of thoughtfulness, consideration, polite gestures, encouragement, and providing. Very often an internal dialogue can go on for years about our resentment over the other person's lack of appreciation for our feelings about them. If this is so for us, it must be the case for others as well. There are people, therefore, in our life who are walking around with an endless mental stream of thoughts about us, having to do with our lack of appreciation of their feelings for us.

This whole arena of anger can be offset and prevented when we see the enormous value of simply acknowledging the gestures of others toward us. This means to acknowledge all of their communications to us. For instance, if friends call us on the phone, we thank them for calling us. The reason for doing this is that it makes the other persons feel complete and secure with us. It is an acknowledgment of their value in our life, and everyone feels pleased when we acknowledge their value.

By this simple mechanism of acknowledgment, it is possible, within a matter of days, to transform all of one's relationships in a rather dramatic way. This acknowledgment does not have to go on in the outer world but can take place within oneself. As we examine our relationships, we can ask ourselves, "What have I failed to acknowledge in those with whom I have daily contact?"

It is a very valuable experience to pick someone in our life who, in our view, is critical toward us and now, within ourselves, begin to look at how we have failed to acknowledge them. We surrender all of our negative feelings about them, and we begin to give them credit, affirming their value to us. Their value may simply be that they are a spur to our emotional growth and development. The nagging spouse or scowling neighbor is trying to say something. Almost always in this sort of situation, such persons are not feeling acknowledged for the contribution they are making to our life. Once their value to us has been acknowledged, the nagging stops.

Expectations

When we stop pressuring others with our expectations, we create an opening for them spontaneously to respond positively to us. We can, in a prophylactic move, offset resentments by shifting what we have done for others from the level of sacrifice to the level of a loving gift. We can then acknowledge ourselves for this move and drop our expectations, which will dissolve the resistances in others.

A simple experiment illustrates this shift. There was a man who brought back two new shirts from Mexico. The new shirts were of a totally different design than the kind of clothes he was accustomed to wearing. The first day that he decided to wear one of the shirts, he noticed he had an inner expectation and a sort of subtle pride in doing something new and different. However, instead of surrendering the pride, he decided to keep it; that is, he purposefully didn't use the letting go technique to surrender the pride and simply let it be there. He wanted to see what would happen, how people would respond. That day, he proudly wore the new shirt and, sure enough, nobody even mentioned it, despite the fact that it was totally different from his usual attire. It must have really stood out, but there was not a single comment. When he went home, he had to laugh at how true was entrepreneur Robert Ringer's term for that kind of a situation as the "boy/girl theory." (Boy wants girl, therefore, girl is disinterested in boy. As soon as boy is no longer interested in girl, girl now wants boy.)

The next morning he decided he would wear the other new shirt, but this time he surrendered all of his vanity and his expectations of being noticed. He let go of that little pride that he was doing something new and different, and he acknowledged the love of all his friends and the important part they played in the happiness of his life. By the time he got through the letting go process, he was totally surrendered on wearing the shirt. He knew he was totally surrendered, because it was okay if they noticed the new shirt, and it was okay if they didn't. That day was suddenly like new shirt day! Almost every person he met commented on the new shirt, asked him where he had gotten it, and he spent the day getting lots of attention. This experiment humorously makes the point: *We get what we want when we stop insisting on it!*

Expectation of others is a form of emotional blackmail. We can feel our resistance when others pull for certain emotional "goods" from us. We can get away from being emotionally blackmailed by looking at how we do it with others, and, then, we can let go of wanting to manipulate their emotional responses toward us.

Another way of preventing anger is by making a decision within oneself no longer to accept invalidation from others or the small aspect of oneself. This decision can be in the form of a firm declaration: "I will no longer accept invalidation from myself or others." When this is coupled with the habit of acknowledging all that is positive within ourselves and others, relationships rapidly change, their potential sources of anger having been removed.

Chronic Resentment

Chronic, unrecognized anger and resentment re-emerge in our life as depression, which is anger directed against oneself. If pushed further into the unconscious, it can re-emerge as psychosomatic illnesses. Migraine headaches, arthritis, and hypertension are frequently cited examples of chronic suppressed anger. These symptoms are very often alleviated as people learn how to let go of their inner anger. For example, in one study, the blood pressure measurements of the participants were taken before and after they received instruction on how to let go of negative emotion. All the people with hypertension showed drops in their blood pressure, both the systolic and diastolic (the upper and lower numerical readings), once they started letting go of the emotional pressure that they had built up over the years. The Stanford University Forgiveness Project confirms the cardiac benefits of relinquishing anger and resentment. In the program, parents of children killed in the Protestant-Catholic violence in Ireland learned how to let go of their bitterness toward the "enemy"; measurements of their cardiac health and physical stamina showed significant improvement (Luskin, 2003). Forgiveness healed their hearts—literally. As we have said before, with muscle testing we can prove instantly that anger and resentment have a deleterious effect on the body, emotions, energy flow, and on the synchronization of the brain hemispheres. Anger kills the angry person, not the so-called "enemy."

The mind would like us to think that there is such a thing as "justifiable anger," which takes the form of moralistic indignation. If we look at moralistic indignation, we will see that it is propped up by vanity and pride. We like to think how right we are in a situation and how "wrong" the other persons are. We get a passing cheap little satisfaction out of that, but our muscle-testing proves what the cost is to our overall emotional and physical economy. The price we pay for chronic anger and resentment is sickness and premature death. Is this worth the small satisfaction of being right?

The cost that we are willing to pay in these kinds of circumstances is sometimes surprising. Let's say we have a situation in which we made a loan to someone

who has never paid us back. We have a chronic
resentment about it and, when we meet the person
socially, we say as little as possible. If we get honest
with ourselves, we will likely see that we are getting
satisfaction out of our being right and the other person's being wrong. In fact, we are enjoying it so much
that a part of us really doesn't want him to pay off the
debt because, then, we would no longer be able to
enjoy the secret pleasure of making him wrong. This
was precisely true in a case involving several hundred
dollars. The inner decision was made on the part of
the lender to be honest about all the little satisfactions
of being right, and making the other person wrong,
and then to surrender on each one of these ego payoffs. Clearly, the ego payoffs were blocking the other
person from repaying the loan. With continual surrender, the whole deal was totally let go, and a shift was
made to view the loan as a gift. Admittedly, this other
person had really needed the money. Why not simply
see it as a gift and let go of the expectation of repayment? Now, instead of resentment, gratefulness pre-
dominated because there had been the opportunity to
help another human being in a moment of real need.
Within 48 hours, a check arrived in the mail for the
entire amount with a note of apology for the delay in
repayment!

　　This experience and many like it demonstrate how
we are all psychically connected. The internal position
we hold about another person is forcing them to adopt
a complementary defensive position. It is, therefore,
not Pollyanna to forgive and forget, but a reasonable
recognition of emotional realities. The inner-actions
between human beings are determined by the config-
urations of the vibrational energies that their emotions

are radiating into space. The energy of the vibration, and the thought form with which it is associated, create a readable record.

Although this common, everyday experience is hardly news to most women, who in our society are characteristically more intuitive, it comes as a shock and surprise to a large percentage of men. In our society, men are characteristically left-brained and given to reason and logic rather than intuition, which is characterized as a right-brain function.

As we continue to let go of negativity and bring about inner emotional healing, there is a greater balance between left and right brain function. The intuitive faculty is also available in men; they are often pleasantly surprised as they begin to recognize its emergence. It is satisfying and surprising to be able, instantly, to "read" a situation that was totally baffling to reason and logic. The ideal situation is to form a working hypothesis with intuition and then to use reason and logic to check it out. This, of course, offsets the anger that arises from misunderstanding and miscalculation, and it increases the skillful mastery of emotions.

Another thing that dissipates anger is our mere willingness to relinquish it. Willingness is our overall decision to find a better way, to stop relying on anger, and to move up to courage and acceptance. This willingness already starts the process of relinquishing anger. As students of the martial arts are well aware, anger indicates weakness and vulnerability; it is seen as a tool that we are handing to our opponent. We can see from muscle testing why this is so. The angry person has already lost half his muscle power and has,

therefore, lost the split second timing that is so decisive to victory in hand-to-hand combat.

It is so prevalent in our society to include the
propensity to anger as a male "macho" attribute. We
hear people swelling with pride as they relate how
they "told that guy off." We can ask ourselves, "Who
needs enemies? Isn't there enough negative influence
in our life without adding one more?" Especially when
we look at the fact that all emotions generate a vibrational energy in the universe, what is the point of sur-
rounding ourselves with negative thought forms about
those we view as enemies? Why go out of our way to
hold onto them as enemies by stockpiling resentments
and negativity in ourselves? Likely, when we review
our own personal experiences, we will see that the
effort involved in converting people we once considered enemies into friends brought gratification and a
later reward. In most cases, they proved to be a positive benefit to our life. We never know whom, in a
later chapter of the book of life, we are going to need
as a friend.

We need to be aware that we have unwittingly
become "injustice collectors." The media reports are
full of this form of chronic resentment. We see "injustice collecting" in international relations where making
the other nation "wrong" is actually a primary objective. We are unconsciously programmed to believe that
"injustice collecting" is "normal." In contrast to this
habitual pattern, which is destructive and weakening,
the letting go technique frees us from keeping close
account of the "wrongs" made against us. Our time
and attention are freed up to see the beauty and
opportunity around us.

Anger is binding, not freeing. It connects us to

another person and holds them in our life pattern. We are stuck in the negative pattern until we let go of the energy of anger and its little payoffs of righteous indignation, feeling wronged, and the desire for revenge. It may not be exactly the same person who constantly recurs in our life. If not that person, then others will appear who have the same quality that triggers our anger and resentment. This will keep recurring until we finally handle our inner angriness. Then, suddenly, people with that quality disappear from our life. Therefore, anger may force someone to be physically distant from us, but psychically it binds them to us more closely, until we fully relinquish the anger and resentment.

Relinquishing anger brings us many benefits. We are free to experience emotional comfort and ease, gratitude for the daily opportunities to grow and heal, mutual caring with another without subtle "strings attached," improvement in health, and more life energy. These breakthroughs allow us to move up to a more effective and effortless state of inner freedom.

9

PRIDE

In common parlance, pride is often thought to be a "good thing." However, if we take a good look at it, we will see that, just like all the other negative feelings we have discussed so far, pride is devoid of love. Consequently, it is essentially destructive. Pride may take the form of over-valuation, denial, playing the martyr, being opinionated, arrogant, boastful, inflated, one-up, haughty, holier-than-thou, vain, self-centered, complacent, aloof, smug, snobbish, prejudiced, bigoted, pious, contemptuous, selfish, unforgiving, spoiled, rigid, patronizing, judgmental, and in milder forms, pigeonholing.

Intellectual pride leads to ignorance, and spiritual pride is the main block to spiritual development and maturation in everyone. Religious pride by self-identification with the righteous and "having the only true way" is the basis of all religious wars, rivalry, and dismal occurrences such as the Inquisition. The biggest downfall of all is religious pride and considering oneself entitled to kill others who don't share one's specific beliefs.

In all of us, the prideful feeling, "I have the answers," blocks our growth and development. It is interesting that the egotistical part of the mind is willing to sacrifice the whole remainder of a person for its own sake. Rather than admit to being wrong, people will literally give up the life of the body itself and sacrifice any aspect of life on the altar of pride (e.g., religious wars and crusades). Male pride about those programs that our society considers masculine blocks the emotional and psychological inner development of most men in our society. Some women are now joining the ranks of chauvinism, which only compounds the problem and intensifies the battle of the sexes.

Vulnerability of Pride

The prideful person is constantly on the defensive because of the vulnerability of inflation and denial. Conversely, the humble person cannot be humiliated for they are immune to vulnerability, having let go of pride. In its place, they have an inner security and self-esteem. Many people try to substitute pride for genuine self-esteem; however, genuine self-esteem does not actually arise until pride is relinquished. That which inflates the ego does not result in inner strength. On the contrary, it increases our vulnerability and overall level of fear. When we are in a state of pride, our energy is dissipated by the constant preoccupation with defending our lifestyle, vocation, neighborhood, clothes, year and make of car, ancestry, country, and political and religious belief systems. There is a tireless preoccupation with appearance and what other people will think, so there is a constant vulnerability to the opinions of others.

When pride and self-inflation have been relinquished, there is an inner security that takes their place. When we no longer feel called upon to defend our image, criticisms and attacks from others diminish and finally stop. When we let go of our need for validation or to prove ourselves right, then the challenges against us fall away.

This brings us to one of the basic laws of consciousness: *Defensiveness invites attack.* An examination of the nature of pride facilitates the letting go of it, as it is no longer valued. It is seen for what it is, in truth: weak. The dictum, "Pride goeth before a fall," prevails. Pride is thin ice, a poor substitute for that rock-like, real strength that comes from courage, acceptance, or peace.

Is there such a thing as "healthy" pride? When we talk of healthy pride, we are referring to self-esteem, an inner awareness of one's true value and worth. This inner awareness is different from the energy of pride. Self-awareness of one's true value is characterized by lack of defensiveness. Once we have consciously contacted the truth of our real beingness—the nature of our inner self with all of its true innocence, greatness, and nobility of the human spirit—we no longer need pride. We just know what we *are*, and this self-knowledge is sufficient for us. That which we truly know never needs defense and is different from the energy of pride that we are discussing in this chapter.

Let's look at some of the kinds of pride with which we have been programmed and see how they bear up under examination. Pride of family, pride of country, and pride of accomplishment are typical examples that come to mind. Is pride really the loftiest of human emotions? The very fact that it is characterized by defensiveness proves otherwise. When we have pride in our possessions or in some organizations with which we identify, we feel obligated to defend them. Pride in our ideas and opinions leads to endless arguments, conflict, and woe.

A higher feeling state than pride is that of love. If we *love* all of the things noted above (family, country, accomplishments), that means there is no question of their worth in our mind. We no longer have to be on the defensive. When true recognition and knowledge replace opinion, which is part of pride, there is no room for argument. Our sheer love and appreciation for something is a solid position that cannot be assailed.

Pride, because it is a vulnerable position, always implies that somewhere there is a doubt that needs to be cleared up, and the opponent quickly centers on that doubt. When all doubts have been removed, opinions and pride disappear. There is a subtle inference of apology in pride, as though the thing in itself was not good enough to stand on its own merit. That which is worthy of our love and respect hardly needs an apologist. Pride infers subtly that there is room for debate and that the worth of something is open to question.

When we truly love something and, thereby, become one with it, it is because we see its intrinsic perfection. In fact, its "faults" are part and parcel of its perfection, for all that we see in the universe is in the process of becoming. In that process, its perfect evolution is part of that perfection. Thus the half-unfolded flower is not an imperfect flower that needs defense. On the contrary, its blossoming is proceeding with precise perfection according to the laws of the universe. Likewise, each and every individual on the planet is unfolding, growing, learning, and reflecting that same perfection. We might say that the unfoldment of the evolutionary process is proceeding precisely according to cosmic laws.

One of the drawbacks about the position of pride, as we have said, is its vulnerability. Vulnerability then invites attack; therefore, in society, we witness that prideful people draw criticism, and their vulnerability is what accounts for the saying, "Pride goeth before a fall." In the biblical account, it was Lucifer's pride that was his Achilles' heel, despite the great standing that he had acquired.

Humility

The attempt to suppress pride out of guilt simply does not work. It is not helpful to label the energy of pride a "sin" and to suppress it in ourselves out of guilt, to hide it, or to pretend that we do not experience it. What happens is that the energy subtly takes on a new form, known as spiritual pride.

We do not feel comfortable in the presence of those who are prideful; therefore, pridefulness blocks communication and the expression of love. Although we love those who are prideful about specific accomplishments, we love them in spite of their pride and not because of it.

Feeling guilty about pride as a spiritual sin only locks it in and, as we have said, is not really the answer. The real answer is merely to let go of it by examining its true nature. Once we see pride for what it is, it is one of the easier emotions to surrender. To begin with, we can ask ourselves: "What is the purpose of pride? What is its payoff? Why do I seek it? For what does it compensate? What do I have to realize about my true nature in order to let pride go without a feeling of loss?" The answer is rather obvious. The smaller we feel within, the more we have to compensate for an inner sense of inadequacy, unimportance, and valuelessness by the substitution of the emotion of pride.

The more we surrender our negative emotions, the less we will rely on the crutch of pride. In its place, there will be a quality that the world calls "humility" and that we subjectively experience as peacefulness. True humility is distinct from the paradox of "pride in one's humility," or "false modesty," seen frequently in the public arena. False modesty is the pretense of self-diminishment with the longing that others will recognize the accomplishments that one is so proud of, but too proud to brag about openly.

True humility cannot be experienced by the person who is said to possess it, because it is not an emotion. As we have said before, the truly humble cannot be humbled. They are immune to humiliation. They have nothing to defend. There is no vulnerability and, therefore, the truly humble do not experience critical attacks by others. Instead, a truly humble person sees the critical verbalization by another person as merely a statement of the other person's inner problems. For instance, if somebody were to say, "You think you're pretty good, don't you?," what the truly humble person would see is that the other person has a problem with envy, and the question has no basis in reality in the first place. There is nothing to be offended by and no need to react. In contrast, for a prideful person, this question would be viewed as an insult and lead to hurt feelings, verbal comeback, or even a violent end in some cases.

Joy and Gratitude

Because pride is sometimes seen as a motivator of achievement, what would be its higher level substitute? One answer would be joy. What is wrong with joy as the reward for successful achievement, rather than pride? Pride carries with it the desire for recognition from others and, consequently, there is a vulnerability to anger and disappointment if it is not forthcoming at some point. If we achieve a certain goal for the pleasure, enjoyment, love of accomplishment, and the inner joy that it brings to us, we are invulnerable to the reaction of others.

We can recognize our proneness to pain by looking at the kind of reactions we are hoping to elicit from others by our choices and behavior. This includes mannerisms, expressions, style of dress, the kind of possessions we choose, the brand name of car we drive, the kind of home we have, the address at which we live, the schools we have attended or which our children attend, or the labels on the products we buy. In fact, if we look at our current society, we see to what an absurd degree this pridefulness has taken place. Labels are now worn on the outside of many clothes and personal articles. It hasn't reached the level of rakes and shovels yet, but it could sooner or later! Nobody has thought of it yet, but we could all carry around rakes and shovels ostentatiously with designer names emblazoned upon them.

This points to another one of the drawbacks of pride: the exploitability to which it exposes us. Pridefulness means that we can be manipulated with great ease. In return for an absurdity, a great deal of money is lifted out of our pocketbooks. The situation is currently comical in that people take great pride in how much they have been exploited. It is a current status symbol among certain circles to brag about how much one has paid for certain things. When we remove the glamour from it, we might say that the person was sort of stupid. They really got suckered in or was naïve and just didn't know any better.

The pride of snobbishness is probably the most supercilious of all. Does ostentation really impress? Actually, no. The response that we see is one of fascination. People get a charge out of the superficial glamour, but underneath they do not truly respect it, because they know what it really is. When we settle for the pridefulness of ostentation, we impress no one.

This dynamic revealed itself during a trip to Canada to visit the home of a wealthy individual who subtly conveyed the price tag of his many possessions. On the same trip, malnourished Canadian Indian children were seen playing around the huge grain elevators that were filled to overflowing, the grain being held there to manipulate a higher world price through artificial creation of a shortage. As this wealthy person talked of his possessions, images of the children with their thin little legs flashed to mind. Far from being impressed with his wealth, there was sorrow for his sense of values and compassion for the lack of self-worth that forced him to compensate in such a pathetic superficiality.

Does that mean that we cannot take pleasure in expensive possessions? No, not at all. What we are talking about is pride. The problem is not that we have possessions, but that we have a prideful, possessive, and self-congratulatory attitude about them. It is the attitude of pride that creates the space for fear. The same wealthy man in Canada mentioned above also had an expensive burglar alarm system. Pride, like all the other negative emotions, engenders guilt. Guilt engenders fear. Fear means potential loss. Pride, therefore, always means a loss of peace of mind.

The opposite of prideful acquisitiveness is simplicity. Simplicity does not mean poverty of possessions; rather, it is a state of mind. Another individual is worth millions of dollars, and she holds title to vast estates and possessions. Yet, as a person, she represents absolute simplicity. Her possessions reflect what the world has brought to her, and she takes joy in their beauty. Consequently, never a single criticism is made of her, nor do others express envy.

It is not what we have that matters, but how we hold it, how we frame it in our consciousness, and its meaning to us. Incidentally, this woman's entire estate is totally devoid of burglar alarms or watchdogs. In fact, when this was brought to her attention, she replied, "Oh, heavens! If somebody really needed something that much, they could have it!" There was a correspondence between the fact that nobody ever stole anything from her and the fact that she was willing to share with others. Her invulnerability to theft was related to her lack of pridefulness about her possessions.

Possessiveness and attachment occur as a consequence of pride. Attachment is, therefore, a potential cause for suffering, because attachment brings about fear of loss and, with loss, we go back into apathy, depression, and grief. If we are prideful of a car and somebody steals it, we will experience anguish, pain, and suffering. If, instead, we loosely hold the car (emotionally speaking), and we enjoy its beauty and perfection and we feel grateful for having it, its loss will bring about only minor disappointment.

Gratitude is one of the antidotes of pride. If we happen to be born with a high IQ, we can be grateful for it rather than take pride in it. It's not an accomplishment; we were born with it. If we are grateful for what has been given us and for what has been fulfilled through our God-given talents and endeavors, then we are in a peaceful state of mind and invulnerable to pain.

It is a comical curiosity of the human mind to watch how it attaches pride to anything that is prefixed by the word "mine." We can have absurd pride over the most trivial things and, once we see the comedy of that, it is not too difficult to let go of the pride involved.

Some people, ironically, have the vulnerability of reverse snobbery. They take pride in "bargains" and thrift store conquests. Their personal opinion of people who pay excessive prices for things is that they are sheep to be sheared and they rehearse the quote, "A fool is soon parted from his money." In this thrift store snobbery crowd, the status symbol is the incredible bargain. In fact, they are often in competition with each other to see who will find the best bargains. It is funny to observe that an article of clothing hanging in a thrift shop has no value at all until it becomes "mine." Instantly, great value is attached to it.

The difficult side of prefixing things with the word "mine" is the pride that goes with that sense of ownership. This makes us feel called upon to defend everything we label as "mine." We can reduce our vulnerability by letting go of the desire to possess; instead of saying "mine," we can use the word "a." Not "my" shirt, but "a" shirt. Thus, we will notice that, if we view one of our thoughts as "an opinion" instead of "my opinion," the feeling tone changes. Why do people get so hot under the collar about their opinions? It is just because of that sense of "mine." If opinions are viewed instead as "only an opinion," then there is no longer the vulnerability to prideful anger.

Opinions

If we look at opinions, we will see that they are a dime a dozen. Everybody on the street has thousands of opinions on thousands of subjects, and their opinions change from moment to moment and are vulnerable to every passing whim of fashion, propaganda, and faddism. Today's "in" opinion is tomorrow's "out" opinion. This morning's opinion is passé by afternoon. We can ask ourselves: "Do I want to spread out my vulnerability to attack by so extensively identifying with all these passing thoughts and calling them 'mine'?" Everybody has an opinion on everything. So what? When we look at the true quality of opinions, we will stop giving them as much value. If we look back on our life, we will see that every mistake we ever made was based on an opinion.

We become much less vulnerable if we put our thoughts, ideas, and beliefs, which are all opinions, into a different context. We can view them as ideas that we like or dislike. Some thoughts give us pleasure, and so we like them. Just because we like them today doesn't mean we have to go to war over them. We like a concept so long as it serves us and we are getting enjoyment out of it. Of course, we discard it quite readily when it is no longer a source of pleasure.

When we look at our opinions, we will see that it is primarily our emotions that are giving them any value in the first place.

Instead of feeling pride about our thoughts, what is wrong with just loving them? Why not just love a certain concept because of its beauty, because of its inspirational quality, or because of its serviceability? If we view our thoughts that way, we no longer need the pride of being "right." If we hold the same view of our likes and dislikes, we are no longer prone to argumentativeness. For instance, if we love the music of a certain composer, we no longer need to defend it. We might hope that our companion would also love it but, if not, the worst that we can feel is mild disappointment at not being able to share something that we personally value and enjoy.

If we try this, we will find that people no longer attack our likes and dislikes and concepts. Instead of defensiveness, what they are getting from us now is appreciation. They understand that we appreciate certain things, and that is why we think the way we do. But they will no longer criticize or attack us. The worst we will get is perhaps a kidding or a quizzical attitude. Where pride is absent, attack is also absent.

This is very valuable in those areas, such as politics and religion, which are so historically prone to elicit argument that they are tactically bypassed in polite society. We will find that if we love our religion, whatever it might be, no one will attack us. If we are prideful, however, we will have to avoid the entire subject, because anger will quickly arise as a by-product of the pride. When we truly value something, we lift it aloft out of the demeaning target range of argument.

That which we truly cherish and revere is protected by our own reverence. If we tell somebody that we do something because we get enjoyment out of it, there is really nothing much they can say about it, is there? If we infer that we do it because we are *right* in doing it, we will instantly see their hackles go up because they, also, have an opinion on what is right.

Our values are preferences. We hold them because we love them, enjoy them, and get pleasure from them. If we hold them in that context, we will be left in peace to enjoy them.

The reason that pride arouses attack is because of the inference of being "better than," which is part and parcel of pride. We see many people with dietary regimens about which they are prideful; consequently, they are in constant arguments over the rightness of their dietary regimens and nutritional opinions. They even try to impose their regimens on family members and friends, touting the moral or health superiority of their dietary practice. In contrast, there are people who follow the same regimens because they enjoy doing so, because it makes them feel better, or because it fulfills certain spiritual disciplines; consequently, they are never heard to be in argument, because they have nothing to defend. If someone tells us that they eat the way they eat because they enjoy it, there is nothing much we can say about it, is there? If, on the other hand, they infer that theirs is the right way of eating and, by inference, that ours is wrong, what they are really saying is that they are better than we are. That always arouses resentment.

If we don't take a prideful stance about our opinions, then we are at liberty to change them. How often have we gotten stuck in performing something we really didn't want to do, because we had foolishly taken a prideful stance on an opinion! Very often we would like to have changed our mind or the direction in which we were going, but we got ourselves boxed in by having taken a prideful position.

That brings up one of the resistances to surrendering pride, and that is pride itself. In the prideful position, one of the underlying problems is fear. We fear that, if we change our position in a certain matter, the opinion of others about us will be adversely affected.

One reason for the need for humility about our opinions is because our opinions change as we get deeper and deeper into any given subject or situation. What seems to be so, upon superficial examination, often turns out to be quite different when we really get into it. This, of course, is to the dismay of the politician who makes promises based on fantasies of what is possible. But as he assumes power, he finds that matters are quite different than he had thought. The problems are far more complex. The situation is really due to the net effect of many powerful forces in society. All that politicians can truly promise us is that they will use the best possible judgment for the good of all, as they get deeper into each matter.

This evolutionary aspect of life is really all that any of us can promise ourselves, and this self-knowledge will protect us from disillusionment. This is the safety of the "open mind" position or what is called "beginner's mind" in Zen practice. When we are open-minded, we are admitting that we are not in possession of all the facts, and we are ready to change our opinions as the situation unfolds. In this way, we do not box ourselves into the pain of defending lost causes.

This is very true even in areas we think are based on strictly factual and observable data, such as the field of science. Actually, science deals with hypotheses, and scientific opinion is constantly in the process of flux and change. Scientific opinion, much to the surprise of laypersons, is also subject to fads, passing popularity, paradigm blindness, and political pressure. For instance, in the field of psychiatry, the subject of the relationship between nutrition, blood chemistry, brain function, and mental illness was not popular in the past. The scientists and clinicians who worked in this area found themselves in the "out" group. As time passed and it proved that there was value in this field of investigation, popular scientific opinion changed. Important discoveries were made, and whole industries came into being to provide products which utilized the basic findings of the relationship between nutrition and brain function. The subject is now accepted as respectable, so clinicians and scientists can do research in that area and be accepted as part of the "in" group. Pride, therefore, is also responsible for holding up scientific progress (e.g., global warming theories).

Pride blinds us to many things that would be profoundly beneficial; to a prideful mind, to accept them would be inferring that we are wrong. The more inwardly powerful we really are, the more flexible we become, so that we are open to all that is beneficial. Pride prevents us from seeing that which is totally obvious. People die by the thousands because of pride. They literally give up their health and life itself. Addicts and alcoholics will go to their death because of the denial inherent in pride: "Other people have the problem—not me!" Pride prevents us from recognizing our own limitations and accepting the help we need to overcome them. Our pridefulness isolates us.

When we let go of pride, help comes into our life to address the problems with which we are struggling. We can experiment and prove the truth of that principle by picking one area in which we are having difficulty and thoroughly surrendering all the pride involved. When we do that, some surprising things begin to happen. Letting go of pride unlocks the door to our receiving that which is the most beneficial to us. Are we willing to let go of pride and feeling superior to others? When we are willing to let go of the pseudo-security of pride, we experience the real security that comes with courage, self-acceptance, and joy.

10

COURAGE

The hallmark of courage is the knowledge and feeling, "I can." It is a positive state in which we feel assured, skillful, adequate, capable, alive, loving and giving, with an overall zest for life. We are capable of humor, activity, confidence, and clarity. In this state, we feel centered, balanced, flexible, happy, independent, and self-sufficient. We can be inventive, creative, and open. In courage, there is a lot of energy, action, letting go, capacity to "be there," to be spontaneous, resilient, resourceful, and cheerful. In this state, we can be very effective in the world.

The Courage to Let Go

The level of courage is very helpful in the mechanism of surrender. In courage, we know: "I can look at my feelings"; "I don't have to be afraid of my feelings anymore"; "I can handle them"; "I can take responsibility for them"; "I can learn how to accept them and be free from them"; "I am willing to take risks, to let go of old points of view and to explore new ones"; "I am willing to be joyous and share my experience with others"; "I experience myself as willing and able."

It is often easy to jump from any of the lower feelings up to courage merely by affirming our courage to look at and handle our feelings. The mere willingness to look at and begin to handle them increases our self-esteem. If, for instance, we have a fear and are unwilling to look at it, then we feel diminished and our self-esteem is lowered. If we are willing to look at that fear, examine it, acknowledge its presence, see how it has inhibited our life, and begin to surrender it, then our self-esteem increases, whether the fear disappears or not.

We all know that it takes courage to face fear. We champion the people who face their fear and attempt to do something about it. Such courage is one of the characteristics of nobility and makes a person truly great. Despite all of their negative programming and despite all of their fear, courageous people go forward in life, with no guarantee and not even the knowledge that things are going to get better. So courage increases our self-respect and brings to us the respect of others. We no longer need to feel ashamed.

Let's look at the example of a man who suffered from a lifelong terror of heights. He had worked on being free of the fear for several years and it had gotten much better, but there was still plenty of it left. This was evident when he went to the Grand Canyon with a friend. At first, he stood back about six feet from the ledge. In previous years, he wouldn't have gone within a block of it. Now he stood there, hesitantly. The friend took his hand, saying, "Come on over to the edge with me." And so he did. He kept surrendering on the fear as he walked forward and found that he could actually stand right next to the edge, although admittedly, not without still feeling considerable discomfort. When they left the edge of the canyon, the friend looked at him approvingly and said, "Well, at least you did it! I know how much courage that took." Even though he had not totally overcome the fear, by transcending an inner barrier, he had earned his own self-respect and the respect of others.

When we have these breakthrough experiences, we begin to perceive our fear differently and we stop being ashamed of it. We stop allowing it to invalidate our true worth. It increases our inner strength and our self-approval. In due time, the underlying fears which require courage to overcome diminish to the point that we move on to acceptance.

Self-Empowerment

On the level of courage, the emphasis is on doing. We already know that we are capable of providing for our own needs and for those of others, and we know that, if we are willing to put forth the effort, we can obtain what we want. Thus, people on the level of courage are the doers of the world. Because we can only give away what we ourselves already have, people on the level of courage are able to be supportive and encouraging of others. This is because they are able to give as well as receive, and there is a balance between giving and receiving that occurs naturally.

The levels of consciousness up to this point are concerned primarily with gain. Now, on the level of courage, there is greater power and energy. We have the ability to give to others, because other people are no longer being looked at primarily as a means of help, survival, or support. When we are in the state of courage, we sense our own inner power, strength, and self-worth. We know that we have the capacity to make a difference in the world, not just gain something from it for ourselves. Because of the inner self-confidence, we are much less concerned with security. The emphasis is no longer on what people have, but upon what they do, and have become.

With courage, there is the willingness to take chances and to let go of former securities. There is the willingness to grow and benefit from new experiences. This involves the capacity to admit mistakes without indulging in guilt and self-recrimination. Our sense of self-worth is not diminished by looking at areas that need improvement. We are able to admit the presence of problems without being diminished. As a result, energy, time, and effort are put into self-improvement.

On this level, statements of intention and purpose are much more powerful and envisioned results tend to manifest. We are much more enterprising and creative, because our energies are not drained by the constant preoccupation with emotional or physical survival. Because of greater flexibility, there is a willingness to examine issues with a view to changing overall meaning and context. There is a willingness to risk shifting paradigms.

A paradigm is a whole worldview, and it is only limited by what we view as possible. As old ways of looking at things are challenged, our worldview begins to stretch and expand. That which was previously considered to be impossible becomes possible and eventually is experienced as a new dimension of reality. There is the capacity to look within ourselves to examine our belief systems, ask questions, and seek new solutions. On the level of courage, we are willing to take self-improvement courses, learn consciousness techniques, and risk the journey within to seek our own true Self, the inner reality. There is a willingness to experience uncertainty, periods of confusion, and temporary upset because, underneath the temporary discomfort, we have a long-term transcendent goal. The mind that is operating on the level of courage makes such statements as: "I can handle it"; "We'll make it"; "The job will get done"; "We can see this through"; "All things shall pass."

If we test a person's muscle strength with kinesiology when in the state of courage, the level of "I can handle it," they will test positive and remain strong to our challenge. Although there is still vulnerability to negative thoughts or energies—such as those that emanate from fluorescent lights or artificial sweeteners—the bio-energy field is more radiant than that of the lower, negative states. Because courage is a stronger, more resilient energy field, physical illnesses are less likely to be a predominant aspect of life. There may be chronic residuals of illnesses that originated from the lower levels of consciousness, but they are generally not stabilized. In courage, there is an overall sense of strength and well-being.

Awareness of Others

The lifestyle on this level shows a balance of work, enjoyment, and love. There is not the necessity for over-ambition or "workaholism," although people on the level of courage are capable of considerable energy output if the situation requires it. Because of the letting go of so much negativity, there is a desire and a capacity to love and to have loving relationships. These now assume equal importance with efforts toward survival. There is vocational security, and in the work area there is concern for the welfare of others. People on this level characteristically state that they want jobs which will be of some benefit to the world. They want to feel that there is more meaning to their job than just a salary. Personal growth is important, and there is the awareness on this level that our life is either positively or negatively influencing those around us.

On the lower levels of consciousness, which are characterized by egotism, there is so much concern with self-gain that there is little energy or thought given to our effect on others. On the level of courage, we no longer identify solely with the small self. The world is no longer seen as the depriving or punishing bad parent. Instead, the world is seen as challenging and presenting opportunities for growth, development, and new experiences. Thus, this level is characterized by optimism and the feeling that with the correct facts, education, and orientation, sooner or later most problems can be worked out satisfactorily.

The lower levels limit our consciousness to personal concern, but on this level social issues become important, and energy is expended to help overcome social problems and to be helpful to those less fortunate. Therefore, generosity becomes possible, not just financially, but also in a generosity of attitude. Pleasure is derived from the championing of causes and from supporting the endeavors of others. This energy creates new jobs, businesses, industries, and political and scientific solutions. Education, although not always in the academic sense, becomes important.

On the level of courage, we really start becoming conscious. It dawns on us that we have the freedom and the capacity to choose. We no longer have to be the victim, and freedom in the psychological, emotional, and spiritual sense is possible. Therefore, much less rigidity is present, and because of flexibility and the capacity of concern and genuine love for others, people on this level make good parents, bosses, employees, and citizens.

There is a capacity to put ourselves in another's place and a concern for the feelings of others, as well as their overall welfare. Although the lower negative feelings still tend to occur, they do not predominate or determine one's lifestyle; that is, we do it even though we're scared. People on this level are the backbone of the country. They are the people we turn to when it is necessary to do so for the common good. They are dependable and can be counted on because of their willingness to accept responsibility. On this level, there is a social conscience and humanitarianism. As the basis of moral decisions, guilt takes a back seat to the welfare of others.

It is from this level that we get such sayings as, "Success breeds success." Because of adequate functioning, there is positive feedback, which reinforces confidence and allows greater self-exploration as well as exploration of the world. Although effort is still required to accomplish goals, it is much less than on the lower levels. There is greater satisfaction and gratification because there is greater reward with less effort than that which would be required to overcome fear. There is much greater capacity not only to seek help, but to be able to utilize it and benefit from it.

Money is used in a much more constructive manner, and there is concern with how the expenditures will affect the lives of others. Money is not spent solely for self-gratification, self-aggrandizement, or self-fortification; rather, it is seen as a tool for accomplishment. This level is the one at which true spiritual awareness becomes possible. Because of the emergence from egotism and the relinquishment of the identification with the small self, there is an experiencing of higher energies and the hope of increased awareness. On the lower levels, God is viewed from the emotional coloration of that level. Thus, in apathy, the whole relationship with God is hopeless, if it can be considered at all. On the level of grief, one feels hopelessly separated from any help from God. When overcome with guilt, the person feels undeserving of any relationship with God, and punishment is expected rather than love. On the level of fear, the fear may be so great that the problem of God cannot even be faced, so that the subject is blotted out of consciousness, and God is viewed as fearful, punishing, avenging, jealous, and angry. On the level of anger, God is viewed as depriving, arbitrary, capricious, and failing. On the level of pride, there is egotism about one's religious or spiritual position, characterized by rigidity, inflexibility, intolerance, proneness to exclusivity, bigotry, clannishness, religious argumentation, and warring.

On the level of courage, we are willing to take responsibility for our religious or spiritual position. The increased awareness often results in the emergence of the spiritual seeker, and the pursuit of truth in its religious or spiritual sense truly awakens. This may result in a reaffirmation of our previous position, but now from a totally new viewpoint—that of choice. It may bring about changes, which may be either slow and gradual, or sudden. On this level, there is the awakening of consciousness and the realization that our beliefs and views are now a result of our choice, not just a result of previous blind programming. There is a search for meaning, and this may occur on the level of ethics and humanitarianism rather than in the area specifically denoted as formal religion. We investigate our social function and role in the world, and we inquire as to the value of our lives, not only to ourselves but also to others.

Carl Jung said that the healthy personality is equally balanced between work, play, love, and an aspect of personality called spirituality, which we could also define as the search for meaning and value. These investigations bring inner upsets but also moments of acceptance and peace. There are moments of intuitive understanding which beckon us on to continue the quest, to find out if there is anything beyond just the physical and material world and its ever-changing phenomena.

This level of consciousness is a good one from which to look at and let go of more negative feelings. On this level, we have the energy, capacity, self-confidence, and willingness to acquire know-how and undergo the necessary steps of learning. On this level, there is a desire for self-improvement and the realization that better states of mind are possible. The level of courage knows that it is not necessary to endure the pain and suffering of the negative emotions or their interference with the satisfactions of life.

In courage, we are no longer willing to pay the cost of negativity. We are concerned about the effects of our negative feelings on the welfare of others with whom we are closely associated. Most people who have learned the letting go technique will continue to use it until they have reached this level of consciousness. On this level, their major life problems are now under control. They are experiencing vocational satisfaction and success. Material wants are supplied. Major problems in relationships have straightened out. They are no longer consciously experiencing pain and suffering, and there is satisfaction from having grown and developed in certain areas.

When we are comfortable, there is a temptation to stop using the technique and only resume it in emergency situations, or when negative feelings again become painful and necessitate our attention. However, there is more yet to be had. Because there is always a feeling going on which can be surrendered, the continuation of the process will lead to greater and greater benefits.

Continual surrender will bring about constant, subtle changes, especially on the levels of subtle awareness in our capacity for love. Previously, we had likened the radiation of love, which stems from our higher aspect, to the energy of the sunlight. We noted that, as the dark clouds of negativity are removed, this energy and our capacity to accept it and radiate it outward, increases progressively.

On the level of courage, our capacity to love is now much stronger, and it has the power to support and encourage others, lending strength to that which is positive and constructive in them. Assisting their development brings us the pleasure of watching their growth and their increasing happiness. This capacity within us can grow ever stronger. It can become ever more powerful and self-rewarding as well as more beneficial to others.

We can utilize courage to reinforce our desire to grow beyond our present state, because on this level, we are already getting inklings that there is something within us that we had hitherto unsuspected. These are indicated by those sudden episodes of perfect stillness and peace in which we have great clarity, understanding, and heightened sensitivity to beauty.

We discover that it was *through* the music—and not because of it—that we experience our mind going suddenly still, and, in that moment of stillness, we were allowed to experience a greater dimension. There may be fleeting seconds in which we feel a complete identification and oneness with others, as though there were no separation.

These are the moments of breaking through into the experiencing of our real inner Self. The memory of those moments is never forgotten. When they first start to happen, we don't know what they mean. We think they are "accidental." "Just due to chance." We attribute the feeling to external events such as the beauty of a sunset, a symphonic passage, or a loving gesture. But, as we investigate further, we find that these were only the circumstances that allowed something else to happen. They were not the cause. They allowed a certain stillness of the mind to take place, and because of that stillness, we were allowed a moment in which we were able to experience something other than the chatter of our own mind with its incessant, restless play of sensations, feelings, thoughts, emotions, and memories.

In the moments when time seems to stand still, we get a glimpse of what is possible. These moments are so rewarding that they are treasured for a lifetime. When they occur, something is experienced that is very impressive. Could it be that, beyond the turbulence of the world and our own mind, there is silence? A realm of peace that is always waiting?

11

ACCEPTANCE

In acceptance, we enjoy the experience of harmony. We feel as though events are flowing. We feel secure. We can be of service to others without a feeling of self-sacrifice. There is the feeling: "I'm okay," "You're okay," and "It's okay." It is a feeling of belonging, connectedness, fullness, loving, understanding, and the feeling of being understood. It is a feeling of caring, warmth, and self-worth. Because of the security of this state, we can allow ourselves to be soft, mellow, and natural. There is joy, and we feel "in tune" and relaxed. There is the feeling that it's all right just to be ourselves.

Everything Is Perfect As It Is

In the state of acceptance, there is the feeling that nothing needs to be changed. Everything is perfect and beautiful the way it is. The world is to be enjoyed. There is compassion for others and for all living things. In this state we are automatically nurturing and supportive of others without any feeling of sacrifice. Because of the inner security and feeling of abundance, there is generosity and ease of giving, with no expectation of return or record keeping, such as, "Here's what I am doing for you." When we are in a state of acceptance, we love our friends instead of being critical, and we are willing to love them in spite of their limitations, which we willingly overlook.

The way people appear to us from this space is that everyone is actually doing the best they can with what they have at the moment. We see that all of life is evolving towards its perfection, and we are in sync with the laws of the universe and consciousness.

In this state we really begin to understand love. On the level of acceptance, love is experienced as a stable state, a permanent condition of a relationship. The source of love is seen to be within ourselves, emanating from our own nature and reaching out to include others. In the state of desire, by contrast, we speak of being "in love," as the source of happiness and love is thought to be outside of ourselves. When we are in the lower energy level of desire, we are looking to be loved. It seems to be something we "get." On the level of acceptance, however, our lovingness radiates out naturally from the essence of our being, because many of the blocks to its awareness have been surrendered.

We discover that this lovingness is our inner nature and that it appears spontaneously and automatically when the blocks are removed. This is what the great teachers mean by our true inner essence, our true Self. It is the aim of our inner Self to transcend the ego, that composite of all our negative feelings, programs, and thoughts, so that we are able to experience the inner essential nature.

There are many pathways that carry us to the state of acceptance, and this is the gateway which leads eventually to the next highest states, described as the consciousness levels of love and peace. To many people who have been surrendering for periods of time, this ultimate objective progressively supersedes all others. To dwell in states of unconditional love and imperturbable peace becomes the inner aim, more important than any other achievement.

Acceptance of Self and Others

On the level of acceptance, because of the major change in the way we perceive others, we now become aware of the inner innocence behind the frantic, fear-driven struggles that have obscured it in ourselves and in our neighbors, friends, and family. The great teachers have said that the negativity which we see in a person or in society is really due to blindness, ignorance, and unconsciousness. This inner innocence, once it is perceived in others, is also perceived in ourselves. All that we did was done because we just didn't know any better at the time. If we had known a better way at the time, we would have done it that way. "It seemed like a good idea at the time," we say. We see that same blindness operating in others, and we can look past their character defects and see the innocent child within.

Once we see our innocence, there is an identification with others and a loss of feeling alone and stressed. We are able to see innocence even behind the most rash and apparently horrible behaviors. We look inside a person and see the frightened animal that just doesn't know any better. We are aware that, if cornered, it will surely attack us and bite. It just doesn't realize that our intentions are peaceful, and so it flails out wildly.

In the state of acceptance, it is possible to forgive
our own past, as well as that of others, and to heal past
resentments. It is also possible to see the hidden gift in
past events about which we have been resentful—
including their possible karmic significance. From this
level, it is possible to create a different context from
which to view the past and thereby heal it. With the
final completion of the level of acceptance, we feel
secure about the future and can move on to the levels
of love and peace. Reason and logic become tools for
the fulfillment of that potential.

Another characteristic of the level of acceptance is
that we are no longer concerned with moralistic judgment, with "good" and "bad." It just becomes obvious
what works and what doesn't work. It is easy to see
what is destructive and what is optimal, without judging anything as "evil." There is the elimination of guilt,
which accompanies all judgments against others and
ourselves. We then see the meaning of the statement,
"Judge not, lest ye be judged."

In acceptance, we have let go of the inner guilt-
monger that found fault with even our most basic
human drives. We can enjoy our physicality without
moralistic aversion or compulsive self-gratification. We
accept that others have come to their understanding of
life and their ethical views in a way that makes sense to
them, even if their beliefs and behaviors are quite different from ours. When we see the innocence in everyone,
we can truly fulfill "loving our neighbor as ourselves,"
and, thus, letting go has allowed us to reach a lofty goal
without even the conscious attempt to do so.

The level of acceptance is characterized by the attitude of selflessness and service. This results from the
surrendering of the negative feelings that create the

small self, which removes our identification with it. Instead, inner harmony and peace are experienced as the nature of our greater Self. Because the negative programs have been relinquished, there is the emergence of greater creativity, inspiration, and intuition. There is certainty that our own personal needs will be met; therefore, there is a shift in relationship so that the focus is on the welfare and happiness of others. This is facilitated by the fact that, at this level, there is no longer neediness in the form of dependency on other people, because there is nothing we feel we need to "get" from them. In a relationship of loving acceptance, minor imperfections are no longer given serious importance and are overlooked.

In acceptance, there is a decreased preoccupation with "doingness," a growing focus on the quality of beingness itself, and the perfection of our own inner capacity for caring and lovingness. Although negative feelings may still arise, they are less and less frequent and are handled with greater ease. In general, functioning is now easy, and the daily activities become hardly noticeable because of their effortlessness.

Personal Responsibility

The hallmark of this state is the taking of responsibility for our own consciousness. Interest in meditation and the various methods of inner contemplation is common. Spiritual and ethical matters become important. We may, for instance, attend religious retreats if we are religious, or we may engage in spiritual or humanitarian endeavors if we are oriented toward those spheres.

The world is seen to be harmonious, and any alteration of that appearance is realized to be a projection onto it of our own inner conflicts. On this level, there is the awareness that all negative feelings are our own problem, and there is no longer looking outside of ourselves for their resolution.

There is a seriousness regarding the growth of our own consciousness and self-awareness, and a focus on honing the quality of that consciousness itself. On this level, we may begin to develop an interest in the philosophy, scientific research, and spiritual classics that explore the highest potential of human mind and spirit. What becomes increasingly important is what we are *becoming*, not what we have or do. On this level, we take on the challenge of fulfilling our greatest inner potential and nurturing the potential and dreams of others.

If muscle-tested in this state, we test strong; we are relatively immune to negative influences, such as the weakening vibrations of fluorescent lights, synthetic fabrics, or artificial sweeteners. There is a strong commitment to health and wellness, and bettering ourselves on all levels. Health issues are often considered to be problems at the psychological, emotional, or mental levels, and resources are sought and found which help to resolve the issues at all of those levels. The power of self-healing is now available.

In acceptance, we are free to be in the present. Once we have accepted our own true nature and the ways of the universe as they are reflected in our world, there is no longer regret about the past, nor is there fear of the future. Fear of the future no longer exists when the past has been healed. This is because in the usual ego-oriented state of consciousness, the ego tends to project the past upon the future, and a past that is viewed negatively becomes fearful when projected upon the imaginary future. Our letting go of the lower energies of guilt, fear, anger, and pride has alleviated the weight of the past and cleared the clouds of the future. We face today with optimism and are grateful to be alive. We see that yesterday is gone, tomorrow has not yet come, and we have only today.

In summary, then, the consciousness level of acceptance is one that we all long to achieve, for it enables us to find freedom from most of life's problems and to experience fulfillment and happiness.

12

LOVE

On the level of love, we are heartfelt, generous, nurturing, affectionate, steadfast, and forgiving. Love is protective, collaborative, uplifting, holistic, and gracious. It is characterized by warmth, gratitude, appreciation, humility, completion, vision, purity of motive, and sweetness.

Love is a way of being. It is the energy that radiates when the blocks to it have been surrendered. It is more than an emotion or a thought—it is a state of being. Love is what we have become through the pathway of surrender. It is a way of being in the world that says: "How can I be of help to you? How can I comfort you? How can I loan you money when you're broke? How can I help you find a job? How can I console you when you've suffered a major loss in your family?" Lovingness is a way through which we light up the world.

Love in Everyday Life
Everyone has the opportunity to contribute to the beauty and harmony of the world by showing kindness to all living things and, thereby, supporting the

human spirit. That which we freely give to life flows back to us because we are equally part of that life. Like ripples on the water, every gift returns to the giver. What we affirm in others, we actually affirm in ourselves.

Once we become willing to give love, the discovery quickly follows that we are surrounded by love and merely didn't know how to access it. Love is actually present everywhere; its presence only needs to be realized.

Love expresses itself in many ways. The little boy memorizes a ditty taught to him by his father, and he is still able to say it eighty years later. The Navy sailor steers the ship through a terrible typhoon for three days, nonstop, without food and drink, when all of his shipmates are seasick. The doctor loves and prays for every patient without their knowing about it. The mother cleans up the messy pants of a young child with diarrhea, saying, "Honey, it's not your fault; you couldn't help it." The wife gets up early to make coffee every morning just the way her husband likes it. The doggie waits by the door for the owner to return and wags her tail when he comes through the door. The kitty purrs. The songbird sings.

Typically, people think of love as "romantic" love, as in "Honey" and "Sweetheart." But romantic love is only a minor part of a human lifetime. There are many types of love other than personal, romantic love, and they infuse our everyday experience: love of pets, love of family and friends, love of freedom, love of purpose, love of country, love of attributes, love of creation, love as virtue, love as enthusiasm, love as forgiveness, love as acceptance, love as motivator, love as appreciation, love as kindness, love as essence of relationship, love as group energy (for example: Alcoholics Anonymous), love as admiration, love as respect, love as valor, love as fraternal bonds of unity (buddies, classmates, shipmates, teammates), love as friendship, love as loyalty, love as affection, love as cherishing, love as self-sacrificing maternal love, love as devotion.

"Love is a many splendored thing," as the popular song goes. Experientially, this statement is true. When we have surrendered all of the resistances to love and let go of the negative feelings that block love, then the world is radiant with the splendor of love. On the level of love, this radiance is no longer hidden from us.

Love Heals

Love facilitates healing. It transforms life. We see this in the true story about a duck hunter who was suddenly changed by witnessing an act of love. One day, he was out duck hunting, which he often did for recreation. As per his usual experience, he saw a duck flying, shot it, and watched it fall to the ground, badly injured. To his sudden amazement, he watched as the female mate of the injured duck immediately flew down on top of her companion and spread her wings over him, to shelter him. Seeing her love, the heart of a hunter was changed; he never hunted again.

Once you become loving, there are certain things you can never do again. And there are certain things you can do in the energy field of love that are impossible otherwise. Moreover, people do things for you that they would not do for others. Love makes possible the miraculous without labeling it "miraculous." Love has a transfiguring effect.

Sometimes, it is best not to tell people that you love them because they'll get scared and think that you have designs on them or you want something from them. Frankly, some people are afraid and suspicious of love; therefore, you love such people without telling them. Lovingness is a way of being that transforms everything around you because of the radiation of that energy. It happens of its own. We don't have to "do" anything, and we don't have to call it anything. Love is the energy that silently transfigures every situation.

This means that people who are hateful will, in our presence, suddenly become willing to forgive others. We can see the person transform right in front of us. Letting go of anger, they might say, "Well, there's no reason to be so mad at him . . . he's too young to know better." They will find an excuse to defend the person, instead of attacking him. Love empowers us, and the people around us, to do things that we would not be capable of otherwise.

Forgiveness is an aspect of love that allows us to see life events from the viewpoint of grace. We forgive ourselves for the errors we made when we were less evolved. It is helpful to see the ego or small part of ourselves as a cute little teddy bear. The teddy bear is not "bad"; we don't hate or scold the little bear. We love it and accept it for what it is: a cute little animal who doesn't know any better. We transcend the smaller aspects of ourselves by accepting and loving them. We see the ego as "limited," not "bad."

In the energy field of love, we are surrounded with love, and that brings gratitude. We are thankful for our life and for all the miracles of life. We are thankful for the doggies and the kitties, because they represent love. We are grateful for every act of kindness from others, their affection, caringness, and thoughtfulness.

Eventually, we just become love. Everything we do and say, every movement we make, is energized by the lovingness that we have owned within ourselves. Whether speaking to a large audience or petting the dog, the energy of love is felt to be pouring out. We want to share what we hold in the heart as an experiential knowingness, and we hold it in the heart for everyone and everything, that they would be feeling it, too. We pray for that inner experience of infinite love for everyone around us, including the animals. Our life is a blessing to everything around us. We acknowledge to others and to our animals the gift that they are to us.

Love emanates from the heart. When we are in the presence of people who love each other, we pick up that energy. The love of our loved ones, pets, and friends is the love of Divinity for us. When we go to bed at night, we give thanks that we were surrounded with love all day. Each moment is possible only because of love. The writing of this book is possible only because of love.

In the state of love, we wake up every morning and give thanks for another day of life, and we seek to make life better for everyone around us. Because of the presence of love, things go better; the eggs get fried better; the ducky gets saved; the kitty gets fed; and the doggie is adopted from the pound and brought home. We share our love with everything around us, all forms of life: kitties, doggies, other people, *all living things*. Yes, even the villains. If it is our job to watch over the captured villain, we seek to make his life tolerable. We say, "I'm sorry that I have to hold a gun to your head, but that's my job." We try to be as gracious and generous as we can be, without exception.

The more we love, the more we *can* love. Love is limitless. Love begats love. This is why psychiatrists recommend having a pet. A dog, for example, brings love and expands love in the heart of the owner. Love prolongs life. In fact, research documents that having a dog extends the owner's life by ten years! Just think of all the bizarre exercises, diets, and other regimens that people go through to add relatively small amounts of time on to their life, when they can simply get a dog and add ten years! Love has a powerful anabolic effect. Love increases endorphins, which are life-enhancing hormones. You live ten years longer with a dog in your life because a pet dog catalyzes the energy of love, and that energy of love heals and prolongs life.

The energy of love has the capacity to heal our bodies when conditions are appropriate. On the physical level, because of the prevailing positive mental state, physical illnesses often resolve themselves. Some diseases automatically heal without any particular attention being paid to them, and those that still remain usually respond to consciousness techniques. Persistent illnesses that are unresponsive to treatment are viewed as karmically, symbolically, or spiritually significant. Overall, there is a decreasing awareness of the body, which now goes about its business and seems to take care of itself on its own. We are no longer identified *as* a body. There is a loss of interest in dealing with health matters on a purely physical level, and there are times when awareness of the body disappears altogether, unless we focus on it for some particular reason.

Intuitive understanding progressively replaces "thinkingness," which begins to disappear. Over time, "thinkingness" and its mental processes are replaced by spontaneous, intuitive "knowingness." Logic is bypassed. This occurs because, at the highest level of vibration, everything in the universe is connected with everything else. Our understanding unfolds as "revelation" from this inter-connected field. The knowing is holistic rather than limited.

Because of the inner quiet, we have the ability to perceive the thoughts and feelings of others on a nonverbal level. Nonverbal communication with others becomes possible and commonplace. Negative emotions are no longer experienced because the small self has been transcended, absorbed into the greater Self. Emotional phenomena are thereby transformed. Loss, for example, is experienced as transitory disappointment or regret, rather than as grief.

Unconditional Love

By continual surrender, we experience the state of unconditional love (calibrates at 540), which is rare and occurs in only .04% of the population. This energy is miraculous, inclusive, nonselective, transformative, unlimited, effortless, radiant, devotional, saintly, diffuse, merciful, and selfless. It is characterized by inner joy, faith, ecstasy, patience, compassion, persistence, essence, beauty, synchronicity, perfection, surrender, rapture, vision, and openness. We relinquish seeing the personal self as a causal agent. Everything happens effortlessly by synchronicity.

Joy emanates from the inner subjective experience of our own existence. The power of the joy is subjective, not stemming from any source outside of oneself. Thus, the energy of motor performance is inexhaustible. We may dance with ecstasy all night in a candlelit chapel, as if being danced by the Source of Life Itself. In that state, the innate perfection and stunning beauty of all that exists shine forth like a luminous radiance, as the infusion of spiritual energy facilitates the transfiguration from perception to vision, from the linear to the nonlinear, and from the limited to the unlimited. While functioning in the world is still possible at the higher vibrations of love (high 500s), we may end up leaving the ordinary arena of commerce and abandoning our prior social milieu and occupation.

In such states, the "miraculous" is common. What is termed "supernatural" is seen to occur all of the time, inexplicable by reason, logic, or cause and effect. It is clear that no "person" performs miracles. They occur spontaneously on their own when conditions are appropriate. The development of a spiritual ego is avoided by the realization that the phenomena are a gift from beyond our personal self; we are only the channels of Love, not its origin. Spiritual progress is known to be the result of Grace, not the result of our personal endeavors. Gratitude for the state replaces pride of accomplishment. The process of surrender continues ever more deeply, as we let go of all doubt, all belief systems, all perceptions, all positions, all opinions, and all attachments. We become willing to surrender all attachments, even attachment to the exquisite state of Ecstasy, which is beyond description.

Out of humility, all opinions about others are surrendered. In a certain way, nobody can help being other than what they are. Love knows this truth and takes no position. Love augments the positive about others rather than their defects. It focuses on life's goodness in all of its expressions. Unconditional love is a love that doesn't expect anything from others. When we have become loving, we have no limitations or demands on others that they should be a certain way in order to be loved. We love them no matter how they are. Even if they are obnoxious! We feel sorry for the criminals that they saw a life of crime as their best option.

When love is unconditional, there's no attachment, expectation, hidden agenda, or bookkeeping of who gives what to whom. Our love is unconditional for whatever we are and whatever they are. It is given without requirements. No strings are attached. We don't expect anything back when giving. We have surrendered all conscious and unconscious expectations of the other person.

Love illuminates the essence of and, therefore, the lovability of others. This is because love opens the heart. Instead of perception, which perceives, *the heart knows.* The mind thinks and argues, but the heart knows and continues. So even when people make mistakes, we love them. Thoughts tell us one thing, but the heart tells us something else. The mind can be critical and disagree, but the heart is loving no matter what. The heart does not put any conditions on what's out there. Only the mind does that. Love makes no demands.

A key to making Love unconditional is the willingness to forgive. With forgiveness, events and people are re-contextualized as simply "limited"—not "bad" or "unlovable." With humility, we are willing to relinquish our perception of a past event. We pray for a miracle to see the truth about the situation or person, and we surrender all of our opinions about the matter. We look at the payoffs we're getting from keeping our perception of what occurred, and we let go of each little payoff: the pleasure of self-pity, of "being right," of being "wronged," and of our resentments.

Eventually, we surrender the very idea of forgiveness. To forgive someone implies that we're still seeing the person or situation as "wrong" and, therefore, in need of being forgiven. True surrender means letting go completely of seeing it in such a way. When we surrender our perception completely, letting go of all judgment, then the whole situation is transfigured and we see the person as lovable. Since all judgment is really self-judgment, we have liberated ourselves in the process.

On the level of unconditional love, we love everybody and everything—even Adolf Hitler. We look at him as a person who was taken over by negative energies, and we're willing to forgive Hitler, who couldn't help what happened to him. He was overcome by evil. Instead of hating evil, we feel sorrow and compassion that people have become overwhelmed by such negativity. Hitler did what he thought he was required to do by honor. That was his contextualization at the time. He was captured by certain ideals and beliefs current in his time. Even with Hitler, then, we can see that he was dedicated, and he thought he was being of service in what he did. In WWII, the kamikaze pilots were doing what they thought they should be doing for their country. And even though they were trying to bomb and kill us, it isn't necessary to hate them. We can respect their willingness to give up their life for their country. We can see that everybody who violates the law of Love is really a victim of some societal belief system or the pressures of the time.

Oneness

As the state progresses, all of existence takes on a different meaning, and we become aware of the inner beingness and essence of everything, rather than just its form. Because of this change of perception, the perfection of all things stands revealed. This experience is outside of time; there is no past or future. In its highest vibration, love sees no separation between the individual and the rest of the universe. We experience total at-oneness with all things. In this state, the total oneness of all things has a greater sense of Reality than the ordinary perceptions of the self in the world, and it can only be described as profound.

As the inner shifts occur, our lifestyle may or may not show a change to the external observer. However, habits and behavior, although they may appear to be the same, are no longer compulsive or driven. They can often be dropped, altered, or changed without undue discomfort. On the other hand, there may indeed be sudden changes in lifestyle, including major shifts in vocation, because of the change of inner values and expansion of interests and vision. Now that we are connected to a greater dimension, there may be an immersion in it through contemplation, meditation, art, music, movement, reading, writing, teaching, and participation in spiritual groups with similar objectives.

Letting go now becomes more automatic and continuous. Periods of inner stillness and beauty begin to occur with greater frequency and duration. These may occur at a very profound level. Oddly, they may follow episodes of great inner turmoil and struggle. These periods of intense inner work occur because we can no longer tolerate negativity. Now that we have greater power of consciousness, we are able to reach down and handle problems at the deepest levels of consciousness. These may be such problems as those concerning the source of our identity or concept of self.

Breakthroughs of great serenity and peace may also occur after prolonged periods of continual surrender, as seen in the following example. At one point, being in a state of constant joy, an event occurred which brought to awareness a conflict that stemmed from the deepest way in which we can relate to others. It was difficult to look at and experience out, but because the prevailing state had so much high energy to it, it was possible to let the inner conflict come up and let it run its course, to be resolved once and for all. It ran for ten solid days, unceasingly, and for that period of time, the approach was to surrender constantly the conflict and let it go without trying to alter it in any way. For a while, the inner conflict seemed as if it would be unending; however, previous experience with the surrender process had confirmed that every feeling sooner or later runs out, if we just keep letting it go.

Moving temporarily to a small cabin in the middle of the woods intensified the process because there were no other distractions. Then the source of the conflict deepened and even more painful feelings came up in full force. There was a great deal of inner turmoil, at times almost agony and despair. Determined not to give up or allow a block in the flow of the process, finally, the bottom of the pit was reached and up came black despair of overwhelming intensity. In spite of this, there was the knowing that everything would be okay, because the primary identification was not with the despair but with the surrendering itself.

Finally, all of the resistance to the despair was totally and completely let go. Instantly it vanished. The despair, which had been overwhelming and nearly unbearable, vanished in an instant! In its place, there was profound peace beyond description. It was infinite in its dimension, curiously powerful and totally unassailable. There was a profound inner stillness, and all perception of time stopped. Instead of "time," there was only the motion of the phenomena of the world occurring. The next day the experience continued and, in fact, was even stronger.

Then, out of curiosity, there was a re-entry into the world to see what it would be like to experience ordinary life from this state of consciousness. Even while walking down Fifth Avenue in New York City, the same profound stillness, harmony, and peace prevailed. This pervasive peace and stillness seemed to underlie all of the superficial chaos, noise, and confusion of the city. It was as though the power and strength of that dimension of stillness was the power that enabled it all to happen and held it all together in one continuous unity. Within the essence of that stillness was unlimited power, and it was clear that it was this very power that counteracted and balanced the collective negativity of the city. As without, so within. Similarly, it was clear that this same cohesive power is that which also counterbalances the negativity of the personality. If unopposed, that negativity would destroy the person and the body with it.

We said in previous sections that the lower emotions are associated with an accumulation of energy in the lower energy centers of the body called "chakras." As our consciousness rises, due to the letting go of negativity, this energy tends to rise to higher centers so that, at the level of love, the energy has moved up to the heart chakra. As love becomes unconditional and ever-joyous, the personal dimension of love gives way to universal love. In general, we say of a person who has reached the level of love that they are "big-hearted" or "all heart." This phrase expresses the shift of interest and focus of the person's life to that which is loving. This upward shift of focus is accompanied by an overall change of perception, a different point of view than that which characterizes the focus of attention of a person who is involved in the negative emotions.

For example, when a person is in a lower state of mind, an old gentleman carelessly dressed standing on a corner would be perceived as a "bum." With that characterization goes other negative thoughts such as: "He might be dangerous—let's avoid him"; "He's costing us taxpayers—he's probably on welfare"; "The police ought to clear the streets of such derelicts"; "He should be in jail or in a mental hospital."

By contrast, the person who is in a loving state might well see him as an interesting person whose face reflects a lot of life experience, character, and wisdom. He might appear as a liberated soul who has pretty much finished with the world and has evolved into beingness, beyond doingness and havingness.

There was an encounter with just such a man on Fifth Avenue, while in that state of total inner stillness described above. While walking down the sidewalk, the old gentleman perceived that state of inner stillness with one glance and, in return, he became totally open. The eyes gazed widely such that nothing was hidden, and the soul became completely open to be read. It was apparent that he was a man who had realized his own true inner Self and was totally at peace. He was, in fact, part and parcel of that powerful, positive, loving energy that was holding the city together.

With that glance we shared our oneness—our timeless oneness. Though strangers, our souls were united and resounded with each other. The one Self radiated forth. That oneness was the energy counteracting the total negativity of New York City at that moment. In our open gaze, there was a cosmic oneness (calibrates as true). There was an all-silent knowingness that the oneness reflected an infinite energy that was counterbalancing the total negativity of New York City at the time, because the power that was shared was Infinite. Without a counterbalance, the city would self-destruct. It was a silent, prevailing, infinite state of consciousness. It was a profound moment in which one of the laws of consciousness was experientially verified: *Love is the Ultimate Law of the Universe* (statement calibrates at 750).

13

PEACE

In peace, there is no longer any conflict. There is a total absence of negativity and an all-encompassing lovingness that is experienced as serenity, tranquility, timelessness, completion, fulfillment, stillness, and contentment. There is inner quiet and light, a feeling of oneness, unity, and total freedom. The peace is imperturbable. Actions become effortless, spontaneous, harmonious, and loving in their effect. There is a shift of perception of the universe and of our relationship to it. The inner Self prevails. The personal self has been transcended, with all of its feelings, beliefs, identities, and concerns. This is the ultimate state sought by all seekers, whether they are religious, humanist, or have no spiritual or philosophical identification at all.

The Profound Impact of Peace

We have all had moments of profound peace where time and the world seemed to suddenly stop, and we have come in contact with the Infinite. In recent years, there have been a number of books about the near-death experience. Under various circumstances, this experience has happened to people who have died and then returned to the body. Characteristically, their lives have been transformed by the experience, and they never forget it. Their vision of the world, its significance, and their personal significance in it has changed considerably.

In the movie, *Lost Horizon*, once the hero had experienced Shangri-La, although he returned to the world again, he viewed it in a totally different way. He longed, at any cost, to return to Shangri-La where the state of peace prevailed. Once the experience of peace has occurred, we are no longer a victim of the world. We are no longer at its effect as we once were, for we have had a glimpse of the truth about it and of what we really are.

With continual surrender, we begin to experience these states of peace with ever-increasing frequency. At times, they may become quite profound and of greater and greater duration. When the clouds are removed, the sun shines forth and we discover that peace was the truth all along. Surrender is the mechanism that uncovers the true nature of our existence.

When a person is in the state of peace, they test strong with kinesiology, and nothing makes them weak, whether it is mental, emotional, or physical. There is no longer identification with the body as our self, and physical disorders may or may not be healed. We are indifferent to them; physical concerns have lost any significant meaning.

With the experience of inner peace comes great strength. An energy field of total peace is unassailable. The person who has found inner peace can no longer be intimidated, controlled, manipulated, or programmed. In this state, we are invulnerable to the threats of the world and have, therefore, mastered earthly life. When the state of peace has become established, ordinary human suffering is no longer possible because the very basis of that vulnerability has been totally relinquished.

Silent Transmission

We describe the person who has reached that state of peace as "enlightened" and being in a state of Grace. Within and beyond that condition are various advanced states of illumination and levels of realization described by the mystics, sages, saints, and avatars.

There is a silent, nonverbal benefit of being in the actual presence of an enlightened state. Classically, it would be an advanced spiritual teacher, saint, or sage. Seekers travel great distances to be in the physical presence of this energy field. The devotee or seeker receives silent transmission of the high-frequency energy of the teacher's aura, described as "Transmission of No-Mind," "Grace of the Guru," or "Benediction of the Teacher." This transmission happens of its own and is not personal. The state of infinite peace radiates forth unconditionally of its own from the energy field of the teacher or saint. When the Buddha gave his disciple a flower, it was symbolic of the transmission of the energy. If we have been in the presence of a great teacher who radiates this energy, we will never be the same. The most beneficial thing that can happen to us is to have been in the presence of a great teacher, because we pick up the vibration by being in the physical presence of that state of peace and complete surrender. The silent transmission of this realized state is a nonverbal, energetic phenomenon that does not depend upon logic or language. The vibration that is within the aura of the advanced teacher functions as a carrier wave to facilitate our comprehension of the words that are being spoken. But it's the wave of energy and not the words that are the catalytic element. Via silent transmission, the energy from the advanced teacher or saint is incorporated into our aura, our brain function, and our whole being.

It's because this energy of peace is transmitted outward into the world that mankind is still alive. It would have destroyed itself a long time ago without this energy to counterbalance it. That's why our own inner evolution serves all of mankind. By reaching these higher states of lovingness and peace within ourselves, we become a saving presence in the world.

Surrender to Ultimate Reality

The hallmark of this level is desirelessness. There is no need to want for anything because everything manifests in our life spontaneously and automatically, without conscious will or effort. Thoughts held in mind at this level are very powerful and tend to manifest rapidly. The phenomenon of synchronicity is continuous. The mechanisms of cause and effect and the inner working of the universe stand forth clearly revealed, as we are now witnessing the very basis of Reality itself.

These very high states of awareness happen spontaneously and unexpectedly, and they tend to recur and stay for longer and longer durations. Once this has been experienced, our intention automatically becomes to make the state of peace permanent.

How this state occurs and what it is like is demonstrated in the following account, which describes what happened after three and a half years of continual surrender.

It was a cold winter day. Surrender was continuous for eleven straight days at a level of consciousness that had never been reached previously, not even during psychoanalysis. It had to do with the ego's very basis of survival and its identification as an individual. It had to do with how we experience our own existence and the desire to experience our own beingness.

As the days went by, the process seemed endless. A doubt surfaced, "Was this attempting the impossible?" It became clear that the purpose of that doubt itself was a defense mechanism; it was relinquished, and the surrender continued at great depth.

Then, entering a restaurant on that cold rainy Sunday afternoon, sitting down alone at the table, suddenly the world was miraculously transformed. A profound sense of inner stillness and peace occurred. It was greater than anything imaginable. The experience was beyond time. In fact, time had no meaning whatsoever, nor did space exist in the way in which we commonly experience it. All things were connected. There was only one life expressing itself with one Self through all living things. There was no identification with the body and no interest in it. It was no longer any more interesting than any other body in the room. All emotions and events were interconnected, and all phenomena occurred because each thing was manifesting its own inner nature spontaneously, as though movement and growth were the spontaneous unfolding of potential. There was a rock-like quality to the imperturbable stillness. It was obvious that the real Self was invisible—without beginning, without end—

and that there had been only a transitory identification with the body and the story that went with the identification as an individual.

It seemed very strange that one could previously have thought that one was an isolated body separate from others, with a limited beginning and a finite ending. The thought seemed absurd. There was no longer any feeling of a separate self, and the pronoun "I" disappeared and became meaningless. Instead, there was the awareness of being all things. It had always been and always would be. True beingness stood outside of time. The period of time that the body had been on earth seemed like a split second during which the truth of timeless identity had been forgotten, due to being blinded by the smaller self. Then how it had happened revealed itself. There had been a wishful thought to experience separate existence, and this wishful thought had manifested itself as the individual person with an individual identity and a physical body to go with it.

The inner connectedness of all things was starkly obvious. It was the holographic universe as described by the Buddha and by modern advanced theoretical physics, both of whom agree as to the intrinsic nature of the universe. Because everything was perfect, there was nothing to wish for, nothing to desire, nothing to create, and nothing to become. There was only That, the very essence of Beingness out of which existence arises. That Beingness is the Source of existence, yet curiously not its Cause.

There was a profound familiarity to the awareness. It was as though one had always known it, as if one were home at last. There were no emotions or feelings. There was an unawareness of sensations. Even though they seemed to go on, they were no longer personal or of concern.

By way of experimentation, a thought was held for a split-second to see what would happen. Almost instantly there was an effect in the physical world. The thought of butter or coffee, for instance, resulted in the waiter's coming over immediately with the items, and yet no word had been spoken. No words seemed necessary. Communication occurred with anyone on a level of silence.

The body drove the car to a meeting that evening where no one noticed anything different. Everyone seemed to be intensely alive. Their aliveness shown forth from their Beingness, and the Self, which was the same for all, shone forth through their eyes. The body spoke to others, spontaneously carrying on normal conversations and behaving in its usual way. At the time, the body seemed like a karmic wind-up toy run by all of its accustomed patterns and programs, not needing any attention in the slightest. It seemed to know what to do and did it very effectively and effortlessly. All conversations and interactions were merely witnessed as phenomena, not directed. It seemed like a strange vanity to have once believed that there had been a small self as the author of the body's actions. In reality, the body was at the effect of the universe, and there had never been a doer of its actions. Phenomena were as vibrations of the mind that had no separate existence or reality. There was Allness only. Only that Oneness actually existed.

The next afternoon a thought arose. Now that the way to Reality had been revealed, there could be a return to the consciousness of being that individual person, which had formerly been accepted as real. Just as the air in the room does not experience the contents of the room, there was no longer an "I" that experienced "my own existence." In that space, there was no "I" to experience the "I am." To return to individual consciousness meant that a choice would have to be made. In truth, the choice made itself for there was no "I" to make a decision. The desire to experience the individual self became re-energized on its own. The option of letting it go was present, but there was the return of memory of things yet to be finished in the world. As the sense of "I"-ness returned, the choices were witnessed, not actively decided. The process of returning was taking place. It could be allowed or it could be let go. It was allowed, and so the process of return continued. When the next morning dawned, the return was complete, but now with a different sense of personal identity. The truth of the Self had been revealed. The responsibility for having chosen to experience life once again as an individual was accepted, yet without being at the effect of a belief in individual existence. In fact, by conscious choosing, there was complete responsibility for it. Experientially, all of this happened autonomously.

At one time, such states of consciousness as the above were considered to be solely the province of the mystic. At the present time, however, investigation of these states, and the information obtainable from them, is considered to be the leading edge of science, especially that branch of physics concerned with quantum mechanics and high-energy subatomic particles. Investigations of these particles indicate that they are not things in the usual sense but are actually events that occur as a result of energy frequencies. Science now postulates a transcendent frequency beyond space and time. An impressive body of research in many laboratories has demonstrated that the brain perceives by sophisticated mathematical analysis of frequency patterns. These findings have resulted in the so-called holographic paradigm, which states that everything in the universe is connected with everything else, including the human mind. In the hologram, each part contains the whole. Consequently, each individual mind is capable of reflecting the entire universe. This relationship between consciousness and science constitutes a whole field in which there is rapidly growing interest, as is indicated by the publishing of such books as *The Holographic Paradigm, Wholeness and the Implicate Order, The Tao of Physics, The Dancing Wu-Li Masters, Mindful Universe, Psychoenergetic Science* and the publication of articles with titles such as "Field Consciousness and the New Perspective on Reality," "The Enfolding-Unfolding Universe," "The Holographic Model," "Physics and Mysticism," and "The Medium, the Mystic, and the Physicist."

Leading among these researchers are neuroscientist Carl Pribram of Stanford University and the late physicist David Bohm of the University of London, whose theories can be summarized: Our brains mathematically construct concrete reality by interpreting frequencies from another dimension, a realm of meaningful, patterned, primary reality that transcends time and space. The brain is, therefore, a hologram interpreting a holographic universe.

It is interesting that the theories of advanced theoretical physics, which are the product of so-called left-brain activities, now require a new context in order to be comprehended. The context that is evolving from these left-brain scientific researchers matches Reality as witnessed by the mystic, who represents right-brain function. Thus, whichever side of the mountain we choose to climb, we end up at the same point: the peak.

A third way up the mountain is through the mechanism of surrender, and each of us, therefore, has the opportunity to verify for ourselves the ultimate nature of Reality itself, which is the same as that revealed to the mystic or the physicist. We can envision that with each and every surrender, we take another step up the side of the mountain. Some of us will ascend until the view gets better and choose to stop there. Others will go still higher. And, then, there will be those of us who will not be satisfied until we have reached the very Peak and verified It for ourselves, although, at that point, there is no longer an individual person to verify anything, for it has been surrendered completely.

14

REDUCING STRESS AND PHYSICAL ILLNESS

Psychological Aspects and Stress Proneness

Though available to all of us, the state of peace is reached by very few people. The inner experience of most people is marked by constant stress. Most of the stress that results in emotional and physical disorders in our society is psychological in origin. Our response to stress depends on our "stress proneness" and, as we pointed out earlier, this is directly the result of the amount of suppressed and repressed feelings we have accumulated. The more emotional pressure that is surrendered and let go, the less vulnerable we are to the stress response and stress-related diseases.

The main stress to the majority of us most of the time is not due to external stimuli, but to the pressure of our own suppressed emotions. These suppressed emotions become the primary stressor so that, even in a calm external environment, we are still subject to chronic, internal stress.

We can observe that the external stress factors are merely the straws that eventually break the camel's back. The main stress load is what we carry around with us all the time. The psychological programming in our society is so extensive that, for most people, even relaxing and enjoying a vacation is a problem. (Guilt says we "should" be doing something else.) There is disappointment when immediate relaxation does not occur. There is restlessness and the endless pursuit of "fun" activities to avoid the pain of facing our own inner self. Most busy executives begin to secretly look forward to getting back to work while they are on vacation. They may outwardly grumble about their heavy workload, but when they return to the accustomed routine, they feel normal again.

The effects of suppressed and repressed feelings plus stress-precipitating factors are responsible for most emotional and physical illnesses. There is an emotional-psychological component in all diseases and, because of this, it is possible to reverse the disease process by removing the internal stress factors. This accounts for the many recoveries, reported daily, from serious and potentially fatal illnesses by the use of emotional-spiritual techniques. Many cures take place after all medical methods have failed. One reason is that, at this stage of "there's nothing else we can do," the patients give up, and they seek and accept the true basic nature and cause of their illness.

Acknowledging and letting go of suppressed feelings progressively reduces a person's personal stress proneness, thereby lowering the vulnerability to stress-related problems and illnesses. Most people who learn and practice the letting go technique notice a progressive improvement in physical health and vitality.

Medical Aspects of Stress

Stress is our response to a perceived threat (real or imaginary) to our security or bodily equilibrium. The stimulus may be internal or external. It may be physical, mental, or emotional. Basic research into the body's physical response to stress was done by Dr. Hans Selye and Dr. Walter Cannon. Selye described what he called the "general adaptation syndrome." In response to a stressful stimulus, the body first goes through an alarm reaction, then secondly a stage of resistance, and if the stimulus continues, it may result in the third stage of exhaustion syndrome.

The alarm reaction occurs via the pathway of the cerebral cortex → hypothalamus (lower brain) → adrenal glands → blood stream (cortisol and adrenalin). In addition, there is the release of brain hormones and stimulation of the body's sympathetic nervous system. The adrenalin then goes to all of the body's organs and prepares them for fight or flight. Many people, especially in big cities, learn to live off the adrenalin "high" of constant challenges. The threat to survival of the intense competition keeps the adrenalin flowing. Typically, they get depressed on weekends or vacations. They are addicted to excitement and abnormal stimulation. They get used to the semi-euphoria induced by the high levels of cortisol.

The second stage, that of resistance, is the body's attempt to restore homeostatic balance. It involves hormonal changes and shifts in metabolism and mineral balance. Commonly, there is sodium, accompanied by water retention in the tissues. Some executives, for instance, develop swollen ankles as the week goes on, and then on Friday evening they have frequency of urination. They complain of a letdown due to the sudden decrease in the level of the cortisol hormone. In addition to a somewhat euphoric effect, cortisol also has an anesthetic effect; therefore, during the letdown period of low-cortisol production, weekenders may notice physical symptoms that were ignored during the excitement of the work week, and they may complain of many aches and pains over the weekend that weren't experienced while at work.

The third stage is exhaustion. If stress continues unabated beyond the capacity of the body's coping mechanisms, eventually they begin to fail. The state of adrenal exhaustion sets in. The body's defenses have become too weak to counter the effects of stress. There is suppression of the immune system. The body's organs begin to show pathologic changes due to the long exposure to stress hormones. The body's energy stores have become depleted, leading eventually to disease, and finally death of the organism.

During the acute alarm reaction, the stomach's motility halts, digestion stops, and the blood supply to the stomach's lining is decreased. As stress continues, due to imbalance of the nervous system and hormone changes, hyperacidity and over-production of digestive enzymes occur. The heightened digestive enzymes and hydrochloric acid, acting on the weakened gastrointestinal lining, result in ulceration, producing stress ulcers. With continued stress, the ulcers may hemorrhage or perforate and precipitate a medical catastrophe. In other cases, the reaction to chronic, abnormal stress may be failure to produce hydrochloric acid or enzymes, resulting in chronic indigestion and poor nutrition.

Besides the gastrointestinal tract, the cardiovascular system also reacts to stress by an alarm reaction. As the stress becomes chronic, the heart, blood vessels, and kidneys may go through damage resulting in hypertension and/or coronary disease. The stress is eventually responsible for strokes, heart attacks, and hypertension, all of which are major causes of death in the United States.

Energy System Response to Stress and the Acupuncture System

The body has three nervous systems: 1) the voluntary network of nerves under conscious control and distributed primarily to voluntary muscles; 2) the involuntary or autonomic nervous system (sympathetic and parasympathetic), which is usually unconscious and which controls the body's organs and physiological functions, such as heart beat, blood flow and distribution, digestion, and body chemistries; 3) the acupuncture system, which transmits the bio-energy to all the body's structures and internal organs. This third system is least known in Western medicine but long understood in Eastern medicine and society.

In the acupuncture system, there is a flow of vital energies throughout the physical body via the body's invisible energy blueprint. This energy system is described as having 12 main channels over the surface of the physical body, down the twelve major acupuncture meridians. From these channels, there are many tributaries leading into the body's various organ systems. Abnormal distribution of energy into these meridians results in dysfunction of the affected organs and eventually the evolvement of the disease process.

This vital bio-energy is the very flow of life itself. It is very quickly reactive to stress. This bio-energy reacts from instant to instant due to fluctuating factors in our lives, which are the changing patterns of our perceptions, thoughts, and feelings. The conventional measurement of the body's medical reactions is relatively slow. A fleeting thought, which may be accompanied by an emotional pang, does not bring about a measurable change in the body's blood pressure or pulse in response; however, it instantly registers in the bio-energy system where a variety of rapid changes can be observed by scientific, psychic, and clinical methods.

The overall balance of the body's acupuncture energy system is regulated by the activity of the thymus gland. The bio-energy system is intimately connected to the body's immune system via the thymus gland. Chronic stress weakens the body's immune system, suppresses the thymus gland, and throws the bio-energy system out of balance. Strengthening the thymus gland or taking thymus supplements rebalances the bio-energy system. An extensive explanation of this is found in the books *Behavioral Kinesiology* and *Life Energy* by John Diamond, M.D.

Interventions to Alleviate Stress

Research at U.C.L.A. by Liebeskind and Shavit during the 1980s further clarified the relationship among stress, suppression of the immune system, and the development of cancer by showing the intermittent stress on the release of the brain opiates known as endorphins. Stress in the form of intermittent shocks suppresses the immune system. When the immune response is strong, there is the release of the brain's endorphins, so-called anti-cancer "killer" cells, which attack and kill young growing tumor cells. But when the immune activity is suppressed and there is a reduced presence of endorphins, the activity of the anti-cancer "killer" cells diminishes.

The report in *Science* (223: 188–190) states, "Our findings support the view that the central nervous system by modulating immune function exercises some measure of control over the inception and development of disease." The report goes on to say that a feeling of helplessness has been related to reduced anti-cancer killer cell activity and increased tumor growth. Depression in animals, as well as humans, lowers the immune response, and this helplessness has to do with how much control the person and the animal feel they have over stressful events. Those findings help explain why depression and a sense of helplessness are associated with cancer. Further research confirms that the stress response was found to be a principal precondition for physical illness in animals and humans (Sapolsky, 2010).

The overall effect of stress on the immune system results in the blocking of the body's immune system because of the production of auto-antibodies. If these auto-antibodies are themselves blocked, the immune function resumes once again. Therefore, the blocking of the immune system is reversible. For example, research done at the Pasteur Institute in Paris has resulted in the so-called Bogomoletz serum which, when injected intradermally, results in reactivation of the immune system. This treatment is called the I.B.R. (Immuno-Biologic-Rejuvenation) treatment. A small amount of serum is injected within the skin on three successive days and results in rapid reactivation of the immune system.

Reactivation of pro-health body responses is also

seen in non-medical interventions, as in the correlation of meditation practice with a reduction in stress and depression. Research done on college students, for example, found that meditation led to a decrease in their inflammatory stress reaction, which was linked to the alleviation of their depression. The study found that students who participated faithfully in a six-week meditation training experienced improved immune system functioning. The students in a control group, who received only educational information about stress without the inner technique, showed little to no physiological or psychological improvement (Pace *et al*, 2009).

Unpublished research studies during the 1980s, for which I served as clinical advisor, showed a greater effectiveness of inner techniques in contrast to purely medical methods of stress reduction. The medical methods such as progressive relaxation have a positive effect; however, the ameliorative effect on heart rate and blood pressure is greater and more sustainable if inner mechanisms are consciously applied.

These scientific results will not be surprising to people who have learned to use inner technologies such as the letting go technique, which is a process of internal surrender that can be applied to any and all situations. They report that they are better able to handle stress because they are calmer in difficult situations after learning how to let go of negative feelings as the feelings arise.

Kinesiologic Testing

Kinesiology or muscle-testing is a rewarding subject for studying the direct relationship between the mind and the body. The basic testing procedure is now relatively widely known and is both highly informative and simple to learn. Diagnosticians use kinesiologic methods to test the balance of the acupuncture system, the acupuncture meridians, and the overall functioning of the body's bio-energy system.

Kinesiology deals primarily with muscle-testing, as sudden drops in bio-energy are indicated by rapid weakening of the body's musculature. This response can be elicited by any negative energy that comes within the aura (vicinity) of the bio-energy system. The stimulus may be physical, such as artificial sweeteners, fluorescent lights, synthetic foods and fabrics, and certain rhythms produced by heavy metal or rap music groups. The most notable stimulus for our understanding is, however, the immediate weakening effect of a negative thought or feeling. *A negative thought or feeling instantly weakens the body and creates an imbalance of the body's energy flow.*

Because this kind of muscle-testing so beautifully and dramatically illustrates the connection between mind and body, it is worth the effort to know of the procedure and to experience it personally; therefore, we will go into some detail about the testing procedure itself, which is extremely simple and requires only two persons. It is important to note that both the tester and the one being tested must be over the consciousness level of courage (calibration of 200) in order to obtain accurate responses from the testing procedure (see Appendix B); that is, those who are dedicated to truth are shown the truth.

Kinesiologic Testing Technique

The test subject stands with one arm stretched out to the side and raised to shoulder height. The second person serves as a tester. Using two fingers, the tester presses down quickly for a few seconds on the back of the testee's wrist to get a feel for muscle strength. At the same time that the tester presses down, he asks the test subject to resist with all his strength. It is important in doing this that the tester does not smile at the subject, and there should be no talking or music at that moment. It is best to have the test subject view a neutral object such as a blank wall or shut the eyes. After several trials, the tester will get a feel of the strength of the subject's muscles.

For the demonstration, simply have the subject think of an emotionally unpleasant situation or hold in mind an unpleasant person. While the subject holds that unpleasant thought in mind, the tester presses down again for a few seconds to test the strength of the subject's arm, which is still being held out horizontally. At the same time, the test subject again resists with all his strength. It will be observed dramatically that there is a sudden major weakening of the deltoid muscle which, with testing, will indicate a loss of about 50% of muscle strength.

Now have the subject think of someone he loves and re-test. He will instantly go strong. This is a dramatic and highly valuable phenomenon to experience and witness. The test can be repeated with various negative objects held in the subject's other hand, in their mouth, or placed on the crown of their head or at the solar plexus. To do this, have the subject look at a fluorescent light or a television commercial at the moment of testing, or test the difference between the effect of classical music versus heavy metal or rap music; homemade bread versus machine-made bread; sugar versus honey; synthetic fabrics versus cotton, wool or silk; junk food versus organic health food; synthetic vitamin C versus organic rose hips vitamin C. Additional tests can be done for individual reactions to diet sodas, cigarettes, soaps, favorite foods, and other objects with which we come into frequent contact.

As various objects and the effects of thoughts and feelings are tested, it soon becomes obvious that everything in the universe has a vibration and that the vibration has a strengthening or weakening effect. For instance, to demonstrate the weakening effect of a negative energy food such as artificial sweeteners, it is not necessary to place the food in the mouth. It will have the same weakening effect if placed in the opposite hand or on the top of the head.

When a person uses the mechanism of surrender and lets go of a negative feeling, the muscle testing we have described will change from weak to strong. As negative thoughts or belief systems are surrendered, they no longer have the power to deplete our energy.

This is a basic law of consciousness: *We are subject only to what we hold in mind.* The body will respond to what we believe. If we believe that a certain substance is bad for us, then it will usually test weak with muscle testing. The same substance will make another person who believes that it is good for them strong. What is stressful to us, therefore, is primarily subjective. Muscle testing is responsible to unconscious belief systems as well as conscious ones. Testing often reveals that a person unconsciously feels or believes the opposite of what they think they consciously believe. The person, for example, may consciously believe they want to heal but unconsciously be attached to the payoffs of illness. A simple muscle test reveals the truth of the matter.

The Relationship of Consciousness to Stress and Disease

As we have seen, stress proneness and vulnerability are directly related to our general level of emotional functioning. The higher we are on the scale of consciousness, the less we respond with stressful reaction. We can take a simple incident from everyday life and illustrate the differences in reactivity.

Let's say, for example, that we have parked our car and, just as we get out, the car parked in front of us backs up into our car with a thud. Our bumper and the front of the fender are dented. Here is what the different levels of consciousness might sound like:

Shame: "How embarrassing. I'm such a lousy driver. I can't even park a car. I'll never amount to anything."

Guilt: "I had it coming. How stupid I am! I should have done a better job of parking."

Apathy: "What's the use? Things like this always happen to me. I probably won't collect on the insurance anyway. There's no use talking to the guy. He'll just sue me. Life stinks."

Grief: "Now the car is ruined. It will never be the same. Life is grim. I will probably lose a bundle on this one."

Fear: "This guy is probably furious. I'm afraid he'll hit me. I'm afraid to talk back to him. He'll probably sue me. I'll probably never get the car fixed right again. Car repair people always rip me off. The insurance company will probably get out of this one, and I'll be the one left holding the bag."

Desire: "I can make a bundle on this one. I think I will hold my neck and fake a whiplash. My brother-in-law is a lawyer. We'll sue the pants off this idiot. I'll get a settlement on the highest estimate and get it fixed at a cheaper place."

Anger: "The damned idiot! I think I'll teach this guy a lesson. He deserves a good punch in the nose. I'll sue his pants off and make him suffer. My blood is boiling. I feel shaky with rage. I could kill the bastard!"

Pride: "Look where you're going, you fool! Oh God! The world is full of such bumbling idiots! How dare he damage my new car! Who the hell does he think he is? He's probably got cheap insurance; thank God mine is the best."

Courage: "Oh, well, we've both got insurance. I'll take down the data and handle it okay. A nuisance but I can handle it. I'll talk to the driver and get it settled out of court."

Neutrality: "These things happen in life. You can't drive 20,000 miles a year without an occasional fender bender."

Willingness: "How can I help the guy calm down? He doesn't need to feel upset about it. We'll just exchange the necessary insurance information and be okay with each other."

Acceptance: "It could have been worse. At least nobody's hurt. It's only money anyway. The insurance company will take care of it. I suppose the guy's upset. That's only natural. Such things just can't be helped. Thank God I'm not running this universe. It's only a minor nuisance."

Reason: "Let's be practical here. I'd like to take care of it as quickly as possible so I can get on with the day's activities. What's the most efficient way to resolve our problem?"

Love: "I hope the guy isn't upset. I'll calm him down. (Says to the other driver), 'Relax. It's all okay. We've both got insurance. I know how it is. It happened to me just the same way. It was a minor dent and we got it fixed in a day. Don't worry—we won't report it if you don't want to. We can probably deduct it and avoid a raise in the insurance premium. There's nothing to be upset about.'" (Reassures the upset driver, putting an arm on his shoulder in fellow human camaraderie.)

Peace: "Well, isn't that fortuitous? I was going to have the rattle in the bumper fixed, anyway, and the fender already had a little dent. So now I'll get it fixed for nothing. 'Say, aren't you George's brother-in-law? You're just the guy I wanted to see. I have some great business that I think you can handle for me. We'll both benefit. You look like the right person to research it for us. How about a cup of coffee and we can talk it over? By the way, here's my insurance card. Say, that's the same company as yours. What a coincidence. Everything is working out for the best. No problem.'" (Walks off humming with new friend, the incident already forgotten.)

The above illustrates all that we have been saying. It is we ourselves who create stressful reactions as a consequence of what we are holding within us. The suppressed feelings determine our belief systems and our perception of ourselves and others. These, in turn, literally create events and incidents in the world, events that we, then, turn around and blame for our reactions. This is a self-reinforcing system of illusions. This is what the enlightened sages mean when they say, "We are all living in an illusion." All that we experience are our own thoughts, feelings, and beliefs projected onto the world, actually causing what we see to happen.

Most people have experienced all the different levels of consciousness at one time or another but, in general, we tend to operate primarily at one level or another for long periods of time. Most people are preoccupied with survival in all its subtle forms, and so they reflect primarily fear, anger, and a desire for gain. They have not learned that the state of lovingness is the most powerful of all survival tools.

Interestingly, as we said in an earlier chapter, having a pet dog can lengthen a human life by 10 years. The love, affection, caring for another being, and companionship that go along with having a dog mitigate the negative effects of stress. Love stimulates endorphins and life energy, bringing a healing balm to stress-prone lives.

15

RELATIONSHIP BETWEEN MIND AND BODY

The Influence of Mind

The basic dictum to comprehend is that the body obeys the mind; therefore, the body tends to manifest what the mind believes. The belief may be held consciously or unconsciously. This dictum follows from the law of consciousness that states: *We are only subject to what we hold in mind.* The only power that anything has over us is the power of belief that we give it. By "power," we mean energy and the will to believe.

If we look at the Map of Consciousness (see Appendix A), it's easy to see why the mind is more powerful than the body. The energy field of reason (calibrates at 400), with its beliefs and concepts of the mind, is more powerful than the energy field of the physical body (calibrates at 200). Thus, the body will express the beliefs held in mind, consciously or unconsciously.

Our proneness to accept negative beliefs depends on how much negativity we are holding in the first place. A positive mind, for example, will refuse to accept negative thoughts and simply reject them as untrue for oneself. There is a refusal to buy into commonly held negative ideas. We know how easy it is to sell self-condemnation to a guilt-ridden person or fear of some disease to a fearful person.

The idea, for instance, that "colds are catching" is a good example. The thought that "everybody's got a cold" will be subscribed to by a person who has sufficient guilt, fear, and naïveté regarding the laws of consciousness. Because of unconscious guilt, a person unconsciously feels that they "deserve" a cold. The body obeys the mind's belief that colds are caused by viruses, which are "catching" and contagious. Thus, the body, which is controlled by the mind's belief, manifests the cold. The person who has let go of the underlying negative energies of guilt and fear does not have a fearful mind that believes, "A cold is going around; I'll probably get it like everybody else."

These are the dynamics behind disease. The mechanisms are carried out through the mind-induced alterations in the energy flow of the bio-energy system and through the spillover of suppressed energy into the autonomic nervous system.

Thought is powerful because it has a high rate of vibration. A thought is actually a thing; it has an energy pattern. The more energy we give it, the more power it has to manifest itself physically. This is the paradox of much so-called health education. The paradoxical effect is that fearful thoughts are reinforced and given so much power that epidemics are actually created by the media (e.g., the swine flu). The fear-based "warnings" about health dangers actually set-up the mental environment in which the very thing that is feared will occur.

Superimposed around the physical body is an energy body whose form is very much like that of the physical body and whose patterns actually control the physical body. This control is at the level of thought or intention. Advanced sub-atomic quantum physics has shown, similarly, that observation influences sub-atomic high-energy particles.

The power of mind over body has been demonstrated by clinical research. For instance, in one study, a group of women were told that they would be given a hormone injection to bring on their menstrual periods two weeks early. Actually, they were merely given a placebo injection of saline. Nonetheless, over 70% of the women developed early pre-menstrual tension with all of the physical and psychological symptoms.

Another clear demonstration of this law of consciousness is observed in persons with multiple personality disorder. Once thought to be rare, it is now found that multiple personality disorder is relatively common; and so, research into the phenomenon has become increasingly prominent. It has been shown that the different personalities in the one body have different physical accompaniments. There are, for instance, changes in the electroencephalographic brain waves, as well as changes in their handedness in handwriting, pain thresholds, electrical skin response, I.Q., menstrual periods, cerebral hemisphere dominance, language ability, accent, and vision. Thus, when the personality that believes in allergies is present, the person is allergic; but when another personality is present in the body, the allergies disappear. One personality may require glasses and another may not. These different personalities actually have notable differences in intraocular pressure and other physiological measurements.

These physical phenomena also shift under the influence of hypnosis in normal people. Allergies can be made to appear or disappear by simple suggestion. Persons who receive the suggestion of being allergic to roses while under hypnosis will start sneezing when they come out of the hypnotic state and spot a vase of roses on the doctor's desk, even if the roses are artificial. Sir John Eccles, Nobel Laureate, stated that after a lifetime of study it became apparent that the brain is not the origin of the mind, as science and medicine had believed, but the other way around. The mind controls the brain, which acts as a receiving station (like a radio) with thoughts being similar to radio waves and the brain being similar to the receiver.

The brain is like a receiving set, a switchboard that receives thought forms and then translates them into neuronal functioning and memory storage. For instance, until recently it was believed that voluntary movements of the muscles originated in the brain's motor cortex. But now, as Eccles has reported, the intention to move is recorded by the supplemental motor area of the brain next to the motor cortex. The brain is, therefore, activated by the mind's intention and not vice versa.

We see this in the many brain-imaging studies done on people in states of meditation. For example, Dr. Richard Davidson's research during the last decade at the University of Wisconsin (Madison) has demonstrated that compassion and loving-kindness meditation practices stimulated increased activity in the left prefrontal cortex (the seat of positive emotions such as happiness) and the production of high amplitude gamma wave synchrony (sign of expanded awareness, alertness, and insight). What is held in mind has the power to alter brain activity and neuroanatomy.

We are subject to all kinds of effects of the unconscious and conscious beliefs that our mind is holding on all of our bodily systems. This includes our beliefs about the supposed effects of various foods, allergens, menopausal and menstrual disorders, infections and all other diseases that are associated with specific belief systems, coupled with the underlying stress proneness due to the presence of suppressed negative feelings.

Norman Cousins, editor-in-chief of the *Saturday Review* for three decades, demonstrated this principle when he cured himself of serious physical illness by means of laughter. He wrote *Anatomy of an Illness,* a book about his experience of recovery from a crippling arthritic disease through heavy doses of Vitamin C and belly-laughter induced by films featuring the Marx brothers. He discovered that laughter had an anesthetic effect that could alleviate his pain for two hours. Laughing is a method of letting go. Through laughter, Cousins just kept letting go of the underlying emotional pressure and cancelling negative thoughts. This resulted in very positive and beneficial changes within his body and facilitated his eventual recovery.

Disease-Prone Beliefs

To ascertain our own disease proneness, we can look at the following questions:

Do I worry about my health, holding fear thoughts in mind about what might happen to me?

Do I get a secret feeling of fear, excitement, and danger when I hear about a new disease that is currently being reported and in vogue?

Do I spend time on constant checkups, reading about diseases, getting frightened by TV stories about them?

Am I interested in hearing about the diseases of famous people?

Do I believe that the environment and foods are full of hidden dangers, or that foods contain additives which are poisonous and will cause disease?

Do I believe that certain diseases "run in our family"?

Do I stop or want to stop (but don't dare) to witness auto accident victims?

Do I like hospital TV programs?

Do I like TV programs that include hitting, shouting, fist fights, killing, torture, crime, and other forms of violence?

Am I a guilt-ridden person?

Am I holding a lot of anger?

Do I condemn other peoples' behavior? Am I prone to be judgmental?

Do I hold resentments and grudges?

Do I feel trapped and hopeless?

Do I say of myself, "Whatever is going around, I'll probably catch it"?

Am I concerned with acquisitions and status symbols instead of the quality of relationships?

Do I carry a lot of insurance and still worry that it's not enough?

In summary, the way to change our bodies is to change our thoughts and feelings. We must let go of negative thoughts and belief systems and shed the stress of negative emotions that give them energy. We have to cancel the negative programming that comes from the world, as well as our own belief systems.

We can see the deleterious effects of fearful negative programming in people who become subject to fear of foods, chemicals, and substances in the environment. Each day a new chemical or substance is announced to have harmful effects. The more fearful we are, the more quickly we become programmed, and then the body responds accordingly. Fear of substances, foods, air, energies, and stimuli of all kinds has gotten to the point where there is almost an environmental paranoia. Some people become so phobic about the environment and everything in it that their world gets smaller and smaller. They become more fearful every day. Some people even succumb to the point where they flee the world and live in artificial bubble enclosures, victims of their own minds.

This can happen to a reasonable person, even to a physician. It started with pollens, ragweed, horse dander, dog and cat hair, dust, feathers, wool, chocolate, cheese, and nuts (all believed to cause allergies). Later, sugar was added (hyperglycemia) plus food additives (cancer), eggs and dairy products (cholesterol), and organ meats (gout). Next on the "harmful" list came food dyes, saccharine, caffeine, coloring matter, aluminum, synthetic fabrics, noise, fluorescent lights, insect sprays, deodorants, food cooked at high temperature, minerals in the water, chlorine in the water, nicotine, cigarette smoke, petrochemicals, car exhaust fumes, positive ions, low level electric vibrations, acidic foods, pesticides, and foods with seeds.

The world shrank so small that there was nothing safe to eat. Nothing could be worn. There was no air to breathe. The body had all the allergies, reactions, and diseases to prove it. Going out to dinner became an enjoyment of the past, since there was nothing on the menu that could be eaten, except lettuce (thoroughly washed, of course), and it was imperative to wear white gloves when picking up restaurant utensils!

Then, with the learning of one core truth, the whole pattern unraveled. "What is held in mind tends to manifest"—including *unconscious* beliefs. The culprit was not the world but the mind. All of the negative programming and fearful conditioning was in the mind, and the body obeyed the mind. This law of consciousness reversed the spiraling paranoia. As each internal belief was looked at and surrendered, all of the negative bodily reactions, diseases, and symptoms disappeared. In other words, it was not poison ivy leaves that caused an allergic reaction but the mind's belief that poison ivy was an allergen. As the mind let go of its programming, the body's reactions cleared.

On kinesiologic testing, there was a complete reversal of the reaction patterns. What had formerly produced a weak muscle response no longer had any effect. The overall stress proneness level obviously became much lower, to the point that the body failed to react at all to what would, otherwise, be considered negative stimuli (e.g., fluorescent lights, artificial sweetener).

Comparison with Other Techniques

As we have seen, stress arises from within as a response to a stimulus. The stressor actually is the pressure of the suppressed and repressed emotional energies, which are a reflection of our general low-level consciousness. Thus, it is the content of our con-

sciousness that has to be changed to eliminate and
prevent stress. The commonly prescribed treatments
for stress are similar to the treatments in the field of
medicine. They try to fix the damage done by the disease we already have, rather than cure the internal
cause of the disease.

Conferences on stress, for example, routinely
include the following topics:

Aromatherapy.

Physical exercise workshop.

Acupuncture for stress disorders.

Bio-feedback.

Chiropractic.

Stress regulation.

Nutrition.

Fitness and exercise profile.

Homeopathy.

Autogenic training.

Holistic healing.

Massage and body work.

Flotation tanks.

Dental balance.

Unwinding technique by use of body movements.

As we can see from the above, the common
approaches deal only with the consequences and resultant damage from the stress syndrome. None of them
deal with the basic causes. They all involve relatively

complicated and time-consuming procedures, and they do not lend themselves to on-the-spot application. As an example, let's say that we are giving a speech or lecture. We are on the spot. It is impractical to stop in the middle of a speech and do breathing exercises, go into hypnotic trance, stick ourselves with acupuncture needles, or hitch up to a bio-feedback machine. How handy is a flotation tank in the middle of a family argument?

Because these approaches are temporary, time-consuming, and often expensive, people try them for a short while with enthusiasm, but then their enthusiasm wears off because basically nothing has really changed. The same basic perceptions of the world persist. The same emotional pressures are there. The personality remains the same. Life circumstances have not changed. One's level of consciousness is not altered. The person's psychology is the same. Expectation continues as before and life, therefore, continues as before.

Without a change of consciousness, there is no real reduction of stress. Only the consequences are ameliorated. All of these after-the-fact techniques and treatments do help and often alleviate a given condition and bring some relief, but they leave the basis of the problem untouched. One can follow all of these techniques and yet remain the same stress-prone person. In our experience, the conscious use of the mechanism of surrender is more effective in addressing chronic stress-related illnesses. Illnesses begin to heal spontaneously because the underlying emotional cause has been removed, and further treatments often become unnecessary.

In the uncommon case of persistent illness that is

not cleared by the surrender of negative thoughts and feelings, unknown factors such as karmic proclivities may be operating. In such cases, we surrender the desire to change or control our experience of life, and we await further inner discovery about the source and significance of the illness. Surrender at great depth is complete when a person has let go of needing or wanting a physical healing to occur. A state of peace about the situation is reached when all three aspects of illness—physical, mental, and spiritual—have been addressed and the final outcome or wished-for recovery has been surrendered. Peace comes with total inner surrender to *what is*.

16

THE BENEFITS OF LETTING GO

Emotional Growth

The most obvious and visible effect of letting go of negative feelings is a resumption of emotional and psychological growth and the solving of problems, which often have been long-standing. There is pleasure and satisfaction as we begin to experience the powerful effects of eliminating the blocks to achievement and satisfaction in life. We soon discover that the limiting thoughts and negative beliefs, which we had naively held to be true, were all merely the result of accumulated negative feelings. When the feeling is let go, then, the thought pattern changes from "I can't" to "I can" and to "I'm happy to do it." Entire areas of life can open up. What used to be awkward or unexpressed can become effortless and joyously alive.

Illustrative of this progression is the experience of an intelligent, successful, middle-aged, professional man who all his life had been unable to dance. He wanted to dance in the worst way, and several times during his life had attended dancing classes. But each time, he found himself to be stiff, awkward, and self-conscious. By sheer willpower, he did manage at times to go through the motions on the dance floor, but never enjoyed it and always felt ill at ease. His movements felt stiff and calculated, and the whole experience was lacking in satisfaction, doing nothing for his self-esteem.

After about a year of working with the mechanism of surrender, he was at a party with someone who kept insisting that he get up and dance. "You know I can't dance," he said. "Ah, come on and try it," she entreated. She persisted and said, "Forget about your feet. Just watch me and do what my body does." Reluctantly, he agreed, and he kept letting go of his feelings of resistance and anxiety.

On the dance floor he let go completely. In an instant, his inner feelings ascended the scale from apathy to love and, to his amazement, he suddenly began to dance like he had always dreamed of and envied! The realization of "I can do it!" hit him, and he went from love, to joy, and even to ecstasy. His delight radiated to everyone. Friends stopped to watch. From a state of high joy, he suddenly went into the experience of oneness with his dance partner. He suddenly saw his own Self looking out of her eyes and realized that there was actually only one Self behind all the individual selves. He and she became telepathically connected. He knew her every step a split second before she took it. They were in perfect harmony and danced as though they had practiced and danced together for years. He could hardly contain his joy. The dancing became effortless and began to happen of its own, without any conscious thought on his part. The longer they danced, the more energy he felt.

It was a peak experience that was to change this

man's life. He went home that night and danced some more. Free-style disco dancing had always terrified him more than any other because there was no form to be memorized. It necessitated spontaneity and a free feeling, which is just what he had specifically been unable to experience previously. At home he turned on the disco music and began to dance for hours. He watched himself in the mirror, fascinated by the body's surrender and the inner feeling of freedom.

All of a sudden, he remembered a previous lifetime in vivid detail. He had been a great dancer in that lifetime, and now he began to remember the specific instructions that had been given to him by his teachers in that lifetime. When he followed their instructions, the results were amazing! He discovered that there was a vertical gravitational center of balance within himself, and he began to rotate about it in perfect balance. The movement was effortless, and he became merely the witness of the dancing. It was no longer any feeling of "I." There was just the joy and the dancing itself. Now he instantly understood the very basis of the Sufi dancing of the whirling dervishes. Their ability to whirl and spin without dizziness or fatigue— that certain state of consciousness—ensued from the surrendering of the individual self.

The breakthrough that this man experienced on the dance floor then transferred itself to many other previously blocked areas of his life. Where there had been limitation, now there was rapid expansion. These changes were very obvious to his friends and family, whose positive feedback increased his self-esteem and his desire to keep letting go of the negative feelings and thoughts that had blocked the experience of joy in life.

This experience has been cited in some detail for a

number of reasons. It illustrates the scale of consciousness that we presented in a previous chapter. For fifty years, this man had been at the lowest end of the scale in this area of his life, with the accompanying belief, "I can't." The inhibition decreased his self-esteem and resulted in avoidance. For years, he managed to avoid social affairs where there would be dancing. He was angry at himself for his inhibition, and he would feel angry when anyone tried to get him to dance. In a matter of seconds and minutes, he experienced every emotion of the whole scale and went all the way to the top. At that point, there was the emergence of a higher consciousness with sudden spiritual awareness of a very high order. With higher consciousness came understanding and the release of psychic ability (telepathic communication, synchronicity, and past life recall). As a result, his life showed a behavioral change, and its momentum removed an endless series of blocks and limitations. There was a positive social response, and the positive feedback reinforced the growth motivation that was already in progress.

The rate of emotional growth reported by those who use the mechanism of surrender is related to the consistency with which they surrender their negative feelings, and there is no relationship to age. People have ranged in age from the teens to the eighties with equal benefit.

Repressed and suppressed feelings require counterenergy to keep them submerged. It takes energy to hold down our feelings. As these feelings are relinquished, the energy that had been holding down the negativity is now freed for constructive uses. Consequent to letting go, there is an increase in available energy for creativity, growth, work, and interpersonal relationships. The quality and enjoyment of these activities increase. Most people are too exhausted to bring a really high quality into their experiences unless the negative programs opposing them have been resolved.

Problem Solving

The effectiveness of the letting go mechanism in problem solving often is quite astonishing. Understanding the process involved here is very important, because it is quite different than the world's usual methods. The approach that brings fast and easy results is the following: *Don't look for answers; instead, let go of the feelings behind the question.* When we are surrendered on the feeling behind the question, we can let go of any other feelings that we might also have about what seems to be the problem. When we are finally and fully surrendered on all components, the answer will be there waiting for us. We won't have to look for it. Consider how simple and easy this is as compared to the mind's usual long, drawn-out, inefficient attempts at problem solving. Usually the mind hunts and pecks endlessly, fumbling around with first this possible answer and then that one. The reason the mind can't decide is because it is looking in the wrong place.

Let's see how the system works with a common everyday example. Let's say that we disagree with our mate on which movie to see. We look to see what the feeling is behind the problem. In this case, let's say that we find the feeling of anger and resentment, specifically that we feel resentful about the lack of romantic time spent together. What we really want tonight is affectionate time spent together. As we let it be okay inside ourselves that what we really want is affectionate togetherness, it suddenly dawns on us that we don't want to go to a movie at all. We just want to be together. Or the opposite might happen. We might find that the feeling behind wanting to go to a movie is fear, because we want to avoid spending the evening talking to and being close to our mate. We see that the feelings we have built up are unpleasant. We have resentment, so we let go of wanting to modify that feeling, and we just let it be there. It's okay to have that resentment. As we surrender our resistance to the resentful feeling, we feel less guilty; we admit to our mate that we have had a resentment. A dialogue starts going, and the other person's feelings are cleared up as well. We both feel relieved and closer, and we then say, "To heck with the movies. Let's stay home, make love, and go for a walk in the moonlight."

This approach is rewarding in all decision-making. When we first clear out the underlying feelings, the decisions are more realistic and wise. Think of how often we have changed our mind and regretted past decisions. That is because there was an unrecognized and un-relinquished feeling behind the decision. When the action that was decided upon is taken, the underlying feeling shifts. Then, from the viewpoint of the new feeling space, the decision turns out to be wrong. This happens with such regularity that most people develop a fear of decision-making, because it turned out to be wrong so often in the past.

Problem solving using the mechanism of surrender can often be lightning quick with problems of long standing. To discover how fast it can work, let's try it out. Take several problems of long standing and stop looking for the answers. Look to see what the underlying feeling is that produced the question in the first place. Once that feeling is let go, the answer will present itself automatically.

Lifestyle

A lot of our activities and attachments are based on fear and anger, guilt and pride. As these negative feelings are relinquished in any given area, we move up to courage. On that level, changes in life begin to occur. Or, if we choose to continue the same activity, the motivation is different and, consequently, we will experience different results than in the past. The emotional payoff will at least be different. Instead of grim satisfaction, we may experience joy. We may find ourselves doing the same activity as before, but now we do it out of enjoyment rather than obligation. We do it because we want to, not because we have to. The energy requirement will certainly be much less.

One delightful discovery we will make is that our capacity for love is far beyond what we ever dreamed. The more we let go, the more loving we become. More and more of our life will be spent doing things that we love to do, with people for whom we feel increasing love. As this happens, our life becomes transformed. We look different. People respond differently to us. We are relaxed, happy, and easy-going. People are attracted to us because they feel comfortable and happy around us. Waitresses and cab drivers suddenly mysteriously become attentive and courteous, and we will wonder, "What has come over this world?" The answer to that question is "*You* have!"

As we let go the negative, we come into our own power. It happens of its own. Happiness was in there all along and now it shines forth after the blocks to it have been surrendered. We are now influencing everyone with whom we come into contact in a favorable way. Love is the most powerful of the emotional energy vibrations. For love, people will go to any lengths and do things that they would never do for any amount of money.

When the negative blocks and "I can'ts" are removed, whole new areas of life open up to us. Success stems from doing what we like to do best, but most people are tied down to what they imagine they have to do. As limitations are relinquished, whole new avenues of creativity and expression become available.

Let's take the example of a young woman with a lot of natural musical talent who was spending most of her time at a boring job, which she felt she had to stick to for financial reasons. What she really liked to do was play musical instruments when she was alone at home. It was something that she did strictly for personal enjoyment. Because of the lack of self-confidence, she seldom played for other people, even close friends. After she began to let go of her inner limitations—all of the low-energy feelings that were blocking her expression—her abilities and confidence grew so rapidly that she began to play in front of public gatherings. Her talent was well received, and a busy musical career ensued. She made a professional recording that was sufficiently successful that she could cut back to working part time, and she began to pour more time and energy into what was now a blossoming career that brought her great joy and satisfaction. Although she had known nothing about business, she now started her own musical business and, within a year, was distributing the recordings nationally, then in Europe. To her delight, she found that she was very successful by doing what she liked to do best. Her increasing vitality and happiness were apparent to everyone, and success spread to other areas of her life.

Another example is that of a middle-aged engineer with no creative ability who had always hated poetry. After learning to let go of his negative feelings, suddenly he found himself writing Haiku (a formal Japanese poetry style). He began writing reams of it effortlessly and later developed the capacity for automatic writing.

Still another example is that of a sixty-year-old woman who decided to return to college part time, even though she already had a full-time job. Eventually, she attained her bachelor's degree, then her master's degree, and finally a Ph.D., becoming an important executive with great responsibilities.

There are literally thousands of examples that could be cited of the rapid expansions that take place in people's life when the "I can'ts" are surrendered. Life situations, often of long standing, may be suddenly resolved.

Paradoxically, such breakthroughs and expansions may be upsetting to friends and family members because of the shift of balance. Things that we had done out of constriction, fear, guilt, or a sense of duty may be suddenly thrown overboard. New levels of consciousness change perception and new horizons open up. Many of the motives that drive people may suddenly become meaningless. Such things as money, fame, esteem, position, prestige, power, ambition, competitiveness, and the need for security diminish. They are replaced by the motivations of love, cooperation, fulfillment, freedom, creative expression, expansion of consciousness, understanding, and spiritual awareness. There tends to be more reliance on intuition and feelings than on thinking, reason, and logic. People who are very "yang" may discover their "yin" side, and vice versa. Rigid patterns give way to flexibility. Safety and security become less important than discovery and exploration. Personal lives pick up momentum, and movement replaces stuck-in-a-rut life patterns.

One surprising observation about the mechanism of letting go is that major changes can take place very rapidly. Lifetime patterns can suddenly disappear, and long-standing inhibitions can be let go of in a matter of minutes, hours, or days. Rapid changes are accompanied by an increased aliveness. The life energy set free by the letting go of negativity now flows into positive attitudes, thoughts, and feelings, with a progressive increase of personal power. Thoughts are now more effective. More is accomplished with less effort. Intention is made powerful by the removal of doubts, fears, and inhibitions. With the removal of negativity, dynamic forces are unloosed, so that what were once impossible dreams now become actualized goals.

Resolution of Psychological Problems: Comparison with Psychotherapy

In general, letting go is often more rapid than psychotherapy. It is often more liberating and stimulating to the growth of consciousness and awareness. Psychotherapy, however, is better designed to elucidate underlying patterns. The two may work well together. The mechanism of letting go facilitates and speeds up psychotherapy, and it elevates its goals. Psychotherapy may be more gratifying intellectually because of its verbal nature and its focus on the "whys" behind behavior. However, that is also its limitation. Too often intellectual insight is all that's really achieved, and the emotional working through is slow, often painful, and ultimately avoided. The mechanism of letting go, on the other hand, is concerned with the emotional "what" from moment to moment, without involving the intellect. The "why" becomes apparent of itself once the "what" has been relinquished. It's one thing to analyze the causal basis of depression and quite another to enter fully into the depth of hopelessness by letting go of your resistance to the feeling. By allowing the full feeling of it and by letting go of every sensation, every thought, and every little payoff you are getting from it, you are free. It's not necessary to probe the "why" of depression to become free from the "what" of it.

The goals of letting go are far beyond those of psychotherapy. The ultimate aim of letting go and surrendering is total freedom. The goal of therapy is readjustment of the ego to a more healthy balance. The two systems are based on different paradigms of reality. The objective of psychotherapy is to replace unsatisfactory mental programs with more satisfactory ones. In contrast, the objective of letting go is the elimination of limiting mental and emotional programs. It is the attainment of an unconditioned mind and, ultimately, transcendence of the mind itself to higher states of consciousness of love and peace.

In therapy, there is dependence on therapists and their training and techniques, and there is also reliance on a psychological theory to which the therapist and the patient both subscribe. Scientific research reveals that the results of therapy are not related to the therapist's school of psychotherapy, training or technique; instead, the results are related to the interaction between them and the degree of the patient's desire to improve, as well as the patient's faith and confidence in the therapist. Therefore, psychic factors are operating of which psychotherapy is unaware.

With the mechanism of letting go, there is no patient role and no dependency on another person or theory. The very wellsprings of neurotic patterns automatically unfold as they are acknowledged, relinquished, and disappear. Their basis is often at depths untouched by psychotherapy. Except for the few holistic frameworks (e.g., Jungian analysis, transpersonal psychology), therapy can be based on a limited understanding of the total mind. It commonly addresses itself only to a portion of the ego. It ignores and does not comprehend the great forces that determine, drive, and control the mind. Since the purpose of most psychotherapy is a well-adjusted ego, there is no conception of what is beyond the ego.

The purpose of letting go, in contrast, is the elimination of the ego. The ego is fearful and limited and, when it is surrendered, the inner Self stands forth, and what was always more powerful is revealed. Many psychotherapies have no real knowledge of the Self and are, therefore, blind to Reality Itself. As for efficacy, psychotherapy is like a horse and buggy, while the mechanism of surrender and letting go is like a space ship. In the time it takes for therapy to slowly poke about a limited area, letting go has already moved far beyond it into a whole new dimension.

Letting go has a peculiar advantage in that the surrendering of one negative feeling also relinquishes the energy behind many other negative feelings, so there is a constant across-the-board effect. For instance, a successful and well-educated man had a life-long terrible fear of heights, an intense phobia. At the time that he learned how to utilize the mechanism of surrender, he had many pressing problems in his life. After learning how to surrender, he was busy with letting go of his feelings and fears about major life problems and never got around to specifically working on his lifelong fear of heights. When he was later in a situation involving standing on a roof, he was amazed to discover that his fear had greatly lessened. He was delighted and went to the edge of the roof where he sat dangling his feet. He was now able to get up on ladders and go on the roof for an hour with no discomfort. This illustrates that, as one fear is relinquished, all fear is diminished non-specifically.

Psychotherapy aims at the amelioration of neurotic patterns. Letting go, however, is designed to undo the underlying causes of all neurotic formation. It undoes the basic structure of maladaptive feeling and behavior. Psychotherapy seeks for an improvement in neurotic balance. Letting go, however, eliminates it all together.

A limitation of most psychotherapeutic frameworks is that the therapist is constricted to what the world calls a healthy, functioning ego with all its restrictions. In this paradigm, a healthy patient is considered to be one who shares the same illusions and limitations condoned by society and the therapist. By contrast, the purpose of the mechanism of surrender is to transcend the illusions of the world and reach the ultimate truth behind it—which is Self-Realization—and to discover the very basis of the mind itself, the source of all thought and feeling.

The goal of letting go is the elimination of the very source of all suffering and pain. This sounds radical and startling and, in fact, it is! Ultimately, all negative feelings stem from the same source. When enough negative feelings have been relinquished, that source reveals itself. When that source itself is let go of and dis-identified with, the ego dissolves. The source of suffering, therefore, loses the very basis of its power.

Each of us has a limit to the amount of negative feelings we have stored up. When the pressure behind an emotion has been let go, that emotion no longer occurs. For instance, if fear is constantly surrendered for a period of time, eventually it runs out. It then becomes difficult or almost impossible to feel further fear. It takes progressively more and more of a stimulus to elicit it. Finally, the person who has surrendered a great deal of fear actually has to search for it diligently. The energy of fear simply isn't there anymore. Anger also progressively diminishes so that even a major provocation fails to elicit it. A person with little fear or anger feels primarily love all of the time and experiences a loving acceptance of events, people, and the vicissitudes of life.

The goal of surrender is transcendence. Psychotherapy accepts levels of behavior as healthy that, from the viewpoint of total freedom, are unacceptable. For instance, in psychotherapy, minimal fear, anger, and pride might be considered necessary or acceptable levels of functioning and perhaps even "healthy." But as we have seen, the innate destructiveness behind those lower states is ultimately not acceptable—given the power of surrender to transcend them totally. Beyond the "acceptable level of functioning" awaits our greater destiny: total freedom.

17

TRANSFORMATION

Although letting go seems simple and easy, its ultimate effects are profoundly powerful. A quick little surrender done in an almost off-handed manner can sometimes bring about a major change in our life. We can picture it being similar to the wheel of a ship. If we make even a one-degree change in the ship's compass, we will notice very little difference; but, as the ship sails over the sea hour after hour, day after day, a one-degree change in the compass will end up taking us to a very different place many miles from where the original course would have taken us.

In this chapter we want to look at the effect that the mechanism of surrender has on those areas of life with which most people are concerned: health, wealth, and happiness. We will discuss these areas as they are usually experienced by the majority of people, and make a contrast to the changes that will occur as the practice of letting go progresses. These changes are quite obvious when we watch the lives of others who use the technique. They will become obvious in your own life as well. Sometimes you will not be aware of them; therefore, it is suggested that you keep a list of goals and check off the gains as they occur, so that you remain conscious and aware of the progress. This self-awareness step is to circumvent a peculiarity of the mind. When we decide on a specific technique to improve our life, and when improvement occurs, the mind has a peculiar tendency to discount the very technique that brought about the change. It is as though the mind's ego is so vain that it doesn't want to give credit where credit is due.

This proclivity of mind to discount inner progress is sometimes quite comical. For instance, a man who had been stuck in the same job position for 23 years began using the technique of letting go. Within a couple of months, he suddenly jumped to the position of Vice President and, by the end of the year, he was President of the company. When asked if he was pleased with himself about what he had accomplished by using the inner technique, his mind totally discounted it and ascribed his gains to "shifts in business patterns." His marriage had also improved and the mind, again, ascribed the improvements to external reasons: "My wife's attitudes finally changed." The relationship with his son also improved, and the mind again circumvented the inner transformation and said it was due to the fact that his son was "getting older."

In the discussions that follow, it will be noted that the transitions from one state to a higher state are not difficult to make. They may only seem "difficult" to us because of current perceptions. It's important to keep in mind that, as we surrender, our perceptions will change. Our goals will automatically be elevated. What now seems impossible will become old hat after we have been practicing the technique a while.

We will also notice that, as the mind contrasts the

lower level of life with the higher level, a peculiar resistance to the description of a higher level of functioning will occur at times. The mind will get critical and try to save face by ridiculing a higher state. This is a golden opportunity because this is the very attitude that prevents a person from reaching that higher state of life. The very process of reading this material is invaluable, for it will reveal precisely what the blocks are and exactly why these goals are impossible at the present time. As resistances, criticisms, and disparagements come up, we can begin surrendering them and letting them go right now in the process of reading about them. It is a great opportunity to identify the inner blocks to fulfillment. As Pogo said, "We have identified the enemy, and it is us."

As a professional psychotherapist and psychiatrist with many decades of clinical experience and training, these higher levels of functioning were considered to be impossible for most people. However, learning how the mechanism of surrender works on the practical level and watching hundreds of families, friends, patients, and ex-patients transform their lives has totally changed this view. Now, higher levels of functioning are seen to be automatic, easy to achieve, and available to everyone, often in a surprisingly short period of time. As a matter of fact, some of these levels of success and happiness will seem impossible, but the higher level will already have occurred by the time you have finished reading this book. You can tell yourself right in the beginning that these high levels of functioning are not only possible, but they are an inherent birthright. They are the natural state of which you have been deprived by all the programming that the mind has been subjected to since birth.

Before reading on, it is advisable to sit quietly and make an inner decision to let go resisting higher levels of functioning. This means to make a decision to stop denying the higher levels to yourself, and to make a decision to let go of all blocks to happiness, success, health, acceptance, love, and peace. By doing this, the deed is already done, for you have set the whole experience into a context that will automatically begin to unfold.

Health

The average person is preoccupied with the body, its functioning, performance, appearance, and survival. The average mind is beleaguered with worries, fears of sickness, suffering, disease, and death; therefore, the mind sets about defending the body in a great variety of ways. This leads to over-attention to diet, weight, exercise, and the health of the environment. With such inner tension, by the end of the day the average person frequently feels like a victim: drained, empty, and exhausted.

One consequence of this preoccupation with the body is self-consciousness. Within the field of awareness, the body's presence is prominent, and there is a mental fixation with what it is doing, its whereabouts and movements, its survival, the attitudes and approval of other persons toward the body, its appearance and behavior.

Underlying all of this concern is the unconscious equation, "I am a body." This is a very limited level of consciousness. In fact, in the spiritual world this is called "being unconscious." Because it is a false identification due to a marked narrowing of awareness, it is like wearing blinders. It is like having a pimple on the nose and thinking that the whole world now revolves around that pimple, and going through the day with that pimple most prominent in our mind.

Be aware of how much energy is drained by this constant preoccupation with the body. Our mind has been continuously programmed with a countless variety of belief systems about the body: what it needs, what will be good for it, and its infinite number of vulnerabilities. This leads to constant preoccupations with all kinds of health preventive measures, including health food fads, the endless reading of labels for potentially poisonous ingredients, the fear of being near someone smoking a cigarette, the fear of dusts and pollens and all of the supposed contaminants of the environment. There is an obsession with offsetting all of these "dangers" by various countermeasures.

As we have seen from previous discussions, these vulnerabilities are merely the product of the mind, and the body will react to what is held in mind. This was demonstrated in our discussion of multiple personalities where the body reflected in each instant what that particular personality and mind believed.

As we begin letting go of all these fears, cancelling the belief systems and reaffirming that our true Self is Infinite and not subject to limitations, we move into a higher state of health, wellness, and vital energy. A helpful way to phrase it to ourselves is, "I am an Infinite Being, not subject to _____." We put into the blank space whatever disease or substance that the mind has been programmed to see as a possible "danger" for us.

After letting go of the endless variety of bodily fears, concerns and belief systems, physical illnesses begin to resolve automatically. There is an increase in the feeling of aliveness and personal freedom. In the state of total surrender, the body is barely perceived at all. It is only peripherally in awareness, and there is no preoccupation with it. It functions effortlessly, smoothly, and with very little attention.

A surrendered person can eat anything or go anywhere and is no longer subject to fears of contaminants, pollutants, drafts, germs, electromagnetic frequencies, carpet, smoke, dust, animal dander, poison ivy, pollen, or food dyes. Our perception of the body shifts, and it now seems to be like a puppet or a pet. This shift of perception is from "I *am* the body" to "I *have* a body."

It becomes progressively obvious that the body is not experiencing itself at all. On the contrary, it is the mind that is experiencing the body. Without the mind, the body cannot be perceived at all. The arm cannot experience its arm-ness. Only the mind can experience the arm-ness. This, of course, is the very basis of anesthesia. When the mind is asleep, the body has no sensation. It slowly dawns on us that, in fact, the body doesn't have any sensation; only the mind is capable of that function.

This is a very important shift of consciousness because now the preoccupation is not with the body and defending it. The focus of attention now shifts to the mind, which is where the greater power lies. As we shift our thoughts, feelings and perceptions, we begin to notice that the body follows suit. We recognize that people are not really responding to our body at all but to our inner attitudes, our energy state, and our level of awareness. One day it dawns on us that everyone and everything in the world are responding to our level of consciousness, our intention, and to the inner feeling we have about them. We register the magnetism of saintly people such as Mother Teresa, the Dalai Lama, and Mahatma Gandhi. We see that they are beloved not because of their physical appearance, but because of the inner radiance of love and peace they emanate. The shift of focus from the physical level to the level of consciousness begins to bring rapid results.

The persistent surrender of negative feelings and attitudes means that the associated guilt is also being constantly relinquished. A consciousness that is not guilt-ridden tends no longer to attract disease. In the unconscious, guilt requires punishment and sickness, with its attendant pain and suffering, as the mind's most frequent means of self-retaliation. This self-retaliation may take the form of an accident, cold, attack of the flu, arthritis, or any of the multiple diseases that the mind has invented. These diseases take epidemic forms due to television and media publicity. When a prominent figure shares with the public some serious illness, there is a sudden jump in the incidence of that illness. The unconscious grabs hold of a disease and utilizes it to settle the score. With the constant surrender of inner guilt, there is less and less of a score to be settled. Therefore, a person who is free of negativity and guilt tends to be free of disease and suffering.

The healing can be dramatic. There was the case, for example, of a magazine publisher who was in a hopeless state of advanced multiple sclerosis. The medical profession had done what it could and had given her up as a terminal, hopeless case. At that point, she came upon a technique of relinquishing guilt by studying the "Workbook" of *A Course in Miracles*. In working with this home-study course, which consists of contemplating exactly one short lesson a day for 365 days, she began to undo all of her guilt and resentment through the mechanism of forgiveness. By constantly forgiving and undoing the negative feelings, and therefore undoing her inner guilt, the disease of multiple sclerosis reversed itself. As of this writing, she has been recovered for years and is in radiant glowing health, happy with her life.

Health and well-being, then, are generally the automatic consequence of the letting go of guilt and other negativities, as well as the letting go of our resistance to the positive states of health and well-being. Through the surrender mechanism, the whole gamut of illnesses can be resolved into wellness.

As was said earlier, there may be uncommon cases in which illness or infirmity continues unabated due to unknown factors, such as karmic proclivities. Continual surrender brings healing at the level of inner being so that, even while the body appears to suffer limitation and others may see it as "tragic," the person is at peace and radiates an inner well-being that uplifts others. Through surrender at great depth, such persons have let go of self-pity, guilt, and resistance to life circumstances. They have transcended the view that their illness is a barrier to personal happiness and see it as a vehicle of blessing to others. In recent years, public examples of this phenomenon have included the late Pope John Paul II, who approached his unremitting Parkinson's disease as a spiritual opportunity to become one with, and even to take on, the suffering of others.

Wealth

This is an important subject, not only because it has such a direct effect on our life, but also because it so quickly and easily makes obvious our feelings, thoughts, and attitudes about money. To the mind that holds limiting belief systems and negative thoughts and feelings, money is a "problem." It is a source of endless worry and anxiety, hopelessness and despair, or of vanity, pride, arrogance, intolerance of others, jealousy, and envy. At its worst the end result of all the negativity is a feeling of financial limitation, lack, and deprivation. In this area, the feeling "I can't" due to fear and limitation is often skirted by simply avoiding the whole issue of money and resigning oneself to a low social economic status as "inevitable."

The unconscious brings to us what it thinks we deserve. If our view of ourselves is small, limited, and miserly—due to accumulated guilt—then the unconscious will bring those economic conditions into our life. Our attitudes about money can be discovered when we look at the many things that it means. For example, we see the degree to which it stands for security, power, glamour, sexual attraction, successful competition, self-worth, and our value to others and the world.

It is very useful to sit down with pencil and paper and, under the heading "Money," begin to delineate what its real meanings are in all the various avenues of life. Then, write down the feelings that are associated with each area and begin to surrender on each negative feeling and attitude. As we do this, we have the surprising discovery that money in and of itself is not the most basic issue. More important than money itself are the emotional gratifications that we hope will be ours with the use of that money.

Let's say that, behind the desire for money, we discover that one of our goals is to be respected and valued. In that discovery, we have just found out that it isn't money itself that we are interested in; rather, it is our self-respect and a feeling of inner worth. We see that money was just a tool to achieve something else and that, as a matter of fact, it isn't money that we want at all but the self-respect and esteem we thought it would bring us. It will also dawn on us that the goals which we thought money would bring us *can be achieved directly.* The higher our inner self-esteem, the less we need the approval of others. As we uncover these awarenesses, money takes on a different meaning in each area of life. Money now becomes subservient to higher goals rather than an end unto itself.

Without being conscious of what money means to us emotionally, we are at the effect of it. We are being run by our unconscious beliefs about money and all of its associated programs. It is like the millionaire who keeps piling up more and more millions. There never seems to be enough. Why is that? It is because he has never stopped to look at what money really means to him. If we obsessively chase after money or other symbols of wealth, it is because our inner self-worth is so small that it takes a huge amount of money to compensate for it. The inner insecurity is so extensive that no amount of money can overcome it. It might be said that the smaller we feel inside, the greater amount of power, money, and glamour must be accumulated in order to try and compensate for the inner smallness.

When we are in a surrendered state, we are free

from that inner smallness, insecurity, and low self-esteem. Then, money becomes merely a tool to achieve our goals in the world. We have an inner security, knowing that there will always be sufficient abundance. We will always get what we need when we need it, because we have an inner feeling of completion, fulfillment, and satisfaction. Money, then, becomes a source of pleasure rather than a source of anxiety.

On a certain level, we may even appear to be indifferent to money. When we need it to complete a project, it just magically seems to appear from somewhere. We feel nonchalant about it because we are connected to the source of our own power. When we re-own the power that we have given to money and see that it is our own power, we are no longer concerned about money, nor do we need to accumulate a great deal of it. Once we have the formula for gold, we don't need to carry a bag of it on our shoulder with all of its attendant worries and anxieties.

The problem with excessive accumulation of money, of course, is the constant fear of losing it. It is tragi-comic to watch someone who is worth 50 million dollars practically have a nervous breakdown because, through a business oversight, he lost 10 million dollars. The man was actually in a panic. Emotionally, he was frightened that he would not be able to survive on the planet with only 40 million dollars. The person who suffers from inner poverty is relentlessly driven to accumulate on the material level. With this inner poverty, there is the whole attitude of selfishness or its correlates of vanity and false pride.

It is very common for people who use the letting go technique suddenly to come into abundance. Struggling actors now have starring roles in Hollywood. A playwright on the edge of poverty becomes the producer of a smash Broadway hit. Paradoxically, some people have grown so nonchalant about money that they have chosen to get rid of a lot of money and live a much simpler life. They are no longer interested in money; they have mastery over it. The inner satisfactions that they had sought by means of money are now satisfied directly, so that inner happiness is independent of outer wealth. In this state of inner freedom, one is independent of the outer world and no longer at the effect of it. This is because one transcends that which one has mastered.

Happiness

In the sections on Health and Wealth, we have already touched upon important areas relating to overall happiness. Now we will focus more on inner emotional life because that is where we all really live. The purpose of health and wealth is, after all, merely because we presume, and to some extent it is true, that they result in happiness. Happiness can be experienced directly, however, and on this level it is relatively independent of health or wealth.

Let's take an objective look at the average view of happiness. To begin with, the happiness is extremely vulnerable. A chance remark, a critical comment, a raised eyebrow, or a car cutting into line ahead of us are all sufficient to blow the average person's happiness in an instant. The threat of a job loss, a feeling of distrust in a relationship, a foreboding remark by a doctor, or an impertinent cab driver, are sufficient to ruin the day for many of us. Why is our happiness so fragile that commonplace occurrences can "ruin" the whole day?

In the section on the anatomy of emotions, we have already looked at the reasons for this. As a result of negative feelings, thoughts, and attitudes, together with the constant judgment and criticism of other people, we often feel separated from others. Because of this feeling of inner aloneness and separation, relationships take on the form of attachments, with all the fear, anger, and jealousy that accompany any threat to those attachments. The inner negativity results in such commonly held beliefs as, "You are born alone and you die alone." Nothing, in fact, is farther from the truth. As recent books on near-death experiences reveal, it is during life that one often feels alone and, at the moment of death, there is an absolute feeling of oneness and connectedness (Eadie, 1992; Neal, 2011).

Because of attachments, dependencies, and inner smallness, we may feel weak and limited. The guilty intolerance of our inner thoughts and feelings are projected onto the world, making the world look like a fearful place. Because these fears are held in mind, fearful events and experiences are literally brought into our life experience. Fear results in chronic anger and makes us prone to attack and to inner emotional chaos. Pain and suffering occur, with periodic despair and proneness to emotional upset. The ego-mind, which sees everyone as separate, is envious of anyone else who appears happier, more successful, or with a better relationship, a better body, or better connections. Soon, because of a lack of inner clarity about goals, there is confusion leading to self-pity, envy, and further resentment. Self-condemnation gets endlessly projected onto the world, taking the form of condemnation from others, which increases further the guilt and feeling of smallness.

For some of us, the only escape is through grandiosity, intolerance, bigotry, arrogance, and anger, which take the form of cruelty, over-bearingness, brutality, and insensitivity to the feelings of others. Often the insensitivity comes with self-excuses, such as: "I am an upfront person who speaks my mind," or "I am the frank type; you always know where you stand with me." These comments are a cover-up for insensitivity, which might be better described as gauche. The low self-esteem results in criticism of self and others, constant competition and comparison, analyzing, contempt, intellectualization, doubt, and fantasies of revenge. When all of those mechanisms fail, there is the recurrence of apathy and feelings of hopelessness and victimization. In such a state, we become progressively alienated because there is so much of ourselves that we must hide. Our behavior leads to isolation from others and an imbalance due to over-valuation of the areas of life that do seem to work.

Because of this inner chaos, the average person must of necessity stay unconscious at all times. It is interesting to watch the means that the mind has invented to accomplish this end. We watch as a person gets up in the morning and flips on the radio or the television to immediately get the mind off the self and its mental chatter. Despite the extra amusement, thoughts and feelings tend to arise until the mind becomes preoccupied with the projects of the day, work, and various schemes of accomplishment or pleasure. It starts the preoccupation with the body—all of the brushing, washing, perfuming, powdering, deodorizing and carefully selecting the clothes for the day. The choosing of clothes brings up all the schedules of the day, its busyness with activities that have all been crowded into the day: the endless appointments, phone calls, errands, social engagements, home responsibilities, and emails. On the way to work or the day's activities, there is the chatting with companions, listening to the car radio, making the cell phone calls, sending text-messages, and reading the morning newspaper on the subway. Once at the destination, there follows the preoccupation with the external events of the day: the business, the deals, the bargains, the arrangements, the worries, the manipulations, the endless search for power, the quest for "strokes," and the ever-present fear of survival. All of this is motivated by the desire to somehow derive meaning and security, and to increase our self-esteem and ensure our self-worth by whatever means.

The franticness of the struggle is not really realized until we are suddenly forced to discontinue it by some external event. Then, we are confronted with the internal emptiness. This calls for the incessant ingestion of novels, magazines, television, and websites. Or, the emptiness is avoided by the constant going to parties, escaping through drugs, numbing out with a few drinks, watching movies, and pursuing other amusements. We tend to do just about anything to avoid facing that feeling of inner emptiness.

There is nothing wrong with any of these activities, in and of themselves. What we want to examine is only the state of consciousness, the state of awareness, and the manner in which the activities are perceived, pursued, and experienced. In a state of inner freedom, these same events and experiences take on a totally different significance.

The identical activities can stem from an inner sense of happiness, self-worth, and completeness. The same goals can be fulfilled through the realization of our inner achievement rather than competition with others. Relationships become sharing and loving rather than jealous, competitive, and driven by the seeking of "strokes" and approval. When we are free of negative drives, we enjoy gratifying relationships because we love people, not because we are attached to them. We can allow the other person to be free, not subject to jealousy and threat. We are not the victims of manipulation by others because we have already found an inner fulfillment.

As negative thoughts, feelings, and attitudes are relinquished, we re-own the power that we had given over to the world. Much of the attraction of the world is due to the glamorization that we have projected onto it. Questions arise for self-reflection: "Is it really all that money that I want, or is it the glamour that I have attached to it? What is it that I want from that job title or from that designation of "Dr." and "Esq." and "Rev."? Is it the responsibility and activities that go along with it, or is it the glamour and esteem associated with it? Do I really love that person, or am I in love with the glamour I have projected onto him or her?"

The more we let go, the more we de-glamorize the world. The more it is de-glamorized, the less it runs us. We are not at the effect of glamour and can no longer be manipulated by it. We are no longer vulnerable to the professional programmers of the media and the political and social arenas. We are no longer at the effect of an inner need for approval from others.

We begin to love people for what they are, not for what they can do for us. We no longer need to exploit others or try to win them over. As our own level of guilt decreases, our self-esteem expands. Relationships are now based on integrity, and we are no longer subject to emotional blackmail. As a corollary, we stop trying to blackmail others with emotional pressure. Because relationships are based on honesty, and they exist and function on a higher plane, there is no longer a fear of alienation or feeling of aloneness. The surrendered person no longer needs others for personal fulfillment but is with them out of choice because of love and enjoyment. Compassion for others and for their humanness transforms life and all relationships.

The State of Inner Freedom

What does life become when one continuously surrenders? What is possible?

In the surrendered state, we are independent of the outer world as a source of satisfaction because the source of happiness has been found within us. Happiness is shared with others so that, in relationships, the surrendered person is supportive, sympathetic, encouraging, patient, and tolerant. There is an effortless appreciation of the worth and values of others and a consideration for their feelings. Power struggles, being "right," and proving our point have been relinquished. There is an automatic nonjudgmental attitude and the supporting of others to grow, learn, experience, and fulfill their own potentialities. There is an easy-going, nurturing acceptance of others. We feel relaxed, vibrant, and full of energy. Life events flow automatically and effortlessly. We no longer respond from a motive of sacrifice or "giving up" something for others; instead, we see ourselves as being of loving service to others and the world. Life events are seen as opportunities rather than challenges. The personality is gentle and open with a willingness to let go and surrender nonstop because of the unfolding and ongoing inner process of continuous revelation.

As the process unfolds, we feel an inner transformation. This leads to a consistent feeling of gratitude, pleasure, and certainty about our goals. There is a living in the present rather than a preoccupation with the past or the future. There is a trusting defenselessness because the power that was projected onto the world has been re-owned. There is an inner feeling of strength and invulnerability leading to an inner serenity.

At first, there is the identification, "I am the body." As the mechanism of surrender continues, it becomes quite obvious that, "I am the mind that experiences the body, not the body." As more feelings and belief systems are surrendered, there eventually comes the awareness, "I am not the mind either, but that which witnesses and experiences the mind, emotions, and body."

Through inner observation, there is the realization of something that remains constant and the same, no matter what goes on in the external world or with the body, emotions, or mind. With this awareness comes a state of total freedom. The inner Self has been discovered. The silent state of Awareness that underlies all movement, activity, sound, feeling, and thought is discovered to be a timeless dimension of peace. Once identified with this Awareness, we are no longer at the effect of the world, the body, or the mind, and with this Awareness come an inner calmness, stillness, and a profound sense of inner peace. We realize that this is what we were always seeking but didn't know it, because we had gotten lost in the maze. We had mistakenly equated ourselves with the outer phenomena of our hectic life—the body and its experiences, the obligations, the jobs, the titles, the activities, the problems, and the feelings. But now we realize that we are the timeless space in which the phenomena are happening. We are not the flickering images playing out their drama on the movie screen, but the screen itself—a nonjudgmental witness of the unfolding movie of life, with no beginning and no end, infinite in its potential. These progressive realizations of our true nature prepare the ground for the Ultimate Realization of the identity of Consciousness with Divinity Itself.

18

RELATIONSHIPS

Because they are so intimately connected with our basic desires for love and security, relationships quickly bring up our innermost feelings. For that reason, they are extremely valuable, no matter whether the relationship is classified as good or bad. In the process of emotional emancipation, everything is equally valuable. It is necessary to remind ourselves that feelings are programs; that is, they are learned responses that often have a purpose. That purpose is directly related to achieving an effect on the other person's feelings and, by doing so, to influence their feelings toward ourselves and to fulfill our own inner goals.

We will look at common emotional reactions and examine what their real purpose is. Emotional reactions have nothing to do with love, for love is a state of oneness with another. Love is not just an emotion that comes and goes. What often passes for love in common human understanding is primarily attachment, dependency, and possessiveness.

Negative Feelings

As we shall see, all emotions toward others involve the basic belief that we are incomplete within ourselves and, therefore, others are viewed and utilized as a means to an end. Although we may not be able to influence the other person in the way we would like, the utilization of the other person still occurs on the level of fantasy and expectation. We also discover that much of what we experience in a relationship is happening only in our imagination. Let's start first with the most negative emotions; we will discover what their underlying purpose is and the other person's likely response.

Anger

The first feelings we will start with are the most negative: feelings of hate, malice, anger, rage, revenge, and violence. It is obvious that the underlying fantasy here is to eliminate, banish, kill, destroy, injure, hurt, frighten, and intimidate. The other person's likely response is to avoid us, to hate us in return, and to bring about a counter-attack. Lesser forms of anger are criticism, criticalness, resentment, sulking, stewing, and negative judgments about others. The emotional purpose is to punish others, make them feel sorry, try to force them to change their feelings or behavior, make them suffer, get even with them, diminish and devalue them. This, of course, also results in the other person's response of counter-criticism, counter-resentment, and avoidance.

To handle this area, we have to realize that almost everyone has these fantasies. Playing ostrich with them, thinking that they are wicked or that we are guilty, will not resolve them. We have to come up to the level of courage and look at our worst feelings, admit that they are part of the condition of being human, and remember that we are only held account-able for what we do with them. It is obvious that these negative feelings take an enormous emotional toll on our own inner selves. That reason alone is sufficient to warrant looking at them and letting go of them.

Looking at the feelings on the level of interper-sonal relationships, we now discover another law of consciousness. *Our feelings and thoughts always have an effect on other persons and affect our relationships, whether these thoughts or feelings are verbalized, expressed, or not.* We will not, at this point, go into the discussion of the mechanics of exactly how this comes about, but it is currently an area of research of modern advanced quantum physics, especially that area con-cerned with high energy subatomic particles and their relationship to thoughts and thought forms.

We can likely intuit the truth of this law of con-sciousness from our own experience. We generally know, for example, when someone is angry toward us, even if they say nothing about it. Sensing their repressed angry feeling, we might ask, "Is something wrong?" Even when they reply, "Oh nothing," we are still aware of the energy of anger and upset.

It is somewhat dismaying to discover the truth of this interfacing at the energetic level, but anyone can discover it by inner investigation. The overall attitudes we hold about another person are influencing that other person's feelings and attitudes about us whether we express them or not. Women in our society are more intuitive than men; they are generally more con-sciously aware that their thoughts and feelings are known by others. True psychics, of course, are merely people who are experts at intuition.

When first discovering the truth of this, we might go through sort of a mild paranoia. Most everyone is brought up to believe that our thoughts and feelings are private affairs and nobody else's business, that all minds are separated, and that emotions happen only within the confines of the body. As we begin to investigate this area, we find that often the set of feelings we hold about another person is mirrored back to us by their attitude and that, when we change our inner attitude about them, their attitude changes abruptly. We are unconsciously influencing others all the time because of the feelings we hold about them. As we become more intuitive, we will laugh at our former naïveté. And, if we research further into the world of psychics and parapsychology, we will discover that thoughts and feelings can be read by expert psychics, even from the other side of the globe.

The only way to get over this initial paranoia is to clean up our own act. Finding out what needs to be cleaned up is simple and easy. Just look at what you would not want others to know about you and begin to surrender it!

With observation, it is quite clear that these intensely negative feelings reverberate and boomerang back to us, and profoundly affect our relationships. The other person merely mirrors back what we are projecting onto them. People who carry a lot of hatred find that they are living in a hateful world and that lots of people hate them. They see external situations and the world as hateful. What they fail to see is that this entire situation is self-created.

We have the secret hope that our angry feelings

towards others will punish and make them suffer. Actually, we are just providing them with justification to hate us back. We have to live with the fear of their retaliation and our own unconscious guilt, which often results in physical sickness. It will be discovered that all of our anger and resentment are due to our perception, that is, to the way in which we are viewing a given situation. When the inner feelings are relinquished, the way in which we see the situation changes, and we are often surprised by the abruptness with which feelings of forgiveness suddenly arise and the relationship becomes transformed, even though on the external level we did or said nothing to express this inner change.

This happens with great frequency when our intention is to overcome our resentments. *A Course in Miracles* is based on that precise process of changing our view of a situation by the willingness to see it differently and to be forgiving. This is what was meant by Jesus Christ when he spoke of the miraculous power of forgiveness.

Interestingly enough, there is a scientific basis for Jesus Christ's admonition to bless and love our enemies. On the level of energy, the lower feelings have a lower vibration frequency and lower power. When we are in lower energy state such as anger, hate, violence, guilt, jealousy or any other negative feelings, we are psychically vulnerable to the other person. In contrast, forgiveness, gratitude, and loving-kindness have a much higher energy vibration and much greater power. When we shift out of a lower to a higher energy pattern, we create a protective shield on the energetic level, as it were, and we can no longer be psychically vulnerable to that other person. When we are in a state of anger, for instance, we are vulnerable to the energy depletion brought about by the other person's counter-anger. Paradoxically, if we really want to affect other people, then we ought to really love them. Then, their anger at us will boomerang back upon them with no effect upon us! This was the wisdom of the Buddha's statement in the *Dhammapada*, "Hate is not conquered by hate. Hate is conquered by love. This is an eternal law."

Guilt

The next "heavy" area of negativity is guilt. Here the underlying purpose is to placate, to assuage, to escape punishment by self-punishment, and to elicit forgiveness. The most important of these is the wish to elicit punishment from another person, combined with self-punishment. This is not a conscious wish; nevertheless, it is the unconscious purpose of guilt. With a little investigation, this can easily be verified. The next time we are feeling guilty about something particular regarding another person, watch what happens in the next encounter. Almost inevitably, they will bring up the very thing we are holding in mind. For instance, if we are feeling guilty because of lateness to an appointment, that guilt will frequently elicit a critical response from the other person. By the holding of guilt, we bring on to ourselves all the criticalness of others and their belittlement of us; our low self-esteem is channeled back to us through others in the form of their invalidation of our life.

If we hold in mind that we are small and unworthy, we elicit those kinds of responses from others, whose remarks tend to indicate that we are small and unworthy. If we think we are only worth a crust of bread, then that is what we will get. This is what the scriptures mean by the statement, "The poor get poorer and the rich get richer." Poverty on any level, not just financial, comes from inner poverty, just as outer wealth comes from inner wealth. If we want others to stop being critical of us and attacking us, the answer is to begin letting go of guilt and all the feelings that have brought it about.

To help clarify the role of emotions in interpersonal relationships, a very quick way of learning is to presume that the other person is conscious and aware of our inner thoughts and feelings. By doing this, we will not be far from wrong, for they are indeed intuitively aware of our thoughts and feelings, even if they are not consciously aware at a given moment. They will respond to us as if they knew our inner feelings. *The overall relationship will behave as though the other person were aware of our inner feelings.* If we are still holding the fantasy that other people do not know our thoughts and feelings, just notice that dogs quickly do! Do we really think that the human psyche is inferior to that of a dog? If a dog can quickly read our total inner attitude, we can be sure that the intuition of people around us is picking up the same vibration.

Apathy and Grief

The feelings of apathy, grief, depression, sorrow, self-pity, the blues, hopelessness, and helplessness come from the inner program of "I can't." Their purpose is to elicit sympathy, to win back, to gain support, to make others sorry, and to summon help. What is the effect of these feelings on another person? Although there may be an initial attempt to help, eventually this is replaced by pity and finally avoidance. Why avoidance? The avoidance is because of the huge energy demand that we are making on the other person. It is an attempt to drain them by throwing ourselves on their doorstep. This results in the common saying, which sounds hard-hearted but is unfortunately so often true: "When you laugh, the world laughs with you; but when you cry, you cry alone."

Constant grief will drive others away. They begin to resent it unless they are in a very high place themselves and capable of effortless compassion. Chronic grief brings premature aging, a tiredness and weariness about the person, and it can only be overcome when we have the courage to allow it to come up under appropriate conditions and have the willingness to surrender to it and let it go.

Fear

The feelings of fear—whether tension and anxiety, shyness, self-consciousness, caution, holding back, or distrust—have the purpose of escape from the imagined threat, and to put psychological distance from the feared situation or person. Paradoxically, as we have pointed out before, because the fear is powerful, the very process of holding it in mind can make that which is feared come into our life. It is like a self-fulfilling prophecy. The energy of fear generates an inner focus on all the negative things that could happen, and that focus can coalesce the appearance of the very events that we fear the most.

Fear in relationships, therefore, is giving away our power to another person and enabling them to do the very thing that is feared. The way out is to look at the worst possible scenario and look at the feelings they arouse and begin to relinquish them. Like other emotions, fear can be unraveled to its component parts, and the parts are then easily relinquished. For instance, let's say that there is fear of critical attack. We ask ourselves, "What is the worst possible scenario?" With this question, we see that the basis of the fear is pride. When the pride is recognized and relinquished, the fear automatically dissolves. Again, in a relationship in which we are experiencing fear, if we unravel the fear, we may find that it is really a fear of discovery of our inner anger; the fear is that the other person will retaliate against the anger. Again, when we relinquish the anger, the fear will automatically disappear.

The insecure person is fearful and prone to jealousy, clinging, possessiveness, and attachment in relationships, an approach that always brings frustration. The purpose of these feelings is to bind and tightly possess the other, to achieve security by preventing loss and, at times, to punish the other for our own fear of loss. Again, these attitudes tend to bring into manifestation the very thing that we are holding in mind. The other person, now feeling pressured by our energy of dependency and possessiveness, has an inner impulse to run for freedom, to withdraw, to detach and do the very thing that we fear the most. These attitudes lead to constantly wanting to influence others. Because people intuitively pick up our wish to control them, their response is to resist. So the only way to bring about relinquishment of their resisting us is to let go of wanting to influence them in the first place. This means letting go of the inner fears as they come up.

Pride

Feelings of pride are often condoned in our society and take the form of perfectionism, neatness, punctuality, dependability, "good personhood," excessive cleanliness, workaholism, excessive ambition, success, moral superiority, and politeness. In its exacerbated forms, we see arrogance, boastfulness, vanity, smugness, and prejudice; on the spiritual level, there is the righteous killing of "nonbelievers." The underlying emotional purpose of these feelings toward others is to win their admiration, avoid criticism or rejection, gain acceptance, be important, and thereby overcome our own inner feelings of worthlessness. Unfortunately, the feelings that are aroused in the other person are often those of envy, competitiveness, or even hatred and easy exploitation. If we look at pride, we see that it's often a substitute for genuine self-esteem.

It is also of considerable interest to realize that the major relationship to which many people apply these phenomena is the relationship to God. There is the belief, often unconscious, that we can elicit a certain response from God: "God will feel sorry for me"; "God will retaliate against me"; "God will punish me"; "God will be pleased with me"; "God will favor me."

When we have adequate self-esteem, we are motivated by inner humility and gratitude and, therefore, we have no need for the constant eliciting of strokes and pats from others (or God). When we stop wanting to be liked, we find that we are. When we stop catering to others and trying to manipulate their approval, we find that they do respect us. Self-denigration in the forms of placating, flattering, deference, self-effacement, and passivity are all attempts to influence others

by catering to their ego, so as to get favorable treatment and get our own way. False humility merely says
to the other person, "I am a small person; please treat
me that way" and, of course, they promptly do.

As is quite apparent, all of the above emotions are
manipulative of the other person and destructive of
real relationship. They all diminish our self-esteem for
they are all positions of vulnerability. Thus, although
we may think that we feel well and secure at the level
of pride, that pride is always accompanied by defensiveness due to its basic vulnerability. We puff up with
pride whenever we feel insecure. The inflation of
pride is easily susceptible to the puncture of a passing
remark or raised eyebrow.

The Human Condition

All of the negative feelings are essentially forms of
fear: fear of loss of esteem by ourselves or others, or
fear of not surviving and a loss of security. Because
most of the negative feelings are accompanied by a
negative value judgment, they are suppressed,
repressed, or projected. Suppression, repression, and
projection are all destructive dynamics and result in a
progressive stress on and decline of our relationships.

We like to pretend that our innermost feelings are
unknown to others, but are they? We are all connected
to each other on the psychic, intuitive level; so, our
feelings are read and known by others. We may not be
consciously aware of it, but their behavior toward us
reveals that they know our inner attitude and feelings
toward them.

For example, let's say that our external behavior on
the job is exemplary. Why is it, we ask, that the other

person gets the promotion or the recognition, and we do not? The answer is to look at our hidden inner feelings about the boss and the job. Do we really think that he hasn't registered our inner envy, criticalness, and resentment? It is a safe bet to assume that others know our inner feelings and the thoughts that go with those feelings. The kind of thoughts we are having about them is very likely matched with similar thoughts they are having about us. If we realize this principle, a lot of things that happen in our life will start to make sense. We can ask ourselves, "How would I react if I were the other person and knew exactly what my personal inner feelings and thoughts really were?" The answer to that will usually make clear what the other person's behavior is all about. Perhaps we didn't get the promotion because, at the unspoken, energetic level, our boss knew that we were critical of him, resentful of our colleagues, and clamoring for approval and recognition.

Before searching ourselves for negative feelings, it is best to remember that these feelings are not our real inner Self. They are learned programs we have inherited from being humans. Nobody is exempt from them; everyone from the highest to the lowest has or has had an ego. Even the few who are enlightened had an ego at one time before it was finally transcended. This is the human condition. To be able to observe our feelings honestly requires a nonjudgmental attitude.

We first have to be aware of what is really going on inside of us before we can do anything about it. As we let go of a feeling, it is replaced by a higher one. The only purpose for recognizing and admitting a feeling is so that we can relinquish it. To be surrendered means that we are willing to relinquish a feeling by allowing ourselves just to experience it and not to change it. Resistance is what keeps it there in the first place.

We may think that some of the negative emotions are necessary to us; however, upon examination we will discover that this is an illusion. The higher emotions are far more powerful and effective in bringing about the fulfillment of our needs.

Let's ask ourselves, for example, what would we be willing to do for someone we really, truly love? We will instantly see that it is almost anything. There is almost no limit to which we will go for love. Now contrast this with what we are willing to do for someone who has intimidated us. We will see that we grudgingly give as little as possible. While the intimidators may seem to get away with something temporarily on the surface, they really have lost the whole thing, haven't they? Their victory is superficial, temporary, and not even real—a victory in appearance only. In the end, the world turns, and the intimidators sow their own destruction. What we win by the negative emotion is short-lived and inauthentic. It doesn't really satisfy. It's like a forced compliment. Real happiness results from a win-win situation. The price of a win-lose situation is hatred and low self-esteem. Underneath it all, we fool neither ourselves, nor others. Others always know when we are out to exploit them.

If we have difficulty in relinquishing a feeling, it helps merely to look at the intent of that feeling. What is the purpose of it? What is the supposed purposeful effect on the other person? What is their likely response? Do we really want that? If this were the last day of our life, would that really be what we wanted? Well, this *is* the last day of our life—our old life with all its conflicts, anxiety, and fear. That is the price we have paid for holding on to the old.

As we relinquish the negative suppressed feelings from all the programs we have internalized, they are automatically replaced by the higher ones. We become happier and lighter and so do the people around us. Let's review what these higher feelings are and what effect they have on the other person's feelings and behavior in response to us.

Positive Feelings

The higher feelings of courage, willingness, confidence, capability, "can do," zest, humor, competence, self-sufficiency, and creativity have an emotional purpose: effective actions, operation, and accomplishment. The reaction of other persons will reflect back to us cooperation, courage, respect, and a willingness to be with us. Additionally, because we increase their self-esteem, they seek our company. As we look at all of this, we see that there is a wonderful payoff in return for our willingness to let go of the negative feelings that stand in the way of these higher feelings, which effortlessly accomplish our real goals and purpose.

When we are operating on the level of acceptance, enjoyment, warmth, gentleness, softness, trustingness, inner truth, and faith, the emotional purposes to which the other person responds are those of love, enjoyment, pleasure, harmony, peacefulness, understanding, and sharing. Their reaction to us will be one of acceptance, satisfaction, feeling "in tune," feeling understood, and joy. They will automatically return our love. It is rather obvious that these reciprocal feelings bring about success in whatever the venture may be with the other person, whether it is vocational, social, personal, or a simple everyday business interaction.

Connectedness

When our inner feelings are of peacefulness, serenity, tranquility, stillness, openness, and simplicity, the effect on other persons is to increase their awareness along with our own, and to give them a greater sense of freedom, perfection, unity, and at-oneness with ourselves. In their relationship with us, they will feel joined; they will identify with us; they will understand at a deep level; and they will feel in communion with us. As a consequence, they will seek our presence, because in it they feel complete, recognized, and contented. They will experience an increased awareness of their own real Self. They will feel higher in our presence or when they think of us. Their response back to us will be that of love and gratitude for the blessing of our presence. In such a relationship, goals are automatically and effortlessly accomplished. Because we are not holding negativity, there is nothing we wish to hide from the other person, and this openness allows the other person to drop all defenses. Nothing is hidden out of guilt or fear, and there is a very conscious psychic connectedness.

It is on this level that so-called telepathic phenomena occur with regularity. When we are in total harmony with another person, there is no desire on our part to withhold or guard any thoughts or feelings. Because the other person responds similarly, there is an effortless knowing of what is crossing the other person's mind and what their passing feeling states may be. There is a total acceptance of our own humanness and that of the other. If we are really in tune with others, we forgive them when we see a passing jealousy or reactivity. We realize it is only natural. And we know that they, in return, are aware of our passing resentment. Yet, they are overlooking it; they accept our humanness, and they understand the situation. They know us so well that they recognize the likelihood of a passing resentment in certain situations, but they know, also, that we are going to let it go. The people with whom we share a relationship of loving acceptance are okay with our humanness and their own. No matter the surface emotions, we remain aware of the shared alignment to love, acceptance, and harmony with each other and the world.

This level of communication actually can be reached with anyone. It does not have to be someone with whom we are intimately associated. Very often we experience it first with our friends with whom there is less at stake than intimate family members. Another situation where it often occurs in the course of an average life is with an ex-lover. With this person to whom we have revealed so much—now that there is no longer anything romantic at stake—a friendship might develop in which it is no longer necessary to hide anything. There can be truly open communication, honesty, and integrity. We see this not infrequently in couples that have separated or divorced. Once the turmoil has settled down, they get along easily and may even remain the best of friends for many years.

Effect of Positive Feelings

It is obvious that higher states of consciousness have a profound effect on our relationships, because one of the laws of consciousness is *like goes to like*. Our inner states are actually radiated to others. We can positively affect others even when we are not physically with them. Feelings are energy and all energy gives off a vibration. We are like sending and receiving stations. The less negativity we are holding, the more aware we can be of what others are really holding about us. The more we love, the more we find ourselves surrounded by love. The replacement of a negative feeling by a higher one accounts for the many miracles one can experience in the course of life. These become more frequent as one continues to surrender.

As we surrender, life becomes more and more effortless. There is a constant increase in happiness and pleasure, which requires less and less from the outer world to be experienced. There is a diminution of needs and expectations of others. We stop looking "out there" for what we now experience as coming from within ourselves. We let go of the illusion that others are the source of our happiness. Instead of looking to get from others, we now look to give. Others now seek to be with us, instead of avoiding us. In Charles Dickens' *A Christmas Carol*, Scrooge experienced the pleasure of giving instead of looking to get from others. The joy of that transformation is available to us all.

Carl Jung wrote of the phenomenon called "synchronicity," which might also have been called "simultaneity," to explain the occurrence of events that, to the intellect, appear unrelated. As we surrender more and more, this type of experience becomes commonplace. An illustration of this phenomenon is the following experience related by a business executive who had been practicing the letting go technique for about a year.

I was President of a small corporation with about fifty employees. We had built up a promising young man to head one of the divisions of the company. It turned out, however, that this man was very immature. Instead of responding with gratitude and cooperation for all that was done for him, he reacted by becoming grandiose, demanding, and somewhat paranoid. He declared that he was going to barge into the next Board of Directors meeting and cause a big upset with his wild accusations and demands. Although all of his accusations could have been easily refuted, the whole affair sounded like a dreadful experience to live through. For days, he appeared just plain hateful with his threats. The day of the Board meeting, which was to be at 1 P.M., I was driving along the parkway thinking angry thoughts about him. Suddenly I let it all go; I surrendered on him totally. I started to see the frightened child in him, and I started to send him love. All of my anxiety disappeared, and I felt a sympathetic love for him. I looked at my watch and it was 12:30 P.M. When I got to the office, my secretary said that this man had walked into the office and stated that he was calling off the whole thing; he had changed his mind at the last minute. I asked her what time he had walked into the office. She said she had made particular note of the time, as the Board meeting was soon to take place. She looked at her watch when he had made his announcement about his change of heart. The time was exactly 12:32 P.M.

Letting Go of Expectations

When we put pressure on other people in order to get what we want, they automatically resist, because we are trying to pressure them. The harder we push, the harder they resist. Even though, out of fear, they may actually concede to our demands, there is not an inner acceptance and, later on, we will lose what we have gained. This resistance is in all of us. We can be aware of it as it operates unconsciously, and we evade that awareness by making excuses and plausible explanations.

As mentioned in an earlier chapter, in his book, *Winning Through Intimidation,* Robert Ringer called it the "boy/girl theory." (Boy meets girl. As soon as she realizes he wants her, she becomes hard to get. So then if boy decides to withdraw, she now wants him, and he in return acts aloof.) When we refer to this phenomenon to explain sales resistance, one way around it is to take the view that our responsibility is to make an effort, but not try to determine the result. Another way is to surrender the feelings we have about what we want from the other person, and let go of the pressures we are putting on them in the form of expectation and desire. They, then, have the psychic space to become agreeable or even to initiate the desired result on their own, the result we had wished for in the first place.

An example of this dynamic is a man who was working with the letting go technique in the midst of a divorce. He and his wife got into a heated argument over something he wanted. She just kept saying "No" to his request. So in the middle of it, he surrendered on the object that he wanted. It was now okay with him if she didn't give it to him, and it was okay if she did. The instant he let go of it in his mind, she suddenly turned to him and offered, not only to give it to him, but to have it packed and shipped as well.

This illustrates a very simple but decidedly elegant and active way of clarifying relationships. First, look at how you are secretly feeling about a person in a given situation. Presume that the other person is aware of those thoughts and feelings. Then, put yourself in their place and see how you would react. You will see that their behavior is probably just what you would have done in their place. The goal is to let go of all those feelings until you can go up to a positive thinking-feeling space about the matter. Once in a positive space, now see how you would react as the other person who was aware of these new feelings. The likelihood is that their behavior will change just as you would expect. There may be a time delay; but, if you keep watching, the change will likely take place. Even if it doesn't, you will no longer be upset about the situation. Sometimes the "payoff" refuses to show up, but we can say, "This is one that the universe owed me in due time." In fact, it is a part of greatness to know that sometimes a good deed is not returned.

The influence that our thoughts and feelings have is, in the world's literature, called "the law of karma," or "You get what you give," or "You reap what you sow." Often we don't see this law in operation because of the time delay. For instance, an acquaintance borrowed $200 and then failed to pay it back as promised. For over a year, there was a resentment and consequent avoidance of the person because of the emotional discomfort, which was compounded by the guilt at holding the resentment in the first place. Finally, when it became apparent that the only person suffering from the resentment was the person holding it, and that it was costing peace of mind, the willingness to let it go emerged. At that point, the resentment was fairly easy to let go and the borrower was forgiven. The $200 was re-contextualized as a loan to someone who had been in need. Within a few months, there was an unexpected encounter with the person, who said out of the blue, "I have been concerned about the money I owe you. Here's the whole $200." The loan was repaid without even asking for it.

We block receiving what we want from others by our expectations or resentments of them. It is very effective to surrender our expectations of others before we enter into a particular situation with them. Emotions are really subtle attempts to force others and impose our will on them, which they unconsciously resist.

The way to facilitate satisfaction in relationships is lovingly to picture the best possible outcome. Make sure it is mutually beneficial: a win-win situation. Let go of all the negative feelings and merely hold the picture in mind. We can tell if we are really surrendered when we feel okay either way; it's okay with us if it happens, and it's okay with us if it doesn't. Therefore, to be surrendered does not mean to be passive. It is being active in a positive way.

When we are surrendered, there is no longer the pressure of time. Frustration comes from wanting a thing now instead of letting it happen naturally in its own time. Patience is an automatic side effect of letting go, and we know how easy it is to get along with patient people. Notice that patient people usually get what they want in the end.

One resistance to letting go is the illusion that, if

we let go of our wantingness and our expectations, we won't get what we want. We fear that we will lose it if we don't keep pressuring for it. The mind has the idea that the way to get a thing is to want it. Actually, if we examine the issue, we will see that events are due to decisions, and choices are based on our intentions. What we get is the result of these choices, even though they are unconscious, rather than what we think we want. When we surrender the pressure of wantingness, we are clear to make wiser choices and decisions.

We think that our happiness depends on controlling events, and that facts are what upset us. Actually, it is our feelings and thoughts about these facts that are the real cause of our upset. Facts in and of themselves are neutral things. The power we give them is due to our attitude of acceptance or non-acceptance and our overall feeling state. If we get stuck in a feeling, it is because we still secretly believe that it will accomplish something for us.

Sexual Relations

Because of the wide availability of sexual material and opportunities for varied sexual experiences, most people nowadays consider themselves rather sexually liberated. This liberation is primarily intellectual and behavioral; there still exists a great deal of emotional and experiential limitation, as well as sensory restriction. All experience takes place within consciousness itself; therefore, sexual experience, like any other, is determined by our overall level of awareness and inner freedom.

The degree to which our sexual experience has

been restricted becomes apparent the more we relinquish our feelings about it. When we are totally surrendered on sexuality, it is like adding a third dimension to what was before a two-dimensional experience. As one woman put it, "It's like I used to hear only violins, then a cello was added, and then a flute, and so on, so that now the experience is totally full and comprehensive."

Besides the increased emotional pleasure of freedom of expression, letting go brings a change in the sensory experience itself. To most people, men especially, sexual excitation and orgasmic pleasure are primarily a genital sensation. As one gets freer, the locale of the orgasm begins to expand and spread to the whole pelvis and abdomen, the legs and arms, and eventually the whole body. Often, after this accomplishment, there is a plateau that follows, and then suddenly and unexpectedly the orgasmic location expands beyond the body, as though the space around the body was having the orgasm instead of the person. Ultimately, there is no limitation of the orgasm. It seems to expand into infinity and be experienced from no particular center or locale. It is as if there is no individual person present. The orgasm is experiencing itself.

This expansion is facilitated by becoming aware that the facial grimacing and breath-holding are restrictions due to fear of loss of control and attempts to limit the experience. If one breathes slowly and deeply, smiling instead of grimacing, the fear will become conscious and can be surrendered.

Sexuality loses its compulsiveness. Freedom means not just freedom to indulge but freedom not to have sex or orgasm. When we are surrendered, we are not run by the desire for the orgasm. This unleashes creative experiencing and awareness because the mind is not focused on the orgasm itself. To be free from the domination of the desire for orgasm allows sexual experiences that have been described in spiritual literature as "Tantric Sex." Most Westerners read a little about it and perhaps give it a try, but then they give up because they approach it in a way that leads to suppression rather than to greater freedom.

The more truly liberated we become, the more we are motivated by lovingness rather than by desire for gratification. This change of motivation from wanting and hunger to the mutual sharing of pleasure and happiness brings about major changes in the nature of sexual relationships. The intimacy with another person becomes more encompassing and pleasurable. There is greater attunement to the other person's sexuality and intuitive fulfillment of each other's styles of satisfaction. One couple expressed it as follows:

> It is as though we just witness what our bodies are doing. It is as though we are the space in which it is all happening. As soon as one person has a desire or fantasy, the other automatically and without even thinking, moves into the acting out of fulfilling it. It is as though there is a psychic connection. There is an acknowledgement of the inner feelings about the fantasies and a letting go of how the other person might react. There is greater variation and frequency with sexuality, also. It used to be mainly Friday and Saturday nights. Now making love may happen for days at a time, or sometimes weeks go by without it. It is always new. It is never the same. Amazingly, it just keeps

getting better and better. Each orgasm seems better than the last, yet often the lovemaking is so enjoyable that there is no bother to have an orgasm. If it happens it's okay, and it's okay if it doesn't. The intimate time spent together is satisfying and freeing, regardless of any end result.

Another man said:

I never really realized before how much sex ran my relationships. It was really compulsive. I was always afraid I would miss out on a sexual opportunity. I didn't want to miss out on the opportunity for pleasure. Now my pattern is more variable; in fact, now I have no pattern. When it happens, it happens and it's great when it does. When it doesn't, I don't even think about it. I used to have sex on my mind all the time. Women would usually say 'No.' But now that I really don't care that much about it, they usually either suggest it or say 'Yes' if I ask. Now, I find that I am more concerned about them instead of myself. Before, I was really just using them for my own selfish ends and, intuitively, the women knew it. Now I feel a lot of love for them. I really care about their welfare and happiness, even if it's only a single encounter. What a relief not to have to lie anymore.

From the above examples, it is clear that there is a change in consciousness from lack to abundance. When we are self-centered and focused on getting emotional or physical pleasure from sex with another person, then we feel angry, frustrated, and deprived. The more loving we become, the more we receive what others are giving us, and we discover that we are all surrounded by love and opportunities for loving involvements, all of the time. This was the case for one woman, who shared the following experience:

> I was always overweight and not very good-looking. All through my life, I rejected myself. I envied and hated sexually attractive women. I got to hate men, too, because they avoided me. I was full of self-pity. I even tried psychotherapy, but I quit when it became apparent that the psychotherapist seemed more interested in his attractive young women patients than he was in me. I tried various self-help methods and at least got over my self-pity and depression; I was able to get a better job. But, men still weren't interested in me, and I was unsuccessful in the sexual and relational arenas.

Using the mechanism of letting go, she went into all the negative emotions that she had about herself and intimacy; she allowed the feelings to come up one by one, and she let them go. She let go of feelings like wanting attention and acceptance from others, fear of expressing herself, fear of being rejected, and even the fear of being deeply loved. There was the underlying feeling, "I don't deserve love; who could possibly love me?" Within a week of surrendering these feelings, she had a date. She explained:

> I was so excited that I even lost my appetite. We had a great time and then all of a sudden I saw the secret. I was giving love instead of looking for it. My whole life has changed now. Instead of feeling desperate to get attention and love, I

know I have the power to give it. When I enter a room, I see all the lonely, love-starved men. They look just the way I used to, so I know what it is they are feeling and what to say to them and how to express myself. I put myself in their place and watch their hearts melt. I used to scare them away because I was so hungry. Get that? Hungry! That was my problem. Now I feel full, and I share that fullness and what I have learned. My social life has become so enjoyable that I don't have time to eat anymore. I have lost 35 pounds in a year. I never even dieted. I just lost interest. I guess it is because I am getting gratified in a way now that really means some-thing to me. Maybe I am a little wild with the newness of it, but I'll settle down before long. There is one man I'm really interested in now.

Sexuality, then, reflects our overall state of con-sciousness. As we let go of fear and limitations, that area of our life expands and becomes ever more grati-fying, and yet not necessary for happiness. Freedom and creativity replace compulsiveness and limitation. Sex becomes another avenue for greater expression and increasing awareness. The pleasure of communion and nonverbal understanding replaces the former self-centered drivenness for relief from tension and the limited goal of sexual pleasure and ego inflation. The secret, as the woman above stated, is in the awareness that when we seek to give instead of to get, all of our own needs are automatically fulfilled. As one person remarked, "I have heard about many personal prob-lems from my friends who practice this technique, but lack of lovers isn't one of them!"

19

ACHIEVEMENT OF VOCATIONAL GOALS

Feelings and Abilities

Our thoughts determine the extent to which we manifest our talents and abilities, and they set the quality and quantity of our successes and failures. But what is it that determines and influences the direction of our thoughts? As we have seen, it is our feelings that determine and produce the kind of thinking that will lead us to success or failure in any endeavor. Feelings are the key to the expansion or constriction of our talents, abilities, and actions.

Generally, we are knowledgeable and well trained in matters pertaining to the outer world. Yet we are sometimes unknowledgeable and untrained in the inner world, the world of feelings. Because feelings determine thoughts and the thoughts we hold in mind determine outcomes, it is important to clarify the relationship between our feelings and the freeing of our abilities so that they result in successful action.

To summarize what we have said about the scale of consciousness, and to make it simple, we can briefly categorize all feelings as either negative or positive and, of course, the thoughts that will result from them will be either negative or positive.

Negative Feelings Related to Work

These feelings are always unpleasant and range from mildly uncomfortable to painful. They instigate the process of thinking and ideation that leads to "I can't" and "We can't," regardless of the event, situation, or problem in which the person is involved. Negative feelings arise when we dislike what we see, hear, think, or remember. Our reaction to disliking comes in the form of such feelings as anger, grief, and anxiety. Our usual way of dealing with unpleasant feelings is to suppress them, and because of this, we assume that these feelings are part and parcel of our thinking process. This error results because the feelings of dislike are being processed through our thoughts. Suppressing these feelings does not make them disappear. On the contrary, they will re-emerge as negative thoughts. Negativity does not exist within a situation or event; rather, it resides in our reaction to the situation as we see it. When negative feelings are acknowledged and relinquished, the situation can rapidly change in appearance from impossible to easily manageable, workable, and even quite useful.

One of the most prominent negative feelings that blocks success in professional life is that of envy. The underlying dynamic of envy is that when we see someone else getting ahead, this triggers our own sense of insecurity. It's not simply that we see the other person's achievement and feel envy. Rather, the other person's achievement triggers in us a feeling of lack or inadequacy about ourselves. It triggers the feeling, "Maybe I'm not accomplishing what I should be accomplishing," or "Maybe I won't be able to accomplish what I want to accomplish," or "Maybe my accomplishments aren't appreciated by others and go unnoticed."

Envy is painful because it arouses our own sense of inadequacy. And then we often resent the person whose successes have inadvertently provoked this feeling. Unconsciously, this resentment fuels our endless desire for strokes, which, of course, do not come our way because our wantingness repels the very thing we want.

As the cycle progresses, we feel increasingly dissatisfied and unhappy in our job and alienated from our colleagues. There may be the belief, "Everyone is against me." Our family members may grow weary of our constant complaints about the situation at work. We may seek escape at the end of the day through endless television or over-indulgence in food, sleep, drugs, and alcohol.

What's the way out of this cycle of envy and dissatisfaction? As we've said before, the answer is to go *within*. With envy, we are constantly looking at others, evaluating their accomplishments, and comparing ourselves to them. We see the cost of this looking outward in the film, *Chariots of Fire*, when one of the runners turned to see where his opponent was in the race. The moment he took his eye off the finish line to compare himself with another runner, he lost that split second which cost him the whole race. The man who won the race was motivated by the sheer love of running and to do his best. He didn't run to "beat" another. He didn't compare himself to other runners. He ran his best because he loved to run.

When we look within ourselves, we see what the underlying feelings are that prevent our success: competitiveness, self-doubt, insecurity, inadequacy, and desire for approval. Are we willing to look at these feelings? Once our feelings are recognized, it becomes obvious to us that they work against us. They drain our efforts and impede our success in the world. Our self-doubts block the very recognition we seek.

Once we see the cost of negative feelings to our happiness and success, we will become willing to let go of them and the payoffs we get from them. For example, we become willing to let go of the cheap little satisfaction we get from blaming others for our lack of success. We become willing to let go of the sympathy we garner from those who listen to our complaints. When we let go of our feelings of inadequacy, we will find that envy of others disappears. We become like the winning runner in *Chariots of Fire* who loves what he does, delights in his success and that of others, and has boundless energy to excel in the world.

Positive Feelings Related to Work

These are always felt as pleasant and include such feelings as joy, happiness, and security. They instigate a process of thinking and ideation that is exemplified by the thoughts "I can" and "We can," regardless of the event, situation, or problem in which the person is involved.

Positive feelings flow naturally when negative feelings are not in action. Nothing needs to be done to acquire positive feelings, as they are part and parcel of our natural state. This positive inner state is always there, and it is merely covered over by suppressed negative feelings.

When the clouds are removed, the sun shines forth. The freeing up of abilities, creative ideas, talents, and resourcefulness occurs automatically as a result of the positive state of mind that ensues when the negative aspects have been surrendered. Letting go of negativity frees up inspiration to create an endless flow of creative ideas. For example, there was the case of a producer of an award-winning Broadway musical who attributed the success of the hit show to the letting go of negative feelings through the mechanism of surrender. There have been writers, artists, and musicians who came into a sudden breakthrough of inspiration as soon as a negative belief or self-limitation was recognized and surrendered. The same experience has been recounted by scientists who suddenly just "knew" the formula that would cure a disease. It is as if the energy field of creative genius is available and waiting for us as soon as we surrender the clouds of negativity that prevent its revelation to us.

Feelings and the Decision-Making Process

We can simplify the levels of consciousness into three major states: inert, energetic, and peaceful. These three states are related to the decision-making process. The first state—inertia—is reflective of the emotional levels of apathy, grief, and fear. The nature of these feelings is to interfere with our concentration on the situation at hand and engage us instead in concentration on our own thoughts, most of which are in the realm of "I don't know," "I'm not sure," and "I don't think I can." This successive concentration of our own uselessly

cycling thoughts renders us temporarily unable to perceive the full dimension and possibilities of the overall
situation at hand.

While these negative thoughts and feelings are
flowing, it is difficult for us to arrive at any decision.
Sometimes we opt to stall the decision until we feel
better. At other times, we proceed to arrive at a decision that we think will answer our questions or take
care of a situation. Unfortunately, the decision that
results is not sustainable in the long run because it is
based on the feeling state, and when the feeling state
changes, the decision has to be changed with it. This
leads to inner insecurity, ambivalence, confusion, and
a loss of confidence in us by those around us. In the
computer language of "garbage in and garbage out,"
the negative feeling state is the "garbage in," and the
decisions that come out of it must be on the same
level.

The second state, which is higher than inertia, is
that of being "energetic." The emotions underlying this
state are those of desire, anger, and pride. The nature
of these feelings is to interfere less with concentration
than the previous lower state because some positive
thoughts are allowed to flow through and mix with the
negative feelings. This is the state of the "go-getter."
Although things are accomplished, there is unevenness
of performance because of the mixture of positive and
negative thoughts and ideas. Negative feelings such as
ambition, desire, or "proving onself" tend to drive the
"go-getter," and at times the decision-making is compulsive or impulsive.

Characteristic of this level of consciousness is personal self-gain as the primary motivating factor. Therefore, many of the decisions are unsustainable because

they are based on a win-lose situation rather than on a win-win situation. A win-win decision would have occurred had the feelings and welfare of the other persons involved in the situation been taken into account.

Using language relating to the body's energy centers, we say that people on this level are motivated by their "solar plexus" (third chakra). This means that they seek to attain success and to master the world. But they are self-centered and driven by personal motives, with little concern for the welfare of others or of the world in general. Because their decisions benefit primarily themselves, their success is limited to personal gain. Any benefit to the world is purely secondary and the results, therefore, fall far short of greatness.

The third and highest level is the peaceful state, based upon the feelings of courage, acceptance, and love. Because these feelings are purely positive and non-disturbing by their very nature, they allow us to concentrate completely on the situation and observe all of the relevant details. Because of an inner state of peace, inspiration brings forth ideas that solve the problem. In this state, the mind is free of worry, and its ability to communicate and concentrate is unimpeded. From this state come solutions to problems that are placed in a win-win context; because everyone benefits, everyone lends their energy to the project and success is shared by all. This approach not infrequently leads to greatness. It characterizes the noble projects that bring about far-reaching improvements in our society. On this level we discover that when everyone's needs in a situation are met, our own needs are fulfilled automatically. The unimpeded creative mind will work out a solution where everyone gains and no one loses.

If we look at a situation and claim that a win-win solution is not possible, that should warn us that we have some un-surrendered inner feelings blocking a possibly perfect solution. We need to remember the dictum that the impossible becomes possible as soon as we are totally surrendered to the situation.

Feelings and Sales Ability

Inasmuch as selling is a part of many vocations, involving either a product or ideas or our personal services, it is rewarding to look at the relationship between these three basic levels of consciousness and sales ability itself.

The lowest or inertia state is governed by feelings of apathy, grief and fear; it is obvious that sales ability is at its lowest. Sales persons in this state are often told by prospects that they are not interested in the product right now. This leads immediately to negative thinking and self-criticism with thoughts such as, "They don't want my product." The very nature of sales activity exposes sales persons to rejection and disappointment. They may temporarily escape these feelings, by taking coffee breaks or indulging in personal conversation with other employees; however, their feelings have impaired their concentration and diminished their ability to produce resourceful ideas. The low self-esteem creates vulnerability to discouragement, which, in turn, creates expectations of failure. When thoughts of failure are held in mind, failure is precipitated in the sales situation. At this point, by acknowledging the negative feelings and letting go of the payoff from each of them, a person can evolve to the next level.

The next level, the energetic state, is based on feelings of desire, anger, and pride. It includes a greater degree of vigor and drive. This facilitates better concentration on the work goal; however, because the feelings are somewhat driven, there may be excessive verbalization, with more time spent talking to sales prospects than listening to them. This may typically lead to premature closings, pushing too hard, and creating marketing problems. Nonetheless, achievement of sales goals is possible on this level because of the higher energies invoked. One block to success on this level is the focus on self-gain and the underlying viewpoint, "I win; they lose." This self-seeking motive is intuitively picked up by sales prospects and may lead to resistance. The thoughts characteristic of this level are along the lines of: "I want to get them to buy it, so I'll get a good commission."

On the highest or peaceful level, based upon the feelings of courage, acceptance, and love, our ability to concentrate is at its highest. Sales people on this level are able to listen carefully to the other person, and place the sale in a context of what is beneficial to the buyer rather than to the seller. Because the mind is peaceful and creative, they are never at a loss for creative ideas as to what will produce sales or what will turn problems into solutions. The person on this level often converts customers to friends, and the customers tend to become loyal. Achievement of sales goals on this level is assured because what is being held in mind is the positive situation of win-win and the inner certainty that a win-win solution can be created in the situation.

Often, surrendering to what appears to be an impossible situation quickly turns into a positive experience. This is exemplified by the case of someone who had been working in an art gallery. Sales were slow; she hadn't made a sale in weeks. She tried a number of consciousness techniques with herself and worked very hard at it. She utilized visualization, positive thinking, advance sales techniques, and written affirmations; however, nothing came of it. Her frustration mounted progressively, with the accompanying feeling, "I can't." Finally, in desperation, she just let go completely and surrendered all of her pent-up feelings. Inside of herself, she suddenly felt free of all the efforting, trying, and striving. The inner tension disappeared and, instead, she felt at peace as she went to work that morning at the gallery. Within the first hour at work, she sold two copies of a sculpture, which interestingly enough, was titled "Letting Go."

Executives of a number of companies have documented similar breakthroughs. For instance, a partner in one of the country's most prestigious accounting firms, after experiencing success with inner surrender, eventually left the firm in order to share with others what he considered to be the most beneficial thing he had encountered in his life. He wanted to introduce the approach to a number of large corporations. He studied the outcome at one of the largest insurance companies in America. His study found that, within six months of learning the technique, the insurance agents' sales increased by 33% over a control group. He concluded that success in the world is related to our ability to concentrate, which means the ability to keep our attention on one thing at a time without interference of other thoughts or feelings.

A mind that is concentrated on a positive thought has the power to increase the likelihood that the positive thought will materialize in the world of events. The most successful people in the world are those who hold in mind the highest good of all concerned, including themselves. They know that there is a win-win solution to every problem. They are at peace with themselves, which allows them to be supportive of the potential and success of others. They do work which they love, and so they feel continually inspired and creative. They do not seek happiness; they have discovered that happiness is a by-product of doing what they love. A feeling of personal fulfillment comes naturally from their positive contribution to the lives of others, including family, friends, groups, and the world at large.

20

PHYSICIAN, HEAL THYSELF

By popular request, the personal experience of self-healing has been shared many times at lectures, talks, and workshops. Everyone seems to want to hear the story over and over again of how a physician was healed of many diseases. Therefore, this chapter will relate the highlights of recovery and healing, because they illustrate in detail just how the principles and techniques we have been talking about actually work at the pragmatic level.

Lived experience and clinical observation confirm that the majority of human disorders are susceptible to being cured by following certain principles. Many diseases can be reversed unless there is a strong karmic dominance to the contrary.

Paradoxically, those serious cases, where all hope has been given up, often respond promptly and give the best results. This is perhaps because the person has finally let go and is now "sweetly reasonable." They are ready for what Thomas Kuhn calls "a paradigm shift," that is, a willingness to see things differently from an expanded perspective and to be open-minded. Sometimes it takes chronic sickness, suffering, pain, and a confrontation with the fear of death before a person is willing to let go of cherished beliefs and open up to the truth of clinical reality.

Basic Principles

This chapter details the healing and recovery from a multitude of physical illnesses in the life of a physician. We will delineate the basic principles that facilitated the process of self-healing. In doing this, there will be a review of some of the material we have already covered, so as to bring it together into an integrated overall experience. We will start with the basic working concepts:

- A thought is a "thing." It has energy and form.

- The mind with its thoughts and feelings controls the body; therefore, to heal the body, thoughts and feelings need to be changed.

- What is held in mind tends to express itself through the body.

- The body is not the real self; it is like a puppet controlled by the mind.

- Beliefs that are unconscious can manifest as illness, even though there is no memory of the underlying beliefs.

- An illness tends to result from suppressed and repressed negative emotions, plus a thought that gives it a specific form (i.e., consciously or unconsciously, one particular illness is chosen rather than another).

- Thoughts are caused by suppressed and repressed feelings. When a feeling is let go, thousands or even millions of thoughts that were activated by that feeling disappear.

- Although a specific belief can be cancelled and energy to it can be refused, it is generally a waste of time to try to change thinking itself.

- We surrender a feeling by allowing it be there without condemning, judging, or resisting it. We simply look at it, observe it, and allow it to be felt without trying to modify it. With the willingness to relinquish a feeling, it will run out in due time.

- A strong feeling may recur, which means there is more of it to be recognized and surrendered.

- In order to surrender a feeling, sometimes it is necessary to start by relinquishing the feeling that is there about the particular emotion (e.g., guilt that "I shouldn't have this feeling").

- In order to relinquish a feeling, sometimes it is necessary to acknowledge and let go of the underlying payoff of it (e.g., the "thrill" of anger and the "juice" of sympathy from being a helpless victim).

- Feelings are not the real self. Whereas feelings are programs that come and go, the real inner Self always stays the same; therefore, it is necessary to stop identifying transient feelings as yourself.

- Ignore thoughts. They are merely endless rationalizations of inner feelings.

- No matter what is going on in life, keep the

steadfast intention to surrender negative feelings as they arise.

- Make a decision that freedom is more desirable than having a negative feeling.

- Choose to surrender negative feelings rather than express them.

- Surrender resistance to and skepticism about positive feelings.

- Relinquish negative feelings but share positive ones.

- Notice that letting go is accompanied by a subtle, overall lighter feeling within yourself.

- Relinquishing a desire does not mean that you won't get what you want. It merely clears the way for it to happen.

- Get it by "osmosis." Put yourself in the aura of those who have what you want.

- "Like goes to like." Associate with people who are using the same or similar motivation and who have the intention to expand their consciousness and to heal.

- Be aware that your inner state is known and transmitted. The people around you will intuit what you are feeling and thinking, even if you don't verbalize it.

- Persistence pays off. Some symptoms or illnesses may disappear promptly; others may take months or years if the condition is very chronic.

- Let go of resisting the technique. Start the day with it. At the end of the day, take time out to relinquish any negative feelings left over from the day's activities.

- You are only subject to what you hold in mind. You are only subject to a negative thought or belief if you consciously or unconsciously say that it applies to you.

- Stop giving the physical disorder a name; do not label it. A label is a whole program. Surrender what is actually felt, which are the sensations themselves. *We cannot feel a disease.* A disease is an abstract concept held in the mind. We cannot, for instance, feel "asthma." It is helpful to ask, "What am I actually feeling?" Simply observe the physical sensations, such as, "Tightness in the chest, wheezing, a cough." It is not possible, for example, to experience the thought, "I'm not getting enough air." That is a fearful thought in the mind. It is a concept, a whole program called "asthma." What is actually being experienced is a tension or a constriction in the throat or chest. The same principle goes for "ulcers" or any other disorder. We cannot feel "ulcers." We feel a burning or piercing sensation. The word "ulcer" is a label and a program, and as soon as we use that word to label our experience, we identify ourselves with the whole "ulcer" program. Even the word "pain" is a program. In reality, we are feeling a specific body sensation. The process of self-healing goes more quickly when we let go of labeling or giving a name to the various physical sensations.

- The same is true with our feelings. Instead of putting labels and names on feelings, we can simply feel the feelings and let go of the energy behind them. It is not necessary to label a feeling "fear" in order to be aware of its energy and relinquish that energy.

The Healing of Multiple Diseases

In the case of this physician, there were so many illnesses all at one time that it was impossible to remember them all. When giving a lecture, it was necessary to list them on an index card. All of the following illnesses were occurring at age 50:

Migraine headaches. Chronic and frequent.

Blocked Eustachian tubes. Painful earaches.

Near-sightedness and astigmatism. Trifocals were prescribed.

Sinusitis; postnasal drip; allergies.

Dermatitis, various types.

Gout attacks. Necessary to carry a cane in the trunk of the car and to have a restricted diet.

Cholesterol problem. Further restrictions in diet.

Duodenal ulcer. Chronic and recurring for over 20 years, unresponsive to all medical treatments.

Pancreatitis. Intermittent attacks precipitated by the recurrent ulcer.

Gastritis; hyperacidity; intermittent pylorospasm. Therefore, further diet restrictions.

Colitis, recurring.

Diverticulitis. An appendicitis-type condition of the colon. Sometimes hemorrhaged, requiring hospitalization and blood transfusions.

Common problems at the lower end of the gastrointestinal tract. Scheduled for surgery.

Arthritis of the cervical spine (neck). Displacement of the fourth cervical vertebrae.

Low back syndrome, necessitating chiropractic treatment.

Vibration disease (Raynaud's Syndrome). Loss of sensation and impending gangrene in finger tips due to loss of circulation.

Middle age syndrome. Coldness in hands and feet, loss of energy and libido, and depression.

Pilonidal cyst at base of spine. Curable only by surgery.

Bronchitis and chronic cough. Aggravated the headaches, spondylosis, and low back syndrome.

Poison ivy sensitivity. Skin broke out every year. Sometimes required hospitalization.

Athlete's foot. There was the belief system that it came from hotel room floors.

Dandruff. There was the belief system that it came from being in a barbershop.

Inflammation of the cartilage (Tzietze's Syndrome).

A rare disorder, with painful swelling of the junction of the rib and sternum.

Dental and gum problems. Loss of bone around the base of teeth. Surgery was recommended for the gums.

Overall energy imbalance. Kinesiologic testing revealed that *all* of the energy systems were out of balance, and every meridian tested weak.

In retrospect, it is mind-boggling how the body kept on going in the world and functioned as well as it did. Inasmuch as each of the disorders required a further restriction in diet, there were times when lettuce and carrots were about the only "safe" foods. This led to the loss of 25 pounds and a body that looked thin and haggard. Later, some friends revealed that they had made bets on how long that body was going to last. Most of them estimated that it would probably keel over at about age 53.

The inner question at the time was: How could a successful, highly educated professional man, functioning creatively in the world, leading a balanced life, who had been thoroughly psychoanalyzed and experienced many modalities of therapy and healing, still have so many physical ailments? Yes, there was a large workload, but it was balanced with physical exercise and creative work such as carpentry, masonry, woodwork, and architectural design. Moreover, the spiritual life was active, with two hours of meditation every day, before and after work. The endless techniques mentioned in the Introduction were investigated: self-hypnosis, macrobiotics, reflexology, iridology, polarity

therapy, affirmations, astral projection, group inten-
sives, bodywork, relaxation, and so on.

What was the answer to this strange paradox of
someone who had tried a multitude of techniques,
groups, and therapies, but who still had a staggering
array of illnesses? Also, how was it that he operated
so successfully in the world despite this long list of illnesses and the constant pain that went with them?
The answer seemed to be: a very strong will. It carried him through all obstacles and had the power to
push aside anything that interfered with that effective
functioning—in this case, primarily, feelings. With that
kind of willpower, when a feeling was suppressed, it
stayed suppressed.

The scientific ideal is objectivity. Objectivity means
an absence of emotion. The achievement of this ideal
in clinical and scientific work necessitated a suppression of feelings. This was especially intense given the
nature of the clinical practice, which was with severely
ill people. The extent of their suffering and that of
their families seemed nearly endless. It went on relentlessly day after day, year in and year out. The intensity
was compounded by having a compassionate nature
and being attuned to people's suffering. The mounting
pressures of suppressed emotion in all areas of life
obviously contributed to the multiplicity of illnesses.

At a certain point, both the mechanism of surrender and *A Course in Miracles* were investigated and
applied to daily life. Because of the busy work schedule, there was very little time for any new techniques.
Happily, the "Workbook" of *A Course in Miracles*
requires the simple contemplation of a sentence or
"lesson" throughout the day. The power of this technique is the alleviation of guilt by utilizing the mecha-

nism of forgiveness. The mechanism of surrender could also be done silently throughout the day as an inner process. The two tools worked together. Surrendering and forgiving went on simultaneously during the day.

Once the mind knows the way to alleviate its inner pressure, like Pandora's box, it begins to let all the garbage up, and up it came in profusion! Thoughts and feelings, which had hardly been noticed at the time of their occurrence, now returned. Life had been so busy that there had not been the time to handle them. The decompression process began to unfold on its own.

One immediate discovery was that every negative feeling or thought is associated with guilt, and this guilt is so all-encompassing that it is constantly being suppressed. Thus, there is no such thing as just anger. The actual feeling is anger/guilt. There is guilt every time we have a critical thought about someone. The mind's constant judging and criticizing of the world, its events and people, is an unending source of guilt. Guilt itself engenders negative feelings, and negative feelings in and of themselves also engender guilt. It is that deadly combination which pulls us all down and creates such widespread illness and unhappiness. The guilt is so omnipresent that no matter what we are doing we feel somewhere in our mind that we "should" be doing something else. We have lived with so much guilt for so long that we don't even recognize it anymore, and somehow that guilt is projected by the average mind onto the world around it. That is why most people need an "enemy"—an object on which to project their inner guilt. It is also where tyrants get their power, by manipulating people's guilt and finding a satisfactory target for it.

There was also the discovery of a disdain for feelings. Anger surfaced at the imposition of feelings, which can make a person feel like a "victim." To a left-brain orientation, feelings were the opposite of reasonableness, logic, and rationality. Superimposed on this was the male chauvinist idea that emotions were for women, children, and artistic types. Feelings had been primarily a matter of intellectual understanding and clinical analysis. When they came up internally, they had been labeled, pigeon-holed, and filed away.

At the beginning of working with the letting go technique, there was a period of rebellion and actually hating the feelings and experiencing dread over having to deal with them. It seemed degrading to have to suffer through them. This required a shift of self-concept because of the strong identification with the intellect. Now, like it or not, it had to be acknowledged that everyone is a thinking/*feeling* organism. It would not work to keep denying reality.

Before long, it was okay to have feelings. With the letting go technique, the only way out was to acknowledge and relinquish the feelings. This became easier as the physical condition started to improve. Although it can initially be difficult to face feelings in ourselves, the light at the end of the tunnel had shone itself, and this engendered hope.

Within days of using the technique, the physical condition at the lower end of the gastrointestinal tract promptly healed itself and, in fact, the surgery was cancelled. Many of the symptoms that had been active for years, even decades, began to diminish in intensity and frequency as the months went by. Migraine headaches, in particular, became less and less frequent. Lower back pains disappeared. The body began to feel lighter and stronger.

Then, an unexpected crisis came that brought intense emotional pressure. The diverticulitis returned in a severe form with massive hemorrhaging. There was an inner decision of great magnitude: "Either this stuff works or it doesn't." So this time, instead of going to the hospital and getting transfusions, there was complete surrender. All of the sensations going on in the abdomen were acknowledged and not resisted. They were not given a name or a label. Instead of thoughts or words, there was a sense of oneness with the sensations, the cramps, and the pain. There was no resistance to the sensations, no matter how intense. Like being on a razor's edge, every sensation and feeling was recognized and surrendered. This went on for four solid hours. At the end of four hours, the bleeding stopped, the cramps went away, and the diverticulitis was healed. Later, there were some minor recurrences; but each one was handled in the same way, and eventually the attacks subsided and disappeared. So the mechanism of surrender passed the acid test. It succeeded where everything else had failed. With continued application, other disorders began to fade away.

Over time, the experience of "knowing" replaced thinking. Knowing comes on in a totally different manner. It is just standing there for our recognition. One morning upon waking, there was the "knowing" of being cured of poison ivy. At the same time, it was obvious that the very name, the label "poison ivy," was a program and a belief system in and of itself. In any case, there was the "knowing" of being immune to poison ivy, even when going outside, touching it, playing with it, and putting some of it in a flower pot to carry to an interview program that evening! The subject of the interview was: "The Power of Consciousness in Self-Healing."

Another episode of "knowingness" occurred one day when unexpectedly confronted by intense insecticide fumes. Such fumes had been a severe allergy for many years and invariably triggered a severe migraine. On this particular day, however, there was the sudden "knowing" of immunity to fumes. Walking into a recently fumigated home and taking very deep breaths of the fumes without any consequences at all, a sudden elated feeling of freedom prevailed. How wonderful to be free and to experience the power of mind! It was obvious in that moment that we are only subject to those things that we hold in mind. It is not necessary to be a slave or victim in the world.

The same thing happened with a long-standing belief about elevated cholesterol. As the belief and concept of it were cancelled, eating dairy products was resumed with no negative impact on cholesterol. In fact, blood testing showed a progressive lowering of unhealthy cholesterol levels! Moreover, food intolerances and allergies disappeared. It took at least another year, however, for the sugar intolerance and functional hypoglycemia to disappear. For a period of time, it would still recur under periods of stress, especially physical exertion, after eating sugar and sweets accompanied by caffeine.

In the meantime, it was possible to return to a regular diet after many years of severe restrictions. How freeing to eat foods with seeds (not allowed with diverticulitis), all the foods that were supposed to be contraindicated for ulcers and colitis, and even hot fudge sundaes! It took a couple of years for the functional hypoglycemia to disappear, but eventually it was possible to eat all of the sweets that had been forbidden for years.

The whole middle age syndrome was a belief system as well. As this belief system was cancelled and surrendered, the coldness disappeared from the hands and feet. The fatigue, mild depression, and irritability also disappeared. Physical stamina increased and the tolerance for physical work became almost unlimited.

Now that the more major things were out of the way, some of the minor ailments were consciously addressed. The belief in pilonidal cyst was surrendered. In six weeks, it disappeared. The Eustachian tube, which always blocked when flying in airplanes, caused severe pain in the right ear. It took two years to correct itself. There was a continual letting go of all thoughts and feelings about it and, at the same time, the use of visualization in which the angle of the canal with the right temple bone was pictured as changing to a normal angle. This was the only ailment with which visualization was used. At the end of two years, the ailment disappeared, and there was never any further difficulty in clearing the ears with changes in altitude.

In the meantime, the neck pains were progressively disappearing, and this made dancing possible. While dancing and surrendering any resistance to the neck pain, soon the body began to automatically put itself into self-healing postures and movements, as though there were an inner chiropractor manipulating the spine. It was an uncanny sensation, as though invisible healers were realigning the spine.

As this was going on, there were changes in circulation occurring in the hands and feet, and they were no longer cold all the time. The vibration disease in the fingertips, which had been threatening gangrene, now reversed itself. The pads on the fingertips swelled back out and turned pink again. The burning pain in the fingertips disappeared. Sensation returned. Up to that time, the fingers had become so numb that it was not possible to turn the pages of a book.

As the more serious ailments were healed, there was the energy and time to look at even more minor issues. There had been a long-standing belief that people catch dandruff in barbershops. When that belief was surrendered, the dandruff disappeared. A similar process occurred with the belief that correlated athlete's foot with hotel room floors. Upon continual cancellation of that belief, athlete's foot disappeared.

At Thanksgiving time one year, there was the opportunity to test the technique in an acute situation. A huge log dropped on the left foot and broke all the bones across the whole forefoot. Instead of rushing out to get a cast, the letting go technique was used. By Christmas, it was possible to return to the dance floor. At a later time, a severely sprained ankle healed itself in minutes by instantly surrendering the pain.

Healing of Vision

One evening while giving a lecture on the mechanism of surrender and making note of all of the above healings which had been experienced, a member of the audience said, "Doctor, if you healed all of those ailments, then why do you still wear glasses? Couldn't poor eyesight be healed the same way?"

"Well, I never thought of wearing glasses as a disease. I always thought of it as an anatomical-structural defect of the body. But now that you mention it, I don't see any reason why that shouldn't heal."

So, the bifocals were removed and stowed in a coat pocket. Indeed, at that time, eyesight was declining to the point that trifocals had been prescribed and ordered. In leaving the lecture that evening, the same inner knowingness came, that the condition would heal itself with sufficient faith and trust.

Driving home without glasses, vision was blurred. The pace was slow, with headlights on the curb. There was an inner knowingness that we would always see what we *needed* to see but unable to see what we *wanted* to see. During the next six weeks, a great deal was observed and learned about what goes on behind our everyday, ordinary seeing. There is a whole myriad of feelings, varying from curiosity to competition to erotic interest to intellectual titillation. Only about five percent of our vision is absolutely necessary to function in the world.

A peculiar phenomenon occurred; only that which was necessary to see was seen. Reading newspapers and magazines, watching television, or going to the movies were all impossible. It became clear how most of vision is merely escapism. On the road, it was as if Mr. Magoo were behind the wheel. Again and again that same mysterious phenomenon would occur. As soon as it was vital to see something, that's when it would be seen. The edge of the cliff was made visible just as it was necessary to see it. There was a great deal of anxiety, with a constant surrendering of fear. Finally, by the end of six weeks, the fear seemed to run out. Instead, a deep surrender took place. "Well, I will only see that which I am allowed to see." The other emotional objectives which seeing had subserved up to that time were willingly surrendered.

Then, a profound sense of inner stillness and peace occurred and a feeling of oneness with whatever it is that runs the universe. And in that instant, suddenly, vision returned totally and perfectly. What had not been visible or readable now was crystal clear: street signs, fine print in dim light, objects in great detail across the room and at great distance. At the next eye test for a driving license renewal, the evaluator said that the vision was perfect and that glasses would no longer be required. This had never occurred on any previous eye test!

Since telling this story around the country, quite a number of other people have taken off their glasses and gone through the same experience. Interestingly enough, each one said that it took about six weeks. One of the people who accomplished this decided to put his glasses on again. When asked the reason, he said that his wife was so used to seeing him with glasses that he looked homely without them, and so he put on blank ones in order to please her. He did it just because he loved her and wanted to make her happy, which is a very different reason than having to wear glasses because of impaired vision.

Those of us who have had the experience of healed vision agree on one discovery: It is with the mind itself that we see, not the eyeballs! Recently, one of the cases was a woman who had been blind since shortly after birth and had gross derangements of both eyeballs. After hearing the lecture on recovery of vision, she pursued a medical protocol and practiced the letting go technique on her sight. Within two days she began to experience a return of vision. She came up after the lecture and said, "I know you are right. I know that one sees through the mind because that is what is happening to me. I am seeing, and I am seeing with my mind!"

To understand how all of these healings can come about—some of them verging on the miraculous—we have to revise many of our thoughts about bodily processes, the mechanisms of healing, and how medical treatments bring about their results. It was discovered that there is a self-healing power *within* that is activated by continual surrender.

21

QUESTIONS AND ANSWERS

This chapter includes verbatim questions and answers from workshops and seminars that have been given around the world in recent years. In anticipation of the reader's questions, the most typical and frequently asked questions about the mechanism of surrender have been included.

Religious and Spiritual Goals

There are always a number of questions regarding the application of surrender to achieving what are generally referred to as spiritual goals, expansion of consciousness, and religious beliefs. We can answer many of these questions by making a general statement.

The letting go mechanism does not conflict with any religion or spiritual pathway or self-improvement program, nor does it disagree with any philosophy or metaphysical position. It entails no spiritual teachings of its own. Instead, it provides a mechanism so that self-understanding removes the blocks to spiritual advancement. It is also compatible with the humanistic movement. All spiritual pathways and religions emphasize the need for expanding our capacity to love, and this is essentially what the process of surrender is all about. By removing the blocks to love, the capacity to love self, others, and God is expanded.

Surrender also facilitates the basic teachings of all the world's great religions. The essential goal of these teachings is to surrender the "small self," commonly called "ego." The letting go technique facilitates the goal of dissolving the small self by using a simple inner process of surrender. When the small self is transcended, the true inner Self shines forth. Let us take, for instance, the most common short means of expression of this surrendering phenomenon as given by most religions. Typically, they follow this pattern:

Let go and let God.

Be still and know that I am God.

Turn your life and will over to the care of God as you understand Him.

Surrender to what *is,* for God is in all things.

It is obvious that letting go of negativity facilitates the very direction that all religions and spiritual pathways urge us to take. The process of letting go is concerned primarily with feelings, and we have seen that feelings have a profound effect on our thoughts and belief systems. The experience of most people who use the mechanism of surrender is that it facilitates their spiritual and religious goals. Those who do not consciously have any religious or spiritual goals have remarked that it facilitates their capacity for lovingness, which substantially increases their happiness and well-being.

Carl Jung pointed out that, because God is one of the major archetypes in the unconscious, each person has to take a position about God whether they like it or not. Even the atheist has feelings about the concept of God. So whether God exists or not, the subject has to be dealt with sooner or later. Suppressing our feelings about God or consciously being overwhelmed by the subject is not a satisfactory solution. The letting go technique brings resolution to long-standing inner conflicts, both to the atheist and to the believer.

Question: What is the relationship of letting go to the whole concept of sin?

Answer: If we examine the negative feelings that we have been discussing and describe them in religious terminology, we see that what we have really been describing are the so-called "cardinal sins." Inasmuch as the mechanism of surrender is a way of letting them go, it seems obvious that letting go of the attachment to these characteristics facilitates the achievement of religious teachings in our personal life.

Question: I am not a follower of any particular spiritual pathway but have my own personal pathway. How could this technique be helpful?

Answer: Without exception, all spiritual pathways are based upon a method of dissolving the ego. The ego includes the totality of our negative programs. Surrendering is the process *par excellence* for letting go of negative programs. It is, therefore, the best tool to facilitate spiritual understanding.

Question: Will this process interfere in any way with my faith?

Answer: On the contrary: What are the obstacles to faith? You will notice that they are all forms of negativity. Consequently, letting go of negativity would be removing the obstacles to faith.

Question: I am a nonbeliever, but I do have an interest in learning about spiritual matters. Would this approach be of any use to me?

Answer: The mechanism of surrender is a tool only. You can use it to remove the obstacles to making a million dollars; or you can use it to remove the obstacles to the development of spiritual awareness. Most people who continuously surrender report that they discover something within themselves akin to love itself, which is independent of the body, emotions, thoughts, and the events of the world. Have you ever heard of anyone becoming displeased by this discovery?

Question: Does the letting go technique contradict any spiritual or religious teachings?

Answer: A study of the subject reveals that there is no conflict between the letting go of negativity and any spiritual teaching.

Question: I gave up religion many years ago because it created so much guilt I couldn't handle it. What would be the effect of using the letting go technique?

Answer: In clinical observations over the years, guilt emerges as the most frequent reason for which people give up their religion. It is because the goals seem unobtainable. Ask yourself what has made these goals seem unobtainable. It will always be the disparity between what one is taught they should be, as compared to what they perceive they really are. Instead of feeling guilty, try letting go of all the negative feelings that come up and wait and see for yourself what change of attitudes might occur. Again, letting go is a tool. It can be utilized to facilitate your goals in any area of life. How you use it is up to you. A good place to start is to let go of all of your guilt since it fosters an emotional environment for suffering and disease.

Meditation and Inner Techniques

Question: How does letting go and surrendering correlate with the different meditative techniques?

Answer: Almost all meditative techniques have as their goal the quieting of the mind. This is the basis of the dictum from the Book of Psalms, "Be still and know that I am God." As most meditators have discovered, achieving silence of the mind is the main problem of meditation itself. This is because suppressed feelings constantly produce thoughts, which are the main distractions in meditation. Acknowledging and letting go of the energy behind these suppressed feelings, therefore, facilitates the goal of meditation. When the feeling behind the train of thoughts is located and surrendered, then that entire train of thought instantly stops.

By constantly surrendering, it is possible to arrive at an extremely silent state of mind. This can be accomplished as one goes about one's daily activities, thus greatly expanding the capacity to meditate. Most meditative techniques are limited to a specified number of minutes or hours during the day. It is possible by constant surrender to reach high states of consciousness.

Question: I do not follow a spiritual pathway, but I do affirmations and visualizations. Will the letting go technique be of use to me?

Answer: Letting go greatly facilitates the power of affirmations. An affirmation is a positive statement. Its power is limited by the fact that, either consciously or unconsciously, we have multiple negative programs that are saying the very opposite thing to the affirmation. You can discover this for yourself by noticing that, as you write the affirmations, your mind comes up with, "Yeah, but . . . " It is these "Yeah, buts . . . " that limit the power of the affirmation and reduce its effectiveness. If you surrender the obstacles to the affirmation, you will notice a rapid increase in their effectiveness.

Psychotherapy

Question: I am in psychoanalysis. Would the letting go technique be helpful or would it be in conflict with my analysis, which is getting progressively more expensive?

Answer: Therapists who have studied the technique agree with it. Many psychiatrists, psychologists, and therapists have learned it and utilize it in their practices. So far, we have heard only

100% positive evaluations of the results, because the so-called "working through" is facilitated by the patient's capacity to let go of negativity and self-limitations, which allows the therapy to move forward much more rapidly. Psychotherapists, themselves, have found that letting go has greatly facilitated their understanding of patients and the resolution of counter-transference. If therapists know how to acknowledge and let go of negative feelings, then they can avoid the development of many stress-related illnesses during the course of their practice. Thus, the technique is considered to be of assistance in psychotherapy, increasing its effectiveness and the satisfactoriness of its outcome.

Question: I am in group psychotherapy. How would that work with the mechanism of surrender?

Answer: Just as in individual psychotherapy, the capability of surrendering one's inner negative feelings greatly facilitates group work.

Question: I am a Jungian analyst. Would this approach fit in with my work?

Answer: Through surrender, we can free ourselves from being at the effect of the archetypes. The archetypes are obviously a collection of beliefs and feelings and are, therefore, programs like any other. The individual who uses the mechanism of surrender to let go of programmed beliefs and feelings has the power of choice over the archetypal patterns, rather than unconsciously being run by them.

Alcoholism and Drug Addiction

Question: I am a member of Alcoholics Anonymous (A.A.), and I would like to know if others in A.A. have benefited from this technique.

Answer: The common experience is that the technique of letting go greatly facilitates working the 12 Steps of Alcoholics Anonymous, especially the Third Step. The Third Step states, "Made a decision to turn our will and lives over to the care of God *as we understood Him.*" This very step is frustrating to many people in A.A. because there is no how-to. Just how do you turn your will and life over to the care of God or some Higher Power? If we look at will, we see that it is desire. This desire is connected to attachments. The mechanism of surrender, therefore, facilitates freedom from attachments and is almost equal to the Third Step in its intention. Surrendering to God means letting go of one's willfulness. Willfulness is the ego itself.

The obsession to drink is a drivenness, a compulsion due to an attachment. This can be weakened and lessened by the process of surrendering. Drinking is also an escape from the pain of negative feelings; therefore, letting go of negative feelings decreases the psychological need for escape in that particular form. This applies to other drugs as well, which are all attempts to replace a lower feeling with a higher feeling.

The letting go technique does not replace the need for self-help groups or for Alcoholics Anonymous; however, it greatly facilitates success in recovery programs and is certainly compatible with all the anonymous groups, which are based uniformly on the 12 Steps.

Relationships

Question: I've been on a spiritual path for many years and do not understand why I still experience negative emotions.

Answer: There's a common illusion that spiritually evolved, loving people never have any negativity, as though they are already angelic. They get annoyed that they still have negative feelings, and then it's compounded by their guilt and self-frustration. They have to realize that feelings are transitory, whereas their intention to evolve remains constant. Let go of feeling guilty that you are still just an ordinary human despite your angelic ambitions! Having compassion towards your innate humanness, its nervous system, and the brain function that goes with it allows for greater equanimity. Heavenly ambitions do not necessarily make us angels!

Question: I have a colleague at work who doesn't carry his load. Every time I see him, I feel resentful. Then, I feel guilty for resenting him. How would I begin the letting go technique in that situation?

Answer: We notice and accept what our feelings are about a situation, and then we proceed to clear them as a priority rather than indulge in emotionality. In the workplace, many people think they should suppress their feelings of resentment; however, this approach does not handle the problem and the tensions will fester. With the letting go technique, go within yourself and acknowledge the negative feelings as they arise. Let them come up without suppressing them and without venting them. And then shift your attention from the feelings to something else. Let the feelings be there and let them go.

Question: You recommend that we shift attention away from the negative feeling. How is this different from repressing the feeling?

Answer: Repression is an unconscious process by which unaccepted feelings are put out of awareness and not dealt with. In shifting attention, you make a choice not to indulge the negative emotion. You have already acknowledged and accepted the feeling within yourself as part of being human, but you are choosing to let it go because you want something higher, like peacefulness, harmony, and getting the job done. People will sometimes shift their attention by way of actions such as rearranging the furniture a little bit, opening and closing the window shades, making a quick trip to the bathroom, or going for a short coffee break. These actions allow for a moment to shift from the negative to the positive.

Question: I notice there are certain feelings that seem to recur frequently, even though I use the method with regularity.

Answer: The frequent recurrence of negative feelings would indicate the necessity for a period of contemplation about recurrent patterns. For instance, the manner of handling negative emotions may follow parental or family patterns, as well as cultural ones. There is a wide variation among cultures in how to handle feelings. So, look at the unconscious underlying patterns going on with your emotional response, and let go of those patterns.

Question: What if a negative feeling toward someone or a situation persists, despite my intention and effort to let it go?

Answer: Sometimes one is more or less forced to surrender to a situation and presume that it's karmic. With spiritual research, one finds out that it is indeed karmic. Let's say you are paying off the karma of being mean to a lot of people! Now you get a chance to see what it's like to have people be mean to you. Sometimes the only reasonable thing left to do is to surrender to karmic patterns. You don't have to believe in karma as a religious doctrine in order to make this step. It's simply accepting the basic law of human interactions that "what goes around comes around," and most of us have not always been saints!

Question: I'm a teacher and sometimes there are students who annoy me. As their teacher I want to get over the annoyance so I can be helpful to them. What do you recommend?

Answer: First, accept the fact that you are annoyed, and that it's okay to be annoyed. It's the price of human consciousness. Let the annoyance come up fully without calling it anything or making it personal. Instead of resisting it, you ask for more of it. See that it's simply the energy of negativity. That observation depersonalizes it. Then ask yourself, are you willing to let go of this energy? Often the energy will lift.

Question: I have a good marriage but there are moments of annoyance, frustration, and disagreement. How do I deal with feeling frustrated and annoyed at my spouse?

Answer: We've already said that it's okay to be annoyed. That is part of being human. What you do is become familiar with what the other person is processing and their style of expression. There are often different attitudes and preferences. Very common differences are preferences over room temperature, volume settings, and how to spend money. The key is to let go of being judgmental of the other person's preferences or feeling prideful about your own as "the right way." Each accepts the humanness of the other and that, of course, there are sometimes going to be different attitudes.

Question: Such seemingly minor differences often lead to the downfall of a relationship because people blame the other person or want to change their behavior. How can they live peacefully instead?

Answer: You just accept that all relationships have their ups and downs. You have to have a sense of humor about the human condition itself and its seeming contradictions and para-doxes. You want the other person to be happy and comfortable, and you know that you are happy and comfortable when they are happy and comfortable. There is a mutual alignment with a peaceful lifestyle. Let go of judging, blaming, and controlling the other. Let go of expecting them to be different than they are. We all have our foibles. It can be sort of fun to make a list of your own foibles. There can be a decision not to focus on negativity in one's environment or a relationship. People can toler-ate tensions and differences for variable periods of time, and at different ages you can tolerate things more or less.

Question: What about the negative emotions that come up for parents when dealing with children?

Answer: Tolerance for children's behaviors varies depending on cultural context, gender, age, moral views, and other factors. You put up with things in kindergarten that you don't toler-ate in third grade. It is common for parents to have to let go of expectations of their children. What's it like for an expert musician to have a child with no musical skill or inclination? Expectations are subtle pressures on the other person, who will then unconsciously resist. In parenting, you want to relinquish expectations and personal favoritisms. If you're an expert at billiards, can you let go of being disappointed that your kid is lousy at shooting pool?

    Another common issue is over-parenting.

Sometimes a parent confuses loving a grown child with bailing them out of every difficulty. At a certain age, sometimes love means "tough love," that is, letting the child find his own way out of the mess he made so that he has the opportunity to discover his own inner resources.

Question: If I let go of a lot of guilt, wouldn't the technique result in promiscuity?

Answer: On the contrary, promiscuity is based on low self-esteem, exploitation, and lack of love. The letting go of negativity and selfishness, concern for others, a heightened pleasure from their company, and higher self-esteem changes one's perspective of relationships. The capacity for lovingness increases rapidly. Much of promiscuity is an attempt to overcome unconscious fears and seek reassurance. These can all be let go of, so that more mature relationships take their place.

Question: I have been going to sex therapy, which is based on behavioral retraining. Would that be compatible?

Answer: There is no incompatibility. Behavioral retraining is an attempt to replace negative programs with positive ones. Essentially, it is replacing "I can't" with "I can." That is what this technique of letting go is all about.

Question: Will the letting go technique cure impotence or frigidity?

Answer: It is not a cure for anything; it is a self-investigative technique that rapidly opens up awareness of inner feelings, thoughts, and beliefs. Both frigidity and impotency are statements on the behavioral level of "I can't," which in the unconscious means "I won't." They are both resistances to joy, love, expression, and aliveness. The most common causes are repressed guilt, fear, and anger, emotions that spill out through the autonomic nervous system. Impotence and frigidity are expressions of conflict. Most people who use the letting go technique report overall improvements in their sexual life in a variety of ways, and many have reported recovery from sexual inhibitions. Likewise, many have also reported the relief from sexual excessiveness and excessive preoccupation with the subject.

Question: How does the mechanism of surrender relate to the process of aging?

Answer: It facilitates graceful aging. Getting older brings a big change in your lifestyle. Often there is a decline in vision, hearing, and mobility, which means you are increasingly dependent on the care of others for things that you accomplished previously without a second thought. Old age can be annoying. Suddenly, you are incompetent in areas where you once excelled. As you let go of feeling annoyed, however, you see that the incapacities of old age serve a purpose. They get you ready to leave the world. If you were still involved as a "star" in some area of life, you'd resent leaving the world. You wouldn't be very graceful about it. As you decline, it gives you time to adjust, get used to the fact that you'll be leaving, and do any spiritual work that you want to have completed by the time you leave here.

When you surrender to the process of aging as simply part of the human condition, you come to peace with it. You become more loving and appreciative of other people's love and care for you. The more loving you become, you see that everybody is trying to be helpful to you. And it is loving to allow them to be helpful to you. People think, "Oh, I'm being selfish if I allow somebody to be helpful to my life." Actually, it's being generous. Generosity is the willingness to share your life with others. It's a gift to people to allow them to love you.

The Mechanism

Question: How can surrendering be more constant?

Answer: The secret to using this mechanism more often and more consistently is, first of all, the wish to do so. That is Step #1. You have to want to be free of the feeling more than you want to keep it. Sometimes it is just a matter of remembering, and you can use some kind of a cue card to remind you.

Another way is to establish a routine. It is very good to start the day by surrendering your thoughts and feelings about your expectations, to picture the way you would like it to go, and to let go of all negative thoughts that would interfere with the day going in that way. Then, at the end of the day, sit down and surrender anything that came up during the course of the day that you overlooked or didn't have time to pay attention to. This is called "cleaning up," and most people find that they sleep better.

Another way is to keep a notebook where you write down your successes. You might put down the goal of constant surrendering and follow it up with what the results were.

Another way is to let go of your resistance to surrendering and, as you start the day, reaffirm your intention to let go of all negativity that day. You also reaffirm that you are free not to surrender. After all, it is totally a matter of choice. Let go of any feeling of compulsion about it. There isn't any "should."

Question: What do you think is the most frequent cause for our resistance to surrender?

Answer: We think that somehow, if we hang on to that feeling, it is going to get us what we want. If we get stuck in a feeling, it is useful to look at the question of what we think we have accomplished by hanging on to it. We will almost always find that we have a fantasy that it will have some effect on some other person and change their behavior or attitudes toward us. If we let go of that, we become willing to let go of the feeling.

Question: If I surrender all the time, won't I just become passive?

Answer: On the contrary, surrendering will clear the decks for effective action. Passivity is often because of inhibition and a failure to see alternate ways to handle a situation. For instance, a person will say, "In the conference, he got me so mad I just sat there and said nothing." Now it's rather clear what the problem is. The saying nothing was due to the anger and the person's picturing that the only emotional response he could make would be anger. Since this would be inappropriate in a business situation, he said nothing. Had the anger been let go, the person could have been confidently assertive and stated his opinion instead of clamming up.

Question: In therapy, I learned how to express anger, and I think it is a very useful thing. Do I have to give it up?

Answer: If you look at anger, you will see that its basis is almost always fear. We get angry because we have been threatened. The threat arouses fear. The fear means we feel that we are unequal to the situation. Anger biologically is like swelling up to intimidate our opponent. Anger is coming from weakness rather than strength. The person who has surrendered is, therefore, relying on strength rather than weakness. The person who has surrendered does not have to fall back upon anger to handle a situation. Also, anger cannot be counted upon. In addition, it has many destructive effects; for example, it is running you instead of your running it. A totally surrendered person is free to choose to express anger if they wish, but it is done out of choice, not out of necessity. Anger, especially chronic anger, has deleterious effects on the body organs, and research in psychosomatic medicine has indicated that repressed anger is associated with hypertension, arthritis, and a variety of other diseases.

Question: You mentioned that surrender is a natural psychological mechanism of the mind. If that is so, how come we have to learn how to do it?

Answer: Although it is true that surrender or letting go is a natural mechanism of the mind, it must be remembered that the mind has multiple conflicting motivations. Whereas one part of your mind would like to be free of the tension from a feeling, another part of your mind is programmed to believe that hanging on to the feeling will somehow magically bring about some desired end. Unless one is conscious and aware and has mastered the technique, the conflicts of the mind will overrule and dominate. Basically, the technique of letting go gives you the power of choice over the tendencies of mind. Instead of being at its effect, the mind is now under your mastery. It opens up freedom and the capacity for free choice.

Question: I have a hard time with acceptance. What do you recommend?

Answer: Divert your attention to that which is really essential, experientially. Some days it rains; some days it's sunny; some days it's cloudy. You can't change the rain, but you can put on your raincoat. You can be realistic and take the necessary steps to remain dry. There are many aspects of life you can't change, but you can let go of your expectation or need that they be different from what they are. With observation, for instance, you will notice that there is always a war going on somewhere in the world. So to be peaceful, it is necessary to accept that waging war is part of human nature and has been throughout all of recorded time. Mankind has been at war 97% of the time.

Question: I realize that fear and insecurity have driven me all of my life, but it seems like those drives account for my financial success. If I learn how to surrender, will this adversely affect my income?

Answer: When a lower motivation has been let go, the mind automatically replaces it with a higher feeling and a higher motivation. What's wrong with enjoying earning a living instead of being driven by fear? The same activity will continue but now from a pleasurable space, and it will start bringing in many rewards other than just financial.

Question: Without guilt, won't people misbe-have?

Answer: Similar to a previous answer, loving concern for others replaces inhibition due to guilt. The more loving we become, the more harmless we become to others and to society in general. When you are lovingly concerned for the welfare of others, your own welfare will be taken care of and covered.

Question: I have a poor memory. Do you think I could learn this technique?

Answer: There is nothing to memorize in learning this technique. It is simply a way of letting go. As yet, we have not heard of anyone unable to learn it.

Question: Sometimes I think I am letting go, and sometimes I'm not sure. I get confused. What is the problem?

Answer: Look at the resistances to the process of surrendering itself. Are there any negative thoughts, doubts, or feelings about your ability to do the technique? Let all of these resistances come up, accept them, and let them go. Clarify your intention to become a happier, more loving and peaceful person.

Surrender to the Ultimate

Question: You've mentioned "surrender at great depth" as a method by which we experience Ultimate Reality. Can you describe what occurs?

Answer: We might call it the "final run." As you apply the letting go technique to every area of life, without exception, the energy of spiritual work gets stronger and stronger. There is the fixity of attention, the relentless staying with a method, no matter what is going on.

Some people say, "I've done spiritual work off and on for 30 years, and I'm still where I was." They've meditated a little there, prayed a little here, gone to a workshop, heard a speaker, read a book, and it has all been sporadic. That's all right. You are busy in the world and accumulating data that you know you're going to use at a later date.

But then there comes a time when it means to do whatever practice you're doing without exception, all the time. The devotion to the Truth becomes overwhelming. It isn't that you're driving it. You're being pulled by your own destiny; it is by your own karmic commitment that you've chosen the ultimate destiny. At that point, let's say you use the technique of surrender. This means to surrender and let go of everything at the very moment it arises. It happens in 1/10,000th of a second—it's coming, it peaks, and then it leaves. So, every feeling, every thought, every desire, you let go at the peak of it. This becomes continuous, nonstop.

As mentioned earlier, I remember letting go of a severe attachment for 11 days, sitting and doing nothing but letting go of this attachment. Every thought, every feeling, every memory, everything about it—as it arose, it was surrendered. The grief that we feel when we lose a member of our family is not just about losing that person here and now. It's an accumulation of the energy of all the deaths from all the lifetimes. This particular surrender was nonstop for 11 days, morning and night. Finally it stopped. Gone forever. Never again to be subject to that.

So, serious spiritual work is a continuous willingness to let things go as they arise. It is the willingness to surrender wanting to control everything as it arises, the willingness to surrender wanting to change it, and to have it our way. Very often there will be illusions about the nature of Reality that also have to be let go. That there's a good and a bad, a desirable and an undesirable; that's all in the mind. In Reality, the sun shines and then the clouds come; the rain falls and the grass grows up and dies; the stock market goes up and down; age comes and goes; people arise and leave. And, so, there's the ebb and flow. If you are at this one point of the cycle, there's no use in crying about it because the cycle will cycle itself out. By surrendering to whatever is cycling up, it eventually disappears. You disappear it by choosing to be one with it and refusing to want to change it as it arises. Do this continuously, no matter what, nonstop.

This means that you cannot make an exception here, or an exception there. It means continuously, and with everyone and everything. The one or two things you hide behind probably represent a stack. That's why you're hanging on to them. It's not just this annoying person you hate; they represent a whole stack of that energy to you. You can't just skip over your mother-in-law!

Eventually, everything is surrendered that stands in the way of the Presence. The Presence is so obvious, so startling, so overwhelming, that there's no question about it. It is profound, total, all-encompassing, absolutely overwhelming, totally transforming, and completely unmistakable. When everything is surrendered that stands in the way, It is there, shining brilliantly forth.

Instead of viewing this as something in the future, own it now. Enlightenment is not something that occurs in the future, after 50 years of sitting cross-legged and saying "OM." It is right here, in this instant. The reason you're not experiencing this state of total peace and timelessness is because it is being resisted. It is being resisted because you are trying to control the moment. If you let go of trying to control your experience of the moment, and if you constantly surrender it like a tone of music, then you live on the crest of this exact always-ness. Experience arises like a note of music. The minute you hear a note, it's already passing away. The instant you've heard it, it's already dissolving. So every single moment is dissolving as it arises. Let go of anticipating the next moment, trying to control it, trying to hang on to the moment that has just passed. Let go clinging to what has just occurred. Let go trying to control what you think is about to occur. Then you live in an infinite space of non-time and non-event. There is an infinite peace beyond description. And you are home.

APPENDIX A:
THE MAP OF CONSCIOUSNESS®

God-view	Life-view	Level		Log	Emotion	Process
Self	Is	Enlightenment	⇧	700-1000	Ineffable	Pure Consciousness
All-Being	Perfect	Peace	⇧	600	Bliss	Illumination
One	Complete	Joy	⇧	540	Serenity	Transfiguration
Loving	Benign	Love	⇧	500	Reverence	Revelation
Wise	Meaningful	Reason	⇧	400	Understanding	Abstraction
Merciful	Harmonious	Acceptance	⇧	350	Forgiveness	Transcendence
Inspiring	Hopeful	Willingness	⇧	310	Optimism	Intention
Enabling	Satisfactory	Neutrality	⇧	250	Trust	Release
Permitting	Feasible	Courage	⇕	200	Affirmation	Empowerment
Indifferent	Demanding	Pride	⇩	175	Scorn	Inflation
Vengeful	Antagonistic	Anger	⇩	150	Hate	Aggression
Denying	Disappointing	Desire	⇩	125	Craving	Enslavement
Punitive	Frightening	Fear	⇩	100	Anxiety	Withdrawal
Disdainful	Tragic	Grief	⇩	75	Regret	Despondency
Condemning	Hopeless	Apathy	⇩	50	Despair	Abdication
Vindictive	Evil	Guilt	⇩	30	Blame	Destruction
Despising	Miserable	Shame	⇩	20	Humiliation	Elimination

APPENDIX B:
MUSCLE TESTING
PROCEDURE

General Information

The energy field of consciousness is infinite in dimension. Specific levels correlate with human consciousness and have been calibrated from 1 to 1,000. (See Appendix A: Map of Consciousness.) These energy fields reflect and dominate human consciousness.

Everything in the universe radiates a specific frequency or minute energy field that remains in the field of consciousness permanently. Thus, every person or being that ever lived and anything about them, including any event, thought, deed, feeling, or attitude, is recorded forever and can be retrieved at any time in the present or the future.

Technique

The muscle-testing response is a simple "yes" or "not yes" (no) response to a specific stimulus. It is usually done by the subject holding out an extended arm and the tester pressing down on the wrist of the extended arm, using two fingers and light pressure. Usually the subject holds a substance to be tested over their solar plexus with the other hand. The tester says to the test subject, "Resist," and if the substance being tested is beneficial to the subject, the arm will be strong. If it is not beneficial or it has an adverse effect, the arm will go weak. The response is very quick and brief.

It is important to note that the intention, as well as both the tester and the one being tested, must calibrate over 200 in order to obtain accurate responses.

Experience from online discussion groups has shown that many students obtain inaccurate results. Further research shows that at calibration 200, there is still a 30 percent chance of error. The higher the levels of consciousness of the test team, the more accurate are the results. The best attitude is one of clinical detachment, posing a statement with the prefix statement, "In the name of the highest good, _____ calibrates as true. Over 100, Over 200," etc. The contextualization "in the highest good" increases accuracy because it transcends self-serving personal interest and motives.

For many years, the test was thought to be a local response of the body's acupuncture or immune system. Later research, however, has revealed that the response is not a local response to the body at all, but instead is a general response of consciousness itself to the energy of a substance or a statement. That which is true, beneficial, or pro-life gives a positive response that stems from the impersonal field of consciousness, which is present in everyone living. This positive response is indicated by the body's musculature going strong. There is also an associated pupillary response (the eyes dilate with falsity and constrict to truth) as well as alterations in brain function as revealed by magnetic imaging. (For convenience, the deltoid muscle is usually the one best used as an indicator muscle; however, any of the muscles of the body can be used.)

Before a question (in the form of a statement)

is presented, it is necessary to qualify permission; that is, state, "I have permission to ask about what I am holding in mind" (Yes/No). Or, "This calibration serves the highest good."

If a statement is false or a substance is injurious, the muscles go weak quickly in response to the command, "Resist." This indicates the stimulus is negative, untrue, anti-life, or the answer is "no." The response is fast and brief in duration. The body will then rapidly recover and return to normal muscle tension.

There are three ways of doing the testing. The one that is used in research and also most generally used requires two people: the tester and the test subject. A quiet setting is preferred, with no background music. The test subject closes their eyes. *The tester must phrase the question to be asked in the form of a statement.* The statement can then be answered as "yes" or "no" by the muscle response. For instance, the *incorrect* form would be to ask, "Is this a healthy horse?" The correct form is to make the statement, "This horse is healthy," or its corollary, "This horse is sick."

After making the statement, the tester says "Resist" to the test subject who is holding the extended arm parallel to the ground. The tester presses down sharply with two fingers on the wrist of the extended arm with mild force. The test subject's arm will either stay strong, indicating a "yes," or go weak, indicating a "not yes" (no). The response is short and immediate.

A second method is the O-ring method, which can be done alone. The thumb and middle finger of the same hand are held tightly in an O configuration, and the hooked forefinger of the opposite hand is used to try to pull them apart. There is a noticeable difference in the strength between a "yes" and a "no" response.

The third method is the simplest, yet, like the others, requires some practice. Simply lift a heavy object, such as a large dictionary or merely a couple of bricks, from a table about waist high. Hold in mind an image or true statement to be calibrated and then lift. Then, for contrast, hold in mind that which is known to be false. Note the ease of lifting when truth is held in mind and the greater effort necessary to lift the load when the issue is false (not true). The results can be verified using the other two methods.

Calibration of Specific Levels

The critical point between positive and negative, between true and false, or between that which is constructive or destructive, is at the calibrated level of 200 (see Map in Appendix A). Anything above 200, or true, makes the subject go strong; anything below 200, or false, allows the arm to go weak.

Anything past or present, including images or statements, historical events, or personages, can be tested. They need not be verbalized.

Numerical Calibration

Example: "Ramana Maharshi's teachings calibrate over 700." (Y/N). Or, "Hitler calibrated over 200." (Y/N). "When he was in his 20s." (Y/N)."His 30s." (Y/N). "His 40s." (Y/N). "At the time of his death." (Y/N).

Applications

The muscle test cannot be used to foretell the future; otherwise, there are no limits as to what can be asked.

Consciousness has no limits in time or space; however, permission may be denied. All current or historical events are available for questioning. The answers are impersonal and do not depend on the belief systems of either the tester or the test subject. For example, protoplasm recoils from noxious stimuli and flesh bleeds. Those are the qualities of these test materials and are impersonal. Consciousness actually knows only truth because only truth has actual existence. It does not respond to falsehood because falsehood does not have existence in Reality. It will also not respond accurately to nonintegrous or egoistical questions.

Accurately speaking, the test response is either an "on" response or merely a "not on" response. Like the electrical switch, we say the electricity is "on," and when we use the term "off," we just mean that it is not there. In reality, there is no such thing as off-ness. This is a subtle statement but crucial to the understanding of the nature of consciousness. Consciousness is capable of recognizing only Truth. It merely fails to respond to falsehood. Similarly, a mirror reflects an image only if there is an object to reflect. If no object is present to the mirror, there is no reflected image.

To Calibrate A Level

Calibrated levels are relative to a specific reference scale. To arrive at the same figures as in the chart in Appendix A, reference must be made to that table or by a statement such as, "On a scale of human consciousness from 1 to 1,000, where 600 indicates Enlightenment, this _____ calibrates over _____ (a number)." Or, "On a scale of consciousness where 200 is the level of

Truth and 500 is the level of Love, this statement calibrates over _____." (State a specific number.)

General Information

People generally want to determine truth from falsehood. Therefore, the statement has to be made very specifically. Avoid using general terms such as a good job to apply for. Good in what way? Pay scale? Working conditions? Promotional opportunities? Fairness of the boss?

Expertise

Familiarity with the test brings progressive expertise. The right questions to ask begin to spring forth and can become almost uncannily accurate. If the same tester and test subject work together for a period of time, one or both of them will develop what can become an amazing accuracy and capability of pinpointing just what specific questions to ask, even though the subject is totally unknown by either one. For instance, the tester has lost an object and begins by saying, "I left it in my office." (Answer: No.) "I left it in the car." (Answer: No.) All of a sudden, the test subject almost sees the object and says, "Ask, On the back of the bathroom door." The test subject says, "The object is hanging on the back of the bathroom door." (Answer: Yes.) In this actual case, the test subject did not even know that the tester had stopped for gas and left a jacket in the restroom of a gasoline station. Any information can be obtained about anything anywhere in current or past time or space, depending on receiving prior permission. (Sometimes one gets a "no," perhaps for karmic or other unknown reasons.)

By cross-checking, accuracy can be easily confirmed. For anyone who learns the technique, more information is available instantaneously than can be held in all the computers and libraries of the world. The possibilities are therefore obviously unlimited, and the prospects breathtaking.

Limitations

The test is accurate only if the test subjects themselves calibrate over 200 and the intention for the use of the test is integrous, calibrating over 200. The requirement is one of detached objectivity and alignment with truth rather than subjective opinion. Thus, to try to prove a point negates accuracy. Approximately 10% of the population is not able to use the kinesiologic testing technique for as yet unknown reasons. Sometimes married couples, for reasons as yet undiscovered, are unable to use each other as test subjects and may have to find a third person to be a test partner.

A suitable test subject is a person whose arm goes strong when a love object or person is held in mind, and it goes weak if that which is negative (fear, hate, guilt, etc.) is held in mind (e.g., Winston Churchill makes one go strong, and Osama bin Laden makes one go weak).

Occasionally, a suitable test subject gives paradoxical responses. This can usually be cleared by doing the thymic thump. (With a closed fist, thump three times over the upper breastbone, smile, and say "ha-ha-ha" with each thump and mentally picture someone or something that is loved.) The temporary imbalance will then clear up.

The imbalance may be the result of recently having

been with negative people, listening to heavy-metal rock music, watching violent television programs, playing violent video games, etc. Negative music energy has a deleterious effect on the energy system of the body for up to one-half hour after it is turned off. Television commercials or background are also a common source of negative energy.

As previously noted, this method of discerning truth from falsehood and the calibrated levels of truth has strict requirements. Because of the limitations, calibrated levels are supplied for ready reference in *Truth vs. Falsehood.*

Explanation

The muscle-strength test is independent of personal opinion or beliefs and is an impersonal response of the field of consciousness, just as protoplasm is impersonal in its responses. This can be demonstrated by the observation that the test responses are the same whether verbalized or held silently in mind. Thus, the test subject is not influenced by the question as they do not even know what it is. To demonstrate this, do the following exercise:

The tester holds in mind an image unknown to the test subject and states, "The image I am holding in mind is positive" (or "true," or "calibrates over 200," etc.). Upon direction, the test subject then resists the downward pressure on the wrist. If the tester holds a positive image in mind (e.g., Abraham Lincoln, Jesus, Mother Teresa, etc.), the test subject's arm muscle will go strong. If the tester holds a false statement or negative image in mind (e.g., bin Laden, Hitler, etc.), the arm will go weak. Inasmuch as the test subject does not know what the tester has in mind, the results are not influenced by personal beliefs.

Disqualification

Both skepticism (cal. 160) and cynicism, as well as atheism, calibrate below 200 because they reflect negative prejudgment. In contrast, true inquiry requires an open mind and honesty devoid of intellectual vanity. Negative studies of the testing methodology all calibrate below 200 (usually at 160), as do the investigators themselves.

That even famous professors can and do calibrate below 200 may seem surprising to the average person. Thus, negative studies are a consequence of negative bias. As an example, Francis Crick's research design that led to the discovery of the double helix pattern of DNA calibrated at 440. His last research design, which was intended to prove that consciousness was just a product of neuronal activity, calibrated at only 135. (He was an atheist.)

The failure of investigators who themselves, or by faulty research design, calibrate below 200 (usually at 160), confirms the truth of the very methodology they claim to disprove. They should get negative results, and so they do, which paradoxically proves the accuracy of the test to detect the difference between unbiased integrity and nonintegrity.

Any new discovery may upset the apple cart and be viewed as a threat to the status quo of prevailing belief systems. That consciousness research validates spiritual Reality is, of course, going to precipitate resistance, as it is actually a direct confrontation to the dominion of the narcissistic core of the ego itself, which is innately presumptuous and opinionated.

Below consciousness level 200, comprehension is limited by the dominance of Lower Mind, which is capable of recognizing facts but not yet able to grasp what is meant by the term truth (it confuses *res interna* with *res externa*), and that truth has physiological accompaniments that are different from falsehood. Additionally, truth is intuited as evidenced by the use of voice analysis, the study of body language, pupillary response, EEG changes in the brain, fluctuations in breathing and blood pressure, galvanic skin response, dowsing, and even the Huna technique of measuring the distance that the aura radiates from the body. Some people have a very simple technique that utilizes the standing body like a pendulum (fall forward with truth and backward with falsehood).

From a more advanced contextualization, the principles that prevail are that Truth cannot be disproved by falsehood any more than light can be disproved by darkness. The nonlinear is not subject to the limitations of the linear. Truth is a paradigm different from logic and thus is not provable, as that which is provable calibrates only in the 400s. Consciousness research methodology operates at level 600, which is at the interface of the linear and the nonlinear dimensions.

Discrepancies

Differing calibrations may be obtained over time or by different investigators for a variety of reasons:

1. Situations, people, politics, policies, and attitudes change over time.

2. People tend to use different sensory modalities when they hold something in mind, i.e., visual, sensory, auditory, or feeling. Your mother could therefore be how she looked, felt, sounded, etc., or Henry Ford could be calibrated as a father, as an industrialist, for his impact on America, his anti-Semitism, etc.

3. Accuracy increases with the level of consciousness. (The 400s and above are the most accurate.) One can specify context and stick to a prevailing modality. The same team using the same technique will get results that are internally consistent. Expertise develops with practice. There are some people, however, who are incapable of a scientific, detached attitude and are unable to be objective, and for whom the testing method will therefore not be accurate. Dedication and intention to the truth has to be given priority over personal opinions and trying to prove them as being "right."

Note

While it was discovered that the technique does not work for people who calibrate at less than level 200, only quite recently was it further discovered that the technique does not work if the persons doing the testing are atheists. This may be simply the consequence of the fact that atheism calibrates below level 200, and that negation of the truth or Divinity (omniscience) karmically disqualifies the negator just as hate negates love.

REFERENCES

Anonymous, *A Course in Miracles.* Huntington Station, New York: Foundation for Inner Peace. 1975.

Backster, C., *Primary Perception.* Anza, CA: White Rose Millennium. 2003.

Bailey, A., *Glamour: A World Problem.* New York: Lucis Publishing. 1950

Bohm, D., *Wholeness and the Implicate Order.* London: Routledge & Kegan Paul. 1980.

Brain/Mind Bulletin. Los Angeles, CA: Interface Press. 1980–1986.

Briggs, J., and Peat, F.D., *Looking Glass Universe.* New York: Simon & Schuster. 1984.

Briggs, J., *Turbulent Mirror: An Illustrated Guide to Chaos Theory and the Science of Wholeness.* New York: Harper & Row. 1989.

"Cancer United to Helplessness and Immune Suppression," *Brain/Mind Bulletin.* June 21, 1982.

Capra, F., *The Tao of Physics: An Exploration of the Parallels Between Modern Physics and Eastern Mysticism.* New York: Bantam. 1976.

Cannon, W., *Bodily Changes in Pain, Hunger, Fear and Rage.* New York: D. Appleton Co. 1915.

Davidson, R., "Towards a Biology of Positive Affect and Compassion," in Davidson, R., Harrington, A. (Eds.), *Visions of Compassion.* New York: Oxford University Press. 2002.

Deliman, T., *Holistic Medicine, Harmony of Body, Mind, and Spirit.* Reston, VA: Reston Publishers. 1982.

Diamond, J., *Behavioral Kinesiology.* New York: Harper & Row. 1979.

——, *Your Body Doesn't Lie.* New York: Warner Books. 1979.

——, *Life Energy: Using the Meridians to Unblock Hidden*

Power of Your Emotions. New York: Paragon House. 1998.

The Dhammapada: The Sayings of the Buddha. New York: Oxford University Press. 1987.

Dumitrescu, I., Kenyon, J., *Electrographic Imaging in Medicine and Biology.* Sudbury, Suffolk, U.K.: Neville Spearman Ltd. 1983.

Eadie, B. J., *Embraced by the Light.* Placerville, California: Gold Leaf Press. 1992.

"Early Stress Style Linked to Later Illness," *Brain/Mind Bulletin.* June 22, 1981.

Eccles, J., *Evolution of the Brain: Creation of the Self.* Edinburgh, Scotland: Routledge. 1989.

Ferguson, M., *The Aquarian Conspiracy: Personal and Social Transformation in the 1980s.* New York: Tarcher. 1980.

Field, J., *A Life of One's Own.* New York: Tarcher. [1934], 1981.

Frankl, V., *Man's Search for Meaning.* Boston: Beacon Press. [1959], 2004.

Gray, W., LaViolette, P., "Feelings Code and Organize Thinking," *Brain/Mind Bulletin.* October 5, 1981.

Hawkins, D. R., Archival Office Visit Series: "Stress"; "Health"; "Illness and Self-Healing"; "Handling Major Crises"; "Depression"; "Alcoholism"; "Spiritual First Aid"; "The Aging Process"; "The Map of Consciousness"; "Death and Dying"; "Pain and Suffering"; "Losing Weight"; "Worry, Fear and Anxiety"; "Drug Addiction and Alcoholism"; and "Sexuality." Lectures in video and audio. Sedona, Arizona: Institute for Spiritual Research, 1986.

———, and Pauling, L., *Orthomolecular Psychiatry.* San Francisco: W.H. Freeman and Company. 1973.

———, *Power vs. Force: Hidden Determinants of Human Behavior.* Author's Official Revised Edition. Sedona, AZ: Veritas Publishing. [1995] 2012.

"Healer Affects Growth of Bacterial Cultures," *Brain/Mind Bulletin.* April 18, 1983.

James, W., *The Varieties of Religious Experience.* New York: Random House. 1929.

Jampolsky, J., *Love is Letting Go of Fear.* 25th Anniversary Edition. New York: Celestial Arts. 2004.

Jung, C. G., *Collected Works.* Princeton, New Jersey: Princeton University Press. 1979.

———, (R. F. Hull, trans.), *Synchronicity as a Causal Connecting Principle.* Bollington Series, Vol. 20. Princeton, New Jersey: Princeton University Press. 1973.

"Kirlian Photos Predict Cancer," *Brain/Mind Bulletin.* May 7, 1984.

Krippner, S., *Western Hemisphere Conference on Kirlian Photography.* Garden City, New York. 1974.

Kübler-Ross, E., *On Life after Death.* New York: Celestial Arts. 1991.

Lamsa, G. (trans.), *Holy Bible from Ancient Eastern Manuscripts.* Philadelphia: A.J. Holmes Co. 1957.

Liebeskind, J., Shavit, Y., article on endorphins and cancer experiment at UCLA, in *Science* (223:188–190). 1980–1984.

Lloyd, V., *Choose Freedom.* Phoenix, AZ: Freedom Publications. 1983.

Luskin, F., *Forgive for Good.* San Francisco, CA: Harper One. 2003.

Maharaj, N., *I Am That,* Vols. I and II. Bombay, India: Cetana. 1973.

Matton, M., *Jungian Psychology in Perspective.* New York: Free Press. 1983.

Monroe, R., *Journeys Out of the Body.* Garden City, NY: Doubleday. 1977.

Moody, R., *Life After Life.* San Francisco: Harper One. 2001.

Moss, R., *The I That is We: Awakening to Higher Energies Through Unconditional Love.* Millbrae, CA: Celestial Arts. 1981.

"Multiple Personalities," *Brain/Mind Bulletin,* (Vol. 8., No. 16). October 3, 1983.

Neal, M., *To Heaven and Back: The True Story of a Doctor's Extraordinary Walk with God.* Copyright: Mary Neal, M.D. 2011.

Pace, T.W., Negi, L.T., Adame, D.D., Cole, S.P., Sivilli, T.I., Brown, T.D., Issa, M.J., Raison, C.L., "Effect of Compassion Meditation on Neuroendocrine, Innate Immune and Behavioral Responses to Psychosocial Stress." *Psychoneuroendocrinology,* 34: 87–98. 2009.

Sapolsky, R., in Lehrer, J., "Under Pressure: The Search for a Stress Vaccine," *Wired Magazine.* August 2010.

Selye, H., *The Stress of Life.* New York: McGraw-Hill. 1956.

"Three Brains of Eve: EEG Data," *Science News,* (Vol. 121., No. 22). May 29, 1982.

Tiller, W. *Psychoenergetic Science: A Second Copernican-Scale Revolution.* Walnut Creek, CA: Pavior Publishers. 2007.

Wilber, K. (ed.), *The Holographic Paradigm and Other Paradoxes: Exploring the Leading Edge of Science.* Boston: Shambhala. 1982.

ABOUT THE AUTHOR

Biographical and Autobiographical Notes

Dr. Hawkins is an internationally known spiritual teacher, author, and speaker on the subject of advanced spiritual states, consciousness research, and the Realization of the Presence of God as Self.

His published works, as well as recorded lectures, have been widely recognized as unique in that a very advanced state of spiritual awareness occurred in an individual with a scientific and clinical background who was later able to verbalize and explain the unusual phenomenon in a manner that is clear and comprehensible.

The transition from the normal ego-state of mind to its elimination by the Presence is described in the trilogy *Power vs. Force* (1995), which won praise even from Mother Teresa, *The Eye of the I* (2001), and *I: Reality and Subjectivity* (2003), which have been translated into the major languages of the world. *Truth vs. Falsehood: How to Tell the Difference* (2005), *Transcending the Levels of Consciousness* (2006), *Discovery of the Presence of God: Devotional Nonduality* (2007), and *Reality, Spirituality and Modern Man* (2008) continue the exploration of the ego's expressions and inherent limitations and how to transcend them.

The trilogy was preceded by research on the Nature of Consciousness and published as the doctoral dissertation, *Qualitative and Quantitative Analysis and Calibration of the Levels of Human Consciousness* (1995), which correlated the seemingly disparate domains of science and spirituality. This was accomplished by the major discovery of a technique that, for the first time in human history, demonstrated a means to discern truth from falsehood.

The importance of the initial work was given recognition by its very favorable and extensive review in *Brain/Mind Bulletin* and at later presentations such as the International Conference on Science and Consciousness. Many presentations were given to a variety of organizations, spiritual conferences, church groups, nuns, and monks, both nationally and in foreign countries, including the Oxford Forum in England. In the Far East, Dr. Hawkins is a recognized "Teacher of the Way to Enlightenment" ("Tae Ryoung Sun Kak Dosa"). In response to his observation that much spiritual truth has been misunderstood over the ages due to lack of explanation, Dr. Hawkins has presented monthly seminars that provide detailed explanations which are too lengthy to describe in book format. Recordings are available that end with questions and answers, thus providing additional clarification.

The overall design of this lifetime work is to recontextualize the human experience in terms of the evolution of consciousness and to integrate a comprehension of both mind and spirit as expressions of the innate Divinity that is the substrate and ongoing source of life and Existence. This dedication is signified by the statement "*Gloria in Excelsis Deo!*" with which his published works begin and end.

Biographic Summary

Dr. Hawkins has practiced psychiatry since 1952 and is a life member of the American Psychiatric Association and numerous other professional organizations. His national television appearance schedule has included *The McNeil/Leher News Hour, The Barbara Walters Show, The Today Show,* science documentaries, and many others. He was also interviewed by Oprah Winfrey.

Dr. Hawkins is the author of numerous scientific and spiritual publications, books, CDs, DVDs, and lecture series. He co-edited the landmark book, *Orthomolecular Psychiatry,* with Nobelist Linus Pauling. Dr. Hawkins was a consultant for many years to Episcopal and Catholic Dioceses, monastic orders, and other religious organizations.

Dr. Hawkins has lectured widely, with appearances at the Oxford Forum and Westminster Abbey, the Universities of Argentina, Notre Dame, and Michigan, Fordham University, and Harvard University. He gave the annual Landsberg Lecture at the University of California Medical School at San Francisco. He is also a consultant to foreign governments on international diplomacy and was instrumental in resolving long-standing conflicts that were major threats to world peace.

In recognition of his contributions to humanity, in 1995, Dr. Hawkins became a knight of the Sovereign Order of the Hospitaliers of St. John of Jerusalem, which was founded in 1077.

Autobiographic Note

While the truths reported in this book were scientifically derived and objectively organized, like all truths, they were first experienced personally. A lifelong sequence of intense states of awareness beginning at a young age first inspired and then gave direction to the process of subjective realization that has finally taken form in this series of books.

At age three, there occurred a sudden full consciousness of existence, a nonverbal but complete understanding of the meaning of "I Am," followed immediately by the frightening realization that "I" might not have come into existence at all. This was an instant awakening from oblivion into a conscious awareness, and in that moment, the personal self was born and the duality of "Is" and "Is Not" entered my subjective awareness.

Throughout childhood and early adolescence, the paradox of existence and the question of the reality of the self remained a repeated concern. The personal self would sometimes begin slipping back into a greater impersonal Self, and the initial fear of non-existence—the fundamental fear of nothingness—would recur.

In 1939, as a paperboy with a seventeen-mile bicycle route in rural Wisconsin, on a dark winter's night I was caught miles from home in a twenty-below-zero blizzard. The bicycle fell over on the ice and the fierce wind ripped the newspapers out of the handlebar basket, blowing them across the ice-covered, snowy field. There were tears of frustration and exhaustion and my clothes were frozen stiff. To get out of the wind, I broke through the icy crust of a high snow bank, dug out a space, and crawled into it. Soon the shivering stopped and there was a delicious warmth, and then a state of peace beyond all description. This was accompanied by a suffusion of light and a presence of infinite love that had no beginning and no end and was undifferentiated from my own essence. The physical body and surroundings faded as my awareness was fused with this all-present, illuminated state. The mind grew silent; all thought stopped. An infinite Presence was all that was or could be, beyond all time or description.

After that timelessness, there was suddenly an awareness of someone shaking my knee; then my father's anxious face appeared. There was great reluctance to return to the body and all that that entailed, but because of my father's love and anguish, the Spirit nurtured and reactivated the body. There was compassion for his fear of death, although, at the same time, the concept of death seemed absurd.

This subjective experience was not discussed with anyone since there was no context available from which to describe it. It was not common to hear of spiritual experiences other than those reported in the lives of the saints. But after this experience, the accepted reality of the world began to seem only provisional; traditional religious teachings lost significance and, paradoxically, I became an agnostic. Compared to the light of Divinity that had illuminated all existence, the god of traditional religion shone dully indeed; thus spirituality replaced religion.

During World War II, hazardous duty on a minesweeper often brought close brushes with death, but there was no fear of it. It was as though death had lost its authenticity. After the war, fascinated by the complexities of the mind and wanting to study psychiatry, I worked my way through medical school. My training psychoanalyst, a professor at Columbia University, was also an agnostic; we both took a dim view of religion. The analysis went well, as did my career, and success followed.

I did not, however, settle quietly into professional life. I fell ill with a progressive, fatal illness that did not respond to any treatments available. By age 38, I was *in extremis* and knew I was about to die. I didn't care about the body, but my spirit was in a state of extreme anguish and despair. As the final moment approached, the thought flashed through my mind, "What if there is a God?" So I called out in prayer, "If there is a God, I ask him to help me now." I surrendered to whatever God there might be and went into oblivion. When I awoke, a transformation of such enormity had taken place that I was struck dumb with awe.

The person I had been no longer existed. There was no personal self or ego, only an Infinite Presence of such unlimited power that it was all that was. This Presence had replaced what had been "me," and the body and its actions were controlled solely by the Infinite Will of the Presence. The world was illuminated by the clarity of an Infinite Oneness that expressed itself as all things revealed in their infinite beauty and perfection.

As life went on, this stillness persisted. There was no personal will; the physical body went about its business under the direction of the infinitely powerful but exquisitely gentle Will of the Presence. In that state, there was no need to think about anything. All truth was self-evident and no conceptualization was necessary or even possible. At the same time, the physical nervous system felt extremely overtaxed, as though it were carrying far more energy than its circuits had been designed for.

It was not possible to function effectively in the world. All ordinary motivations had disappeared, along with all fear and anxiety. There was nothing to seek, as all was perfect. Fame, success, and money were meaningless. Friends urged the pragmatic return to clinical practice, but there was no ordinary motivation to do so.

There was now the ability to perceive the reality that underlay personalities: the origin of emotional sickness lay in people's belief that they *were* their personalities. And so, as though of its own, a clinical practice resumed and eventually became huge. People came from all over the United States. The practice had two thousand outpatients, which required more than fifty therapists and other employees, a suite of twenty-five offices, and research and electroencephalic laboratories. There were a thousand new patients a year. In addition, there were appearances on radio and network television shows, as previously mentioned. In 1973, the clinical research was documented in a traditional format in the book, *Orthomolecular Psychiatry*. This work was ten years ahead of its time and created something of a stir.

The overall condition of the nervous system improved slowly, and then another phenomenon commenced. There was a sweet, delicious band of energy continuously flowing up the spine and into the brain where it created an intense sensation of continuous pleasure. Everything in life happened by synchronicity, evolving in perfect harmony; the miraculous was commonplace. The origin of what the world would call miracles was the Presence, not the personal self. What remained of the personal "me" was only a witness to these phenomena. The greater "I," deeper than my former self or thoughts, determined all that happened.

The states that were present had been reported by others throughout history and led to the investigation of spiritual teachings, including those of the Buddha, enlightened sages, Huang Po, and more recent teach-

ers such as Ramana Maharshi and Nisargadatta
Maharaj. It was thus confirmed that these experiences
were not unique. The *Bhagavad-Gita* now made complete sense. At times, the same spiritual ecstasy
reported by Sri Ramakrishna and the Christian saints
occurred.

Everything and everyone in the world was luminous and exquisitely beautiful. All living beings
became Radiant and expressed this Radiance in stillness and splendor. It was apparent that all mankind is
actually motivated by inner love but has simply
become unaware; most lives are lived as though by
sleepers unawakened to the awareness of who they
really are. People around me looked as though they
were asleep and were incredibly beautiful. It was like
being in love with everyone.

It was necessary to stop the habitual practice of
meditating for an hour in the morning and then again
before dinner because it would intensify the bliss to
such an extent that it was not possible to function. An
experience similar to the one that had occurred in the
snow bank as a boy would recur, and it became
increasingly difficult to leave that state and return to
the world. The incredible beauty of all things shone
forth in all their perfection, and where the world saw
ugliness, there was only timeless beauty. This spiritual
love suffused all perception, and all boundaries
between here and there, or then and now, or separation disappeared.

During the years spent in inner silence, the
strength of the Presence grew. Life was no longer personal; a personal will no longer existed. The personal
"I" had become an instrument of the Infinite Presence
and went about and did as it was willed. People felt

an extraordinary peace in the aura of that Presence. Seekers sought answers but as there was no longer any such individual as David, they were actually finessing answers from their own Self, which was not different from mine. From each person the same Self shone forth from their eyes.

The miraculous happened, beyond ordinary comprehension. Many chronic maladies from which the body had suffered for years disappeared; eyesight spontaneously normalized, and there was no longer a need for the lifetime bifocals.

Occasionally, an exquisitely blissful energy, an Infinite Love, would suddenly begin to radiate from the heart toward the scene of some calamity. Once, while driving on a highway, this exquisite energy began to beam out of the chest. As the car rounded a bend, there was an auto accident; the wheels of the overturned car were still spinning. The energy passed with great intensity into the occupants of the car and then stopped of its own accord. Another time, while I was walking on the streets of a strange city, the energy started to flow down the block ahead and arrived at the scene of an incipient gang fight. The combatants fell back and began to laugh, and again, the energy stopped.

Profound changes of perception came without warning in improbable circumstances. While dining alone at Rothmann's on Long Island, the Presence suddenly intensified until every thing and every person, which had appeared as separate in ordinary perception, melted into a timeless universality and oneness. In the motionless Silence, it became obvious that there are no "events" or "things" and that nothing actually "happens" because past, present, and future are merely artifacts of perception, as is the illusion of a separate "I" being subject to birth and death. As the limited, false self dissolved into the universal Self of its true origin, there was an ineffable sense of having returned home to a state of absolute peace and relief from all suffering. It is only the illusion of individuality that is the origin of all suffering. When one realizes that one is the universe, complete and at one with All That Is, forever without end, then no further suffering is possible.

Patients came from every country in the world, and some were the most hopeless of the hopeless. Grotesque, writhing, wrapped in wet sheets for transport from far-away hospitals they came, hoping for treatment for advanced psychoses and grave, incurable mental disorders. Some were catatonic; many had been mute for years. But in each patient, beneath the crippled appearance, there was the shining essence of love and beauty, perhaps so obscured to ordinary vision that he or she had become totally unloved in this world.

One day a mute catatonic was brought into the hospital in a straitjacket. She had a severe neurological disorder and was unable to stand. Squirming on the floor, she went into spasms and her eyes rolled back in her head. Her hair was matted; she had torn all her clothes and uttered guttural sounds. Her family was fairly wealthy; as a result, over the years she had been seen by innumerable physicians and famous specialists from all over the world. Every treatment had been tried on her and she had been given up as hopeless by the medical profession.

A short, nonverbal question arose: "What do you want done with her, God?" Then came the realization that she just needed to be loved, that was all. Her inner self shone through her eyes and the Self connected with that loving essence. In that second, she was healed by her own recognition of who she really was; what happened to her mind or body did not matter to her any longer.

This, in essence, occurred with countless patients. Some recovered in the eyes of the world and some did not, but whether a clinical recovery ensued did not matter any longer to the patients. Their inner agony was over. As they felt loved and at peace within, their pain stopped. This phenomenon can only be explained by saying that the Compassion of the Presence recontextualized each patient's reality so that he or she experienced healing on a level that transcended the world and its appearances. The inner peace of the Self encompassed us beyond time and identity.

It was clear that all pain and suffering arises solely from the ego and not from God. This truth was silently communicated to the minds of the patients. This was the mental block in another mute catatonic who had not spoken in many years. The Self said to him through mind, "You're blaming God for what your ego has done to you." He jumped off the floor and began to speak, much to the shock of the nurse who witnessed the incident.

The work became increasingly taxing and eventually overwhelming. Patients were backed up, waiting for beds to open, although the hospital had built an extra ward to house them. There was an enormous frustration in that the human suffering could be countered in only one patient at a time. It was like bailing out the sea. It seemed that there must be some other way to address the causes of the common malaise, the endless stream of spiritual distress and human suffering.

This led to the study of the physiological response (muscle testing) to various stimuli, which revealed an amazing discovery. It was the "wormhole" between two universes—the physical world and the world of the mind and spirit—an interface between dimensions. In a world full of sleepers lost from their source, here was a tool to recover, and demonstrate for all to see, that lost connection with the higher reality. This led to the testing of every substance, thought, and concept that could be brought to mind. The endeavor was aided by my students and research assistants. Then a major discovery was made: whereas all subjects went weak from negative stimuli, such as fluorescent lights, pesticides, and artificial sweeteners, students of spiritual disciplines who had advanced their levels of awareness did not go weak as did ordinary people. Something important and decisive had shifted in their consciousness. It apparently occurred as they realized they were not at the mercy of the world but rather affected only by what their minds believed. Perhaps the very process of progress toward enlightenment could be shown to increase man's ability to resist the vicissitudes of existence, including illness.

The Self had the capacity to change things in the world by merely envisioning them; Love changed the world each time it replaced non-love. The entire scheme of civilization could be profoundly altered by focusing this power of love at a very specific point. Whenever this happened, history bifurcated down new roads.

It now appeared that these crucial insights could not only be communicated with the world but also visibly and irrefutably demonstrated. It seemed that the great tragedy of human life had always been that the psyche is so easily deceived; discord and strife have been the inevitable consequence of mankind's inability to distinguish the false from the true. But here was an answer to this fundamental dilemma, a way to recontextualize the nature of consciousness itself and make explicable that which otherwise could only be inferred.

It was time to leave life in New York, with its city apartment and home on Long Island, for something more important. It was necessary to perfect myself as an instrument. This necessitated leaving that world and everything in it, replacing it with a reclusive life in a small town where the next seven years were spent in meditation and study.

Overpowering states of bliss returned unsought, and eventually, there was the need to learn how to be in the Divine Presence and still function in the world. The mind had lost track of what was happening in the world at large. In order to do research and writing, it was necessary to stop all spiritual practice and focus on the world of form. Reading the newspaper and watching television helped to catch up on the story of who was who, the major events, and the nature of the current social dialogue.

Exceptional subjective experiences of truth, which are the province of the mystic who affects all mankind by sending forth spiritual energy into the collective consciousness, are not understandable by the majority of mankind and are therefore of limited meaning except to other spiritual seekers. This led to an effort to be ordinary, because just being ordinary in itself is an expression of Divinity; the truth of one's real self can be discovered through the pathway of everyday life. To live with care and kindness is all that is necessary. The rest reveals itself in due time. The commonplace and God are not distinct.

And so, after a long circular journey of the spirit, there was a return to the most important work, which was to try to bring the Presence at least a little closer to the grasp of as many fellow beings as possible.

The Presence is silent and conveys a state of peace that is the space in which and by which all is and has its existence and experience. It is infinitely gentle and yet like a rock. With it, all fear disappears. Spiritual joy occurs on a quiet level of inexplicable ecstasy. Because the experience of time stops, there is no apprehension or regret, no pain or anticipation; the source of joy is unending and ever-present. With no beginning or ending, there is no loss or grief or desire. Nothing needs to be done; everything is already perfect and complete.

When time stops, all problems disappear; they are merely artifacts of a point of perception. As the Presence prevails, there is no further identification with the body or the mind. When the mind grows silent, the thought "I Am" also disappears, and Pure Awareness shines forth to illuminate what one is, was, and always will be, beyond all worlds and all universes, beyond time, and therefore without beginning or end.

People wonder, "How does one reach this state of awareness," but few follow the steps because they are so simple. First, the desire to reach that state was intense. Then began the discipline to act with constant and universal forgiveness and gentleness, without exception. One has to be compassionate towards everything, including one's own self and thoughts. Next came a willingness to hold desires in abeyance and surrender personal will at every moment. As each thought, feeling, desire, or deed was surrendered to God, the mind became progressively silent. At first, it released whole stories and paragraphs, then ideas and concepts. As one lets go of wanting to own these thoughts, they no longer reach such elaboration and begin to fragment while only half formed. Finally, it was possible to turn over the energy behind thought itself before it even became thought.

The task of constant and unrelenting fixity of focus, allowing not even a moment of distraction from meditation, continued while doing ordinary activities. At first, this seemed very difficult, but as time went on, it became habitual, automatic, requiring less and less effort, and finally, it was effortless. The process is like a rocket leaving the earth. At first, it requires enormous power, then less and less as it leaves the earth's gravitational field, and finally, it moves through space under its own momentum.

Suddenly, without warning, a shift in awareness occurred and the Presence was there, unmistakable and all encompassing. There were a few moments of apprehension as the self died, and then the absoluteness of the Presence inspired a flash of awe. This breakthrough was spectacular, more intense than anything before. It has no counterpart in ordinary experience. The profound shock was cushioned by the love that is with the Presence. Without the support and protection of that love, one would be annihilated.

There followed a moment of terror as the ego clung to its existence, fearing it would become nothingness. Instead, as it died, it was replaced by the Self as Everythingness, the All in which everything is known and obvious in its perfect expression of its own essence. With nonlocality came the awareness that one is all that ever was or can be. One is total and complete, beyond all identities, beyond all gender, beyond even humanness itself. One need never again fear suffering and death. What happens to the body from this point is immaterial. At certain levels of spiritual awareness, ailments of the body heal or spontaneously disappear. But in the absolute state, such considerations are irrelevant. The body will run its predicted course and then return from whence it came. It is a matter of no importance; one is unaffected. The body appears as an "it" rather than as a "me," as another object, like the furniture in a room. It may seem comical that people still address the body as though it were the individual "you," but there is no way to explain this state of awareness to the unaware. It is best to just go on about one's business and allow Providence to handle the social adjustments. However, as one reaches bliss, it is very difficult to conceal that state of intense ecstasy. The world may be dazzled, and people may come from far and wide to be in the accompanying aura. Spiritual seekers and the spiritually curious may be attracted, as may be the very ill who are seeking miracles. One may become a magnet and a source of joy to them. Commonly, there is a desire at this point to share this state with others and to use it for the benefit of all.

The ecstasy that accompanies this condition is not initially absolutely stable; there are also moments of great agony. The most intense occur when the state fluctuates and suddenly ceases for no apparent reason. These times bring on periods of intense despair and a fear that one has been forsaken by the Presence. These falls make the path arduous, and to surmount these reversals requires great will. It finally becomes obvious that one must transcend this level or constantly suffer excruciating "descents from grace." The glory of ecstasy, then, has to be relinquished as one enters upon the arduous task of transcending duality until one is beyond all opposites and their conflicting pulls. But while it is one thing to happily give up the iron chains of the ego, it is quite another to abandon the golden chains of ecstatic joy. It feels as though one is giving up God, and a new level of fear arises, never before anticipated. This is the final terror of absolute aloneness.

To the ego, the fear of nonexistence was formidable, and it drew back from it repeatedly as it seemed to approach. The purpose of the agonies and the dark nights of the soul then became apparent. They are so intolerable that their exquisite pain spurs one on to the extreme effort required to surmount them. When vacillation between heaven and hell becomes unendurable, the desire for existence itself has to be surrendered. Only once this is done may one finally move beyond the duality of Allness versus nothingness, beyond existence versus nonexistence. This culmination of the inner work is the most difficult phase, the ultimate watershed, where one is starkly aware that the illusion of existence one transcends is irrevocable. There is no returning from this step, and this specter of irreversibility makes this last barrier appear to be the most formidable choice of all.

But, in fact, in this final apocalypse of the self, the dissolution of the sole remaining duality of existence versus nonexistence—identity itself—dissolves in Universal Divinity, and no individual consciousness is left to choose. The last step, then, is taken by God.

—*David R. Hawkins*

For a list of available audio and video recordings
and other publications on consciousness
and spirituality by Dr. Hawkins,
please contact:

Veritas Publishing
P.O. Box 3516
West Sedona, AZ 86340 U.S.A.
Phone: 928.282.8722   Fax: 928.282.4789
www.veritaspub.com